AUTOBIOGRAPHY
IN EARLY MODERN SPAIN

Edited and Introduced by
Nicholas Spadaccini and Jenaro Talens

AUTOBIOGRAPHY IN EARLY MODERN SPAIN

hispanic issues 2

edited and introduced by
Nicholas Spadaccini
and Jenaro Talens

THE
PRISMA
INSTITUTE

PQ
6136
.A98
1988

First Edition
ISSN 0893-2395
ISBN 0-910235-24-4
Library of Congress Catalog Card No. 88-9772

Published by The Prisma Institute
            3 Folwell Hall
            9 Pleasant Street SE
            Minneapolis, MN 55455

The editors of this volume gratefully acknowledge assistance from the Program for Cultural Cooperation between Spain's Ministry of Culture and United States' Universities, as well as the Dept. of Spanish and Portuguese Languages and Literatures and the College of Liberal Arts, University of Minnesota, towards preparation of this work.

COVER: Studio 87501, Santa Fe, New Mexico.
        Manuscript of Alfonso de la Torre, *Visión delectable de la philosophia e artes liberales*, Seville, Juan Cromberger, 1538 (Cromberger first introduced printing into America by starting a press at Mexico City in 1539: the first Hispanic issue). Special thanks to Orlando Romero, History Library, Museum of New Mexico.

Hispanic Issues is a member
of (CELJ) Conference of
Editors of Learned Journals

Library of Congress Cataloging-in-Publication Data

Autobiography in early modern Spain / edited and introduced by
    Nicholas Spadaccini and Jenaro Taléns. -- 1st ed.
p. cm. -- (Hispanic Issues, ISSN 0893-2395 ; #2)
Bibliography: p.
Includes index.
ISBN 0-910235-24-4 : $9.95
1. Spanish prose literature--Classical period, 1500-1700--History and
    criticism. 2. Autobiography. 3. Biography (as a literary form).
    4. Self in literature. 5. Autobiographical fiction. I. Spadaccini,
    Nicholas. II. Taléns, Jenaro, 1946-   . III. Series.
PQ6136.A98 1988
860'.9'492--dc19   88-9772
                                    CIP

HISPANIC ISSUES
ISSN 0893-2395

A semi-annual publication in English touching on theoretical and methodological issues toward a reconfiguration of Spanish literary history and criticism. The series stresses collaborative research, drawing on a network of scholars from the U.S. and abroad. Sample areas of inquiry include: Literary Criticism and Historiography; Historical Function of Cultural Forms; Popular and Mass Culture; Literature and Institutions; Literature among Discourses.

TABLE OF CONTENTS

INTRODUCTION:
THE CONSTRUCTION OF THE SELF.
NOTES ON AUTOBIOGRAPHY
IN EARLY MODERN SPAIN

Nicholas Spadaccini and
Jenaro Talens

"What is your name?" asked King Milinda. The
monk answered: "They say my name is Nagasena."
But although parents give their children names as
Nagasena, Surasena, Virasena or Sihasena, these are
only designations, denominations, conceptual terms of
the usual appellations—simple names. There is not a
real person behind them.
                        —Saraha, *Dohakosha*, lines 70-112

One of the problems related to the social use of discourse since the beginning of time is the question of truth,
a truth that is dealt with in terms of verification outside of
discourse itself. If one remembers how power and rhetoric
were related among the Greeks ("He who has the word,
has the sword," Gorgias used to say), one will understand
the importance that producing the *effect* of having truth
could signify in social life.

Towards the end of the Middle Ages, when the idea of God as center and justification for Truth (the Word that is all words) began to disappear, man needed to look for a new mechanism for the validation of truth. This mechanism was related to the necessity of becoming a kind of substitute for God. By becoming the center of his world, man could justify what he was saying as truth: hence, for a medieval writer truth was validated from writing. Berceo, for example, used to connect his stories (the *Milagros de Nuestra Señora*) to written texts in order to convince the intended recipients of their historicity, all the while erasing himself as transmitter: "This Saint Hugo wrote, much truth there is in it." ("Esto Sant Hugo escripto, mucho es veridat.") The validation comes from the narrating voice itself, which is offered as a witness (eye/ear) of the narrated facts. But in order to be a witness, one needs, first of all, to exist. For this reason the rhetorical first person has two distinct and articulated functions: to construct a self and to use this construction for the validation of truth.

The notion of autobiography, therefore, implies problems of a specific nature and perspective. In this introductory essay we shall focus on two such problems: a) the historical meaning of autobiography, and b) the use of this concept in the History of Literature.

It may be worthwhile to begin our discussion with a multiple question: Who speaks in a text? From where? To whom? In his *Problems in General Linguistics*, Emile Benveniste has dealt with these issues in an attempt to clarify two basic categories of discourse: the category of the person and that of tense. He also goes on to indicate that when the individual appropriates language "it... is turned into instances of discourse, characterized by this system of internal references of which *I* is the key, and defining the individual by the particular linguistic construction he makes use of when he announces himself as the speaker" (220).

We saw what was the story—the life—of a character. Not only can we follow its development and analyze its contradictions; we can also project it on our models of behavior in order to construct a "psychological process" as a kind of metaphor. For our purpose we are interested in seeing how this "life" or story does not exist outside of the text. For through the act of speech that constitutes the text, the subject structures itself and the world as object (see A.J. Greimas and J. Courtés).

The "I" that begins the narrative is an empty sign which refers back to its own discourse rather than to some other kind of reality. Although the "I" states at the initial point that it is going to narrate some event, it has as referent a reality that is "other" than the discourse it is sending forth; what it is really doing is beginning a process through which this empty "I" turns into a full sign thanks to the emission of a discourse in which it inscribes itself as referent and referred; it thus assumes/structures reality through language. As Roland Barthes very clearly pointed out:

> Today, writing is not 'telling'; rather it signifies that one is telling, thereby making the whole referent ("what is being said") contingent upon this illocutionary act. (236)

"What happens" in the narrative is not "something" from the referential point of view; it is only the adventure of language whose advent is still celebrated (Barthes). Through the act of enunciation not only does the subject construct itself and the world as object, but, thanks to a series of textual elements, it locates the text in a context which it also constructs. Benveniste defines personal indexes (the I-you relationship), ostension indexes (this, here, etc.) and the verbal forms determined by the relationship to the ego as elements of internal referentiality. Cristina Peña-Marín expands these elements in the case of a marked text, when it presents itself as "referred to a subject that intends to express its opinions, points of view, narrate an experience or some event related to itself."[1] Thus to Benveniste's indicators of person, space and time, she adds the modalities of enunciation that define, in the first place, the attitude of certainty, doubt, possibility and order for the interlocutor.

Discourse, then, constructs an outside reality in order to validate it. It is a kind of tautology that hides a more important question: how this rhetorical game was instituted to justify discursively what was happening outside of discourse: how power and class differences were distributed as they were, not from the perspective of exploitation, but from one of a truth that relies on the capacity of discourse to construct it. Thus, for example, if "great men" were considered to be models whose lives were worthy of being imitated, and, consequently, narrated (the origin of biography as genre), this idea of model becomes feasible only if related to the capacity of the narrator to be close to truth.

In the sixteenth century, a historical period of expansion and innovation which among students of Spanish culture came to be known as the Renaissance, the necessity to be close to truth accelerated a virtual explosion of writing in the first person. Such writing was tied to the privileged position assigned to experiential knowledge, especially the kind that was gained from what the individual writer had seen or witnessed. Examples of such privileging abound in a wide range of areas, including fields such as navigation, cosmography, medicine and even metallurgy, among others (see José A. Maravall, *La literatura picaresca desde la historia social* 297+). This insistence and emphasis on what is seen extends as well to the "life-stories" or "memoirs" written by Spanish soldiers in the late sixteenth and early seventeenth centuries, although it is more accurate to say that in them the "I" is defined through observation and action, with the interest in writing resting on concrete hopes for material rewards: economic benefits, the attainment of positions in the bureaucracy, and so on (cf. M. Levisi in this volume). For this group of writers, the focus on one's own experiences is paramount, although the same can be said about the fictional autobiographies of *pícaros*, narratives in which the ostentatious use of the "I" points to the *pícaro*'s radical solitude, of his or her lack of solidarity with other individuals or groups (Maravall, *La literatura picaresca* 298+). What is important here is the "dramatic charge of his [the *pícaro*'s] individualism," and the notion that the individual life of any subject is material for a story: "there is no life of any man who roams the world which does not have the stuff of a great story" ("que no hay vida de hombre ninguno de cuantos andan por el mundo de quien no se pueda escrebir una gran historia")—says Vicente Espinel's Marcos de Obregón (Ed. S. Carrasco Urgoiti, I, 230).

The assumption that the life of any individual, however humble or lacking in social status, is material for a story, underlines the emergence of first-person picaresque narratives in Spain, with the publication of *La vida de Lazarillo de Tormes* (1554). Such an assumption is part of Lázaro de Tormes's (pre)text: a manifestation of Lázaro's will to talk about himself on his own terms. Thus, when an anonymous "Your Excellency" asks him to give, in writing, a full account of a certain "matter," the town crier of Toledo is seen shifting the focus of his autobiographic narrative: "I thought it best not to start in the middle, but in the beginning—says Lázaro. In this way the whole story of my life will be revealed, and those who inherited noble estates may see how little is due to their own efforts, since Fortune favored them, but rather how much has been accomplished by those who have rowed hard and skillfully against the tide and reached safe harbor."[2]

However socially humble, the "I" here speaks with authority and knowledge, going about "reconstructing the unity of life across time" (Gusdorf, "Conditions and Limits of Autobiography") for the specific purpose of placing the "matter" into an explanatory context. That is, Lázaro reorders his life across time in order to justify his present situation (a *ménage à trois* involving him and his wife with an archpriest), but the town crier's strategy of self-defense also involves a preemptive attack against his masters, especially those who "inherited noble estates": those who were born into positions of privilege but failed to discharge their social and moral responsibilities to the poor and the less fortunate.

Lazaro's "autobiography" is by no means a religious confession, whereby one either pleads guilty before the Creator or provides an intimate account of a sinner's journey toward some kind of conversion. Similarly, as with the *Lives* of soldiers later, its interest lies in the pivotal role that the individual assumes at the center of experience. This, of course, does not mean that the "writer" seeks to bring the reader into the recesses of his inner self (in the style of what will later be Rousseau's model) or that he concentrates on "the history of his personality"—a *sine qua non* for autobiography according to Philippe Lejeune (*Le pacte* 14). As has been correctly observed by Margarita Levisi (in this volume), even in the religious autobiographies of early modern Spain, "there is no gratuitous self-observation but rather a desire to demonstrate that a higher power has favored them with grace."

Autobiography, then, is not limited to those discourses explicitly referred to as autobiographical (because of their verifiable utterance); they are also inscribed in other texts, even though this inscription may appear in the enunciation. If one agrees with Beckett that it is impossible not to say "I", then one would have to consider the possibility that the lyric tradition is a disguised form of autobiography. Here the *Cancioneros* of the fifteenth century are a good example. For even *if* (or, perhaps, *because*) poems were written at the request of someone else, they were generally accepted as expressing the deep feelings of the buyer—and supposedly author. Thus, there was no truth in the utterance, but rather an effect of truth produced from—and through—the process of enunciation. In short, the autobiographical effect is a rhetorical construct.

Under those circumstances, rather than locating the analysis of autobiographies in the field of utterances one must do so in the sphere of the "production" of meaning, in a territory where the reader is a co-producer of meaning rather than a mere passive receiver. That is why authors of so-called autobiographies in early modern Spain were more interested in convincing readers about the truth of their narratives than about truth itself. Cervantes saw this problem clearly as evidenced by the fact that his entire body of work revolves around the opposition between truth as such and truth as rhetorical construct. He could argue about the difficult task of identifying the borderline separating discourse as reality and reality as discourse, thus leaving both possibilities open: if reality as life ends, literature cannot survive (cf. the episode of Lagartija in *El rufián dichoso*); but life can survive because of its imitation of literature (*Don Quijote*). On the other hand, when he seems not to face reality, because the horizon of expectation does not relate truth to utterance—for instance, in his poetry—Cervantes writes his own profile, inscribing himself on the margins, as a distant and discrete observer. As with the transcriber of Cide Hamete Benengeli in *Don Quijote*, the narrator of *Viaje del Parnaso* tries to efface himself behind the false objectivity of a reader; but it is the human opacity of a real body that inscribes its absence in the text (see the essay by J. Talens in this volume). And it is probably this invisible presence that allows us nowadays to read Cervantes as if we were engaged in conversation with him.

Georges Gusdorf has sought to define autobiography in terms of time and space, in light of certain formal features, and in relation to theories of genre and Literary History (28+). We shall proceed to sketch out at some length his main arguments before returning once again to Cervantes—the most significant writer of early modern Spain to have dealt with some of these very same issues along both theoretical and practical lines. In his essay Gusdorf argues that the recollection of one's life for the specific purpose of narrating it, is peculiar to Western man; that the awareness of the singularity of each individual life is possible only in a cultural landscape marked by the existence of the consciousness of self. In earlier times—in the Middle Ages—"each man [...] appears as the possessor of a role, already performed by the ancestors and to be performed again by the descendants. The number of roles is limited, and this is expressed by a limited number of names. Newborn children receive the names of the deceased whose roles, in a sense, they perform again, and so the community maintains a continuous self-identity in spite of the constant renewal of individuals who constitute it" (30). A condition for autobiography therefore, is humanity's entrance into the domain of history.

The emergence of biography and autobiography is tied to one's desire to endure in memory. Biography is said to be reserved for famous men, for heroes and princes, whose lives are written for the edification of future generations. Such writings are often dictated by the exigencies of propaganda and as a rule involve an exterior presentation of great figures; autobiography, on the other hand, seeks an identification between the artist and the model; the writer is said to tackle himself or herself—the self-image he or she has *as object*. Moreover, unlike biography, the focus of autobiography is often on private history, on the triumphs and reversals of often obscure men or women (31-32). In early modern Spain such is clearly the case with the auto-biograhical *Lives* of *pícaros*, soldiers, and even nuns— from the "saintly" Teresa of Avila to the swashbuckling heroine of *La monja alférez* (c. 1626).

For Gusdorf, "Autobiography properly speaking assumes the task of reconstructing the unity of life across time. [...] The essential themes, the structural designs that impose themselves on the complex material of exterior facts are the constituent elements of the personality. [...] Man [...] is the essential agent in the bringing about of situations in which he finds himself placed" (37). Freed of doctrinal allegiance, Renaissance man is said to seek out hidden aspects of his individual being (see the *Essays* of Montaigne). From this follows that autobiography "is one of the means to self-knowledge" (38), allowing for the re-composition and interpretation of life in its totality through a "second reading of experience [that] is truer than the first because it adds to experience itself consciousness of it" (38).

Moreover, Gusdorf recognizes that, while the avowed plan of an autobiography may be simply to retrace the history of a life and to recall its deepest emotions, in practice the autobiographer is engaged in a work of personal justification rather than in an objective and disinterested pursuit. Thus he argues that, "the recall of history assumes a very complex relation of past to present, a reactualization that prevents us from ever discovering that past 'in itself,' as it was, that past without us. [...] The child, the young man, and the mature man of yesterday are gone and cannot protest; only the man of today can speak" (40).

Gusdorf perceptively argues that narrative confers a meaning on the event which the event may or may not have had when it occurred. In effect, the perspective that the present adds to the past, constructing it as a coherent whole, establishes relationships between elements where they never existed (40-41). This happens in order to make believable and coherent the narration of facts. Thus one can argue that the inscription of the effect of truth in a text is ultimately a rhetorical construct that transforms what we usually call "facts" into what they really are: "interpretations." We can see this, for instance, in *La vida y hechos de Estebanillo González, hombre de buen humor* (1646), through a buffoon's account of some of the key battles of the Thirty Years' War, or in Cervantes's views on autobiography which in some ways anticipate those of Goethe.[3]

Gusdorf's question regarding the conferral of meaning to an event through narrative, could be problematic if one focuses more on an autobiography's origin than on its destination: more on the author than on the reader. The reason is that meaning is not, properly speaking, either inherent to an event or conferred upon it solely by the autobiographer, for the reader also intervenes in its construction. So, what is at play here is a kind of displacement of authority, from author and text to reader and his/her interpretation of the same text. Such an interpretation is framed by the reader's own lived experience, including, in some cases (see the references to Cervantes's Ginés de Pasamonte, below) the experience of reading autobiographical texts and reflecting upon their claims to truth. In short, despite the commonplace claims to historical truthfulness in the autobiographies of early modern Spain—claims which sought to confer legitimacy and plausibility to those narratives—a writer such as Cervantes leaves little doubt that history becomes intelligible through narrative, i.e., in the form of a story. And a story always has a focus; it is told from one or more perspectives, through the use of one or more voices. Now one can argue that in autobiography perpectivism is restricted to the "I'(s)" of an author/narrator, in an autobiographical contract which also incorporates the actor and reader. For Cervantes, however, the structural limitations of such a narrative are made clear: they are dealt with in his discussions of the nature of picaresque autobiographic *Lives*, in the manner in which he addresses their deficiencies along structural and philosophical lines.

It is in *Don Quijote* (I, 22), in the story of the galley slave, Ginés de Pasamonte, that Cervantes begins to tackle

directly intertextual issues connected to picaresque autobiographic *Lives*. The reader is made to witness an exchange
between an aging rural *hidalgo* who has sallied forth in
imitation of the knights errant of books of chivalry—particularly *Amadís de Gaula*—and a roguish galley slave
who purports to have penned the story of his own life in
the tradition of those new literary heroes—the *pícaros*—
who, around 1600, had captured the imagination of the
Spanish urban reading public. A dramatic point to emerge
from the exchange between don Quijote and Ginés revolves around the concept of narrative as it underscores a
distinction between life and literature, history and story. Of
the two interlocutors, it is Ginés who has reflected on the
strategy of story-telling and most especially on the distinction between lived experience and the conscious reading of
that experience as a prelude to the construction of a narrative. His *Life*—we are told—is unfinished, for it deals se-
quentially with episodes spanning a time frame that begins
with his birth and stops at the moment when he was last
in jail where he has left his autobiography pawned for two
hundred ducats. Similarly, after telling don Quijote that he
could not have finished writing his story since he is still
alive, he admits, playfully, that he can easily bring it to
closure on his return trip to jail, for, after all, he knows the
end by heart ("me lo sé de coro"). And this is precisely the
point: he can write the end of his story because he has been
able to conceptualize it. Moreover, that conceptualization
does not assume a confessional tone; the story is not told
from the standpoint of a spiritual awakening—from the
perspective of one who has apologies to make for a life of
crime and sin. In fact Ginés's written account of his life
remains unpublished, so that, unlike the *Lives* of
Lazarillo, Guzmán and others of the "genre," his *Life* does
not reach the public domain in printed form. Yet, while
readers of *Don Quijote* must fill in the volume of gaps and
silences in Ginés's story, there is never any doubt as to the
general directions of the galley slave's story or the masterful conversion of his picaresque experiences—including
those obtained through the mediation of reading—into
narrative.

The same Ginés is made to reappear in the second part of *Don Quijote* in the guise of a puppet master, playing yet another role in the constant game of wit and survival. Ginés the "writer" has moved on to new constructions; he roams the inns and country roads of La Mancha in search of audiences for his theatrical productions. He is, after all, a creator of fictions and his world, however socially confined, is (re)structured by poetry and imagination. In a sense one could argue along similar lines in reference to another of Cervantes's imaginative creatures, Pedro de Urdemalas, the consummate actor/director who constructs for himself a series of otherwise unattainable social roles through the world of the theatre. Pedro the artist is not unlike Ginés: both are highly aware of their social limitations within the framework of an estatist system; of their inherited place in a society that is still highly stratified and which, around 1600, when the monarchical-seigneurial segments of society perceive a potential for displacement of authority, rank, status and power, undergoes a process of "refeudalization" (José A. Maravall, *Culture of the Baroque*). In both cases, the reader is confronted with stories that go against the grain. Ginés's account tests the literary and social conventions of picaresque autobiographic narratives—especially the kind in which a reformed *pícaro* offers his life-history as an example not to be followed—the type which propagates the official institutional position that an individual is capable of salvation within one's own inherited social role. Unlike those stories, Pedro's *Life*—which is inscribed within the framework of a play—highlights the power of an individual's imagination: the creation of multiple roles through the medium and language of theatre.

While one might agree with Gusdorf's subtle suggestion that autobiography is a kind of mirror in which the individual can view his/her own unfinished image or "diagram of a destiny" (40, 47), one must also wonder with Cervantes as to the reliability of that image. As Ruth El Saffar indicates in this volume, Cervantes's characters arrive at a discovery of the self through the story of the other. Those stories are usually related orally, thus allowing for immediate clarification and response from the audience. This kind of dialogue was absent from picaresque autobiographic *Lives* and, as Carlos Blanco Aguinaga was able to show some thirty years ago ("Cervantes y la picaresca"), that absence struck at the very heart of Cervantes's reservations about the picaresque "autobiographic" genre. It is well known that Cervantes's *El Coloquio de los perros* (*The Dialogue of the Dogs*), a story inscribed within the framework of another exemplary novel—*El casamiento engañoso* (*The Deceitful Marriage*)—provides a biting criticism of the structure of picaresque *Lives*—especially the kind initiated by *Guzmán de Alfarache*. That criticism, which is aimed at the limited and singular perspective from which those stories are told and which rejects all attempts to totalize experience, is carried out through the use of multiple narrators and readers. In the end, Cervantes's point becomes quite clear: to write an autobiography, to attempt "to give the meaning of [one's] own mythic tale" (Gusdorf 48) is to struggle with one's own shadow. To grasp the significance of one's own life it is necessary to engage in dialogue. Cervantes was quite aware of the dilemma that such a dialogue entailed for both the autobiographer and for readers of his or her fiction.

Some of the problems connected with a reader's textual interpretation are tackled perceptively by Jorge Lozano who argues that it is subjected not only to the *recuperation* of the semantic information that the text possesses, but also to the *introduction* of all those "elements" included into what he calls textual competence: from the socio-cultural and "ideological" assumption, to the systems of beliefs, the structures of passions, to what Umberto Eco called *sub-codes* (Lozano 27). Here it may be useful to recall a notion advanced by Eco, for whom the recognition of a topic is akin to proposing a hypothesis about a certain textual regularity. It is that regularity that fixes both the limits and the conditions of textual coherence. The reader (the Model Reader, in Eco's case) can reconstruct the topic in certain circumstances because it is indicated explicitly (the title, etc.) while in others the reader has to look for it in keywords (reiteration and the *dispositio*). The difficulty resides in that there is not only one topic, so that the reader must distinguish between *oration topics, discursive topics, narrative topics,* and the *macrotopic* that includes them all. Ultimately, it is important to remember that to speak of coherence when one speaks of discourse is to speak of isotopy. Hence for Eco the recognition of the topic allows for a series of semantic amalgams that establish a determined level of meaning or isotopy. The difference between the two concepts resides in the fact that isotopy is a semantic phenomenon, whereas the topic is a pragmatic one. The notion of autobiography is related to these two different modalities.

One of the first theorists of autobiography to deal with these issues was Philippe Lejeune. And while his positions have been criticized in many respects, we find it useful to refer to them in order to articulate our own proposals. We will begin with his definition of autobiography as: "A retrospective account in prose that a real person makes of his own existence stressing his individual life and especially the history of his personality."[4]

This definition relates elements that belong to four distinct categories:

1. Form of the language: a) narrative; b) in prose.
2. Topic or subject: a) individual life; b) history of a personality.
3. The author's situation: the author (whose name designates a real person) and the narrator are identical.
4. Position of the narrator: a) the narrator and the main character are identical; b) retrospective perspective of the narrative.

The absence of any of the aforementioned elements separates autobiography from a number of related genres: memoirs (point 2); biography (4a); personal story (3); autobiographical poem (1b); diary (4b); self-portrait or essay (1a and 4b). These genres are related to autobiography but do not combine all of the conditions outlined in Lejeune's four categories. Such is the case, for example, with the autobiographical poem which is banished from the realm of autobiography proper because it is written in verse form rather than in prose. Such an exclusion is somewhat extreme and, in a more recent publication (*Moi aussi* 27), the author has sought to modify, however slightly, his earlier position.[5]

For autobiography to be possible, according to Lejeune, there has to be an identity between author, narrator and main character, and it is here that problems arise. In the first place, the identity between narrator and main character is usually indicated by the use of the first person (what Genette, appropriating the terminology of cinematographic semiology, calls *autodiegetic* narration [*Figures, III,* 72]) This criterion for identification functions on the level of the linguistic utterance strictly-intended. It is a *grammatical* identity. The relation to the author puts into play the possibility of identifying the *real* individuals to which the utterance refers. We are at the level of the enunciation on one side and History on the other. The problem of the author—which is obvious in the case of autobiography, hidden in works of *fiction,* but present in all other circumstances—compels one to disassociate the problem of the grammatical person from the one posed by *identity.*

At this point, Lejeune, claiming Benveniste's definition of the personal forms of the pronoun, defines its articulation on the *referential* level as well as on the level of *utterance*:

> a) Reference: The personal pronouns (I/you) have reference only within a discourse, in the very act of the utterance... There is no concept 'I.' 'I' refers, each time it is used, to the individual who is speaking and who is identified *by the very fact* of his speaking.

> b) Utterance: the personal pronouns of the first person express *identity* of the subject of the speech act ("énonciation") and the subject of the utterance ("énoncé").[6]

While the utterance refers to the enunciation, the enunciation is not the ultimate reference point. The identity between the two, which in oral language is resolved simultaneously with the reception of the linguistic message, is carried out in the case of the written text by means of referents external to its own linguistic discourse (graphological traits, vocabulary, etc.). If we accept them as integral parts of a referential and deciphering code, it is to the extent that such a code had been established before the occurrence of the discourse. Person and discourse merge and identify in an intermediate space: the proper name. The reiteration of technical traits in texts that appeared under the same proper name will elaborate the referential code which identifies the subject of the utterance and the subject of the enunciation in the author's discourse. However, it is commonly accepted that such fiction (such proper name) refers to a *real person*, who is physically and historically localizable, and while in reality it is common to fuse both levels, from a theoretical point of view it is essential to keep this dichotomy, inasmuch as the actual problem at stake is based on it. The author (at times *proper name*, at times *anonymous*) is not a concept either, but a function. Such a function often indicates a real, socially-responsible person, as producer of a given discourse while, in fact, it is the discourse that produces that person in the role of *author*.

If the fusion of the dichotomous elements mentioned is carried out in the social practice of reading, it is not for theoretical reasons, but for reasons of convention through a (subconscious) contract in reading. This *contract*, whose point of departure appears to be imposed by logical reasoning (texts *are* written *by* someone), presupposes another kind of relationship which is neither logical nor correct in the absolute. This second type of relationship, in making an individual responsible for the production of the discourse, transforms such discourse (the discourse of *one* individual) into the language of an "I," which is now understood as entity (concept), rather than what it really is, a function. In short, it takes for granted the already widely accepted conception of the "I" as a construct of language.[7]

One of the forms that such a contract adopts is defined by Lejeune as "the affirmation in the text of the identity of the three elements... author, narrator, character, finally referring to the author's name on the book cover" (26). It is an *autobiographical* contract which differs substantially from another kind, the *novelistic*, where an author, from the very beginning of his narrative, either identifies it as a novel, inscribing the term as such under the title, or manages to mark in other ways his distance or separation from his character and from what his character tells (as in the case of Francisco de Quevedo's *Buscón*).

While thus far we have been speaking of *identity*, we have left pending another problem of equal importance, that of *resemblance*. If the former belongs to the level of the enunciation, the latter can be included on the level of the utterance. Both terms are used by Lejeune to differentiate biography from autobiography. Whereas in the former, fidelity (problem of *resemblance*) supports identity, in the latter it is identity that provides the basis for *resemblance*. In any case the final verosimilitude derives neither from the so-called *autobiographical contract* nor from the *novelistic* one; rather it surfaces from the *referential*, so called because it refers to those texts needing an extratextual referent, one to whose *verification* they must submit themselves in order to be accepted. The *referential contract* thus works for texts that are explicitly not fictitious; texts that intend to bring information close to a "reality" that is external to the textual space.

As a variant of the *autobiographical contract* (and therefore within a non-fictional textuality) Lejeune speaks eventually of a *phantasmatic* contract, one which without directly proposing the identity between author, narrator, and main character suggests the reading of the fictional as *phantoms* that reveal a concrete individual: the author. In Lejeune's exposition, *autobiographical, referential* a n d *phantasmatic contract* would differ from the *novelistic contract* in light of the fictional character of the latter.

While Lejeune has refined his initial requirements for authentic autobiography, he has continued to insist on the question of identity between author, narrator and main character, even while granting that the use of *other persons* is not alien to autobiography.[8] Armed with Emile Benveniste's studies as a starting point, he seeks to get at the identity that is hidden behind the "I": "That the 'I' refers to the act of speaking cannot be denied: but the speech act is not the last term of reference: it raises, in turn, a problem of identity which, in the case of direct oral communication, we resolve instinctively from extra-linguistic givens."[9]

In written communication the problem is much more complex, and the function of the personal, the possessive and the demonstrative pronouns consists in the fact that they refer to a noun, or to an entity that is susceptible to being designated by a noun that allows us to solve the problem of identity. Lejeune further develops the two following propositions: a) "The personal pronoun 'I' refers to the utterer at the moment of speech (*l'instance de discours*) in which the 'I' plays a role, but this utterer is himself susceptible of being designated by a name (whether a common name determined in different ways or a proper name)" and b) "The opposition *concept/no concept* acquires its meaning from the opposition of the common name and the proper name (not from a common name and the personal pronoun)."[10]

Here we find a critique of Benveniste, who indicates very well the function of the "I." According to Lejeune, Benveniste forgets its articulation for the lexical category of proper names: "It is in the *proper name* that person and discourse articulate themselves even before they are articulated in the first-person, as shown by the order of acquisition of language by children."[11] By contrast,

> In printed texts, all utterance is assumed by a person who is accustomed to placing his *name* on the cover of a book and on the inside page, above or below the volume's title. It is in that name that is summarized the existence of what one calls the *author*: it is the only mark in the text of an undoubtable outer-text, referring to a real person who thus asks that in the last instance we attribute to him the responsibility of the enunciation of all the written text. In many instances, the author's presence in the text is reduced to this name only. But the place assigned to this name is crucial: by social convention it is connected with the accepting of responsibility of a *real person*."[12]

In the case of authors of autobiographies in early modern Spain, it often happens that the *civil* existence of a real person behind the proper name is not always easily ascertainable, even if there are extra-textual elements to presuppose it. That is, the existence of a proper name can not always assure us that a real person exists behind the mask of discourse. It is a question of homonymy, not of identity. Thus the appearance of the name of the author within the text is not crucial, although it functions as a kind of signature within a typology of forms of repetition (Derrida 389) that would confirm the identity author=narrator=main character in the text.[13] The difference between what is inside and what is outside of the text is thus eliminated; the opposition fiction-reality is resolved in favor of the latter thanks to the presence of the proper name in the text.

Beginning with his definition of what constitutes an autobiographical contract, Lejeune classified all possible cases on the basis of two criteria, the relationship between the name of the character and the author's name, and the nature of the contract established by the author. In the texts considered to be autobiographical in early modern Spain, the *autobiographical contract* is established explicitly from within the text. Moreover, when the character's name equals the author's name, the consequences of this equivalence are enormous, since: "This fact alone excludes the possibility of fiction. Even if the account is completely false, historically, it will be in the order of a lie (which is an 'autobiographical' category rather than [a category] of fiction.)"[14] According to these arguments, even if the story can be put into question, the signature guarantees the identity, that is, it eliminates any vestiges of fiction.

There are problems with Lejeune's thesis, and if we have dwelled on it extensively it is because much of the work done on Spanish autobiography in recent years has given Lejeune what amounts to phantasmatic status.[15] In the next few paragraphs we shall first try to illustrate the kinds of limitations inherent in Lejeune's autobiographical contract by exploring the case of *La vida y hechos de Estebanillo González, hombre de buen humor, compuesto por él mesmo* (1646) (*The Life and Deeds of Stevie González, Man of Good Humor, Composed by Himself*). Subsequently, we shall refocus on the problem of identity from the perspective of psychoanalysis.

To begin, the *Vida y hechos* presents itself to the reader in an ironic way. On the one hand it establishes a clear identification between author, narrator and main character, a characteristic displayed not only in the title itself and in the dedication to the famous general Ottavio Piccolomini, but also in the amoral perspective which informs and shapes the narrative. On the other hand, the attempt to forge an autobiographical contract exposes itself to a potential questioning at the same moment in which *El libro de [la] vida* of Esteban González (The book of Estebanillo's life) inserts itself polemically in the problematic of picaresque narratives. Conversely, in a paradoxical way, at the very moment that Estebanillo's *Vida y hechos* comes closest to the picaresque genre, one notices an attempt to detach itself from it:

> Mine is not the feigned [life] of Guzmán de Alfarache, nor the fabulous [life] of Lazarillo de Tormes, nor the supposed [life] of the Knight of Pincers, but a *truthful relation*, duly documented, seen by eyewitnesses, and attested by others, all of whom I mention by name so that the veracity of my happenings may be ascertained and proven; and [I mention] where, how, and when [such happenings took place] without omitting anything but day, month, and year; and I take away from my account rather than adding to it.

> [Mi vida] no es la fingida de Guzmán de Alfarache, ni la fabulosa de Lazarillo de Tormes, ni la supuesta del Caballero de la Tenaza, sino una *relación verdadera* con parte presente y testigos de vista y contestes, que los nombro a todos para averiguación y prueba de mis sucesos y el dónde, cómo y cuándo, sin carecer de otra cosa que de día, mes y año, y antes quito que no añado. (Eds. N. Spadaccini and A.N. Zahareas I, 133-134)

Mindful of the textual tradition within which he is operating, the clownish narrator playfully warns the "dearest or very cheap reader" ("carísimo o muy barato lector") that his *Vida* is different from those others, since the events narrated in it refer to facts experienced out of the text and are, according to him, ascertainable. Following the model of his Cervantean predecessor—the galley slave Ginés de Pasamonte—the good humored Estebanillo defends his *Vida*'s verisimilitude, that is, the internal truth of the narrative. At the same time he underlines the extrinsic truth of the narrated facts, referring the contemporary reader to a series of sources and witnesses, among them, many of the best-known figures of the Thirty Years' War and most especially those connected to the political interests of the Hapburgs. The *pícaro*-buffoon's *Vida y hechos* lacks a confessional tone and defines itself as a book of jests given to print: "for the expressed purpose of regaling princes, noblemen and people worthy of [social] esteem" ("para que sirva de presente y regalo a los príncipes y señores y personas de merecimiento" [135]).

That is, this picaresque *Vida* lacks doctrinal pretension *(Guzmán)* or stoic or class moralities *(Buscón)* and is published with the mere pretext of entertaining some aristocrats with the memories of a good-humored man who was able to survive in the midst of war thanks to his role as clown. In exchange for the book, the writer expects protection and favor ("amparo y favor"): the protection and money needed to abandon his ignominious buffoonery and enjoy a carefree retirement through the management of a bordello-gambling house ("casa de conversación") in Naples.

Despite his expressed intention to address the *Vida y hechos* to the Flemish aristocracy,[16] the narrator seems to point to the potential autonomy of the text and to its interpretative possibilities by different types of readers (Spadaccini, "La picaresca y el lector"). Thus, the reading subject of Estebanillo's *Vida y hechos* is not conceived merely in terms of a "class" or social group, or as an individual submitted to good or evil. The narrator intends to address his narrative to a concrete reader, although it becomes clear that this project is not carried out in the mimesis of the story. Unlike Cervantes, who offers a true archeology of possible readings (especially if one takes *Don Quijote* into account), in *Estebanillo* one does not get beyond some kind of psycho-social taxonomy:

> The *curious* reader will find here witty sayings; the
> *soldier*, pitched battles and voyages to the Orient;

the *lover*, love entanglements; the [reader] with a
happy disposition, a diversity of jokes and a variety
of pranks; the *melancholy* one, funereal epitaphs
and details of the untimely deaths of the Cardenal
Infante, the Queen of Spain, and the Empress María;
the *poet*, new compositions and humorous ballads;
the *cloistered* [reader will learn of] cardplayers'
tricks, the laws of the underworld, the privileges
[enjoyed by] *pícaros* [who serve] in the tunny fish-
eries, the cunning ways of those who [serve in]
kitchens, the craftiness of sutlers; and, finally, the
prodigious [events] of my life which has had more
twists and turns than the labyrinth of Crete.

Aquí hallará *el curioso* dichos agudos; *el soldado*
batallas campales y viajes a Levante; *el amante*
enredos amorosos; *el alegre* diversidad de chanzas y
variedad de burlas; *el melancólico* epitafios fúnebres
a los tiernos malogros del Cardenal Infante, de la
Reina de España y de la Emperatriz María; *el poeta*
compostura nueva y romances ridículos; *el recogido en
su albergue* las flores de la fullería, las leyes de la
gente del hampa, las preeminencias de los pícaros de
jábega, las astucias de los marmitones, las cautelas
de los vivanderos; y finamente, los prodigios de mi
vida, que ha tenido más vueltas y revueltas que el
laberinto de Creta (Eds. N. Spadaccini and A.N.
Zahareas I, 136).

In *Estebanillo*, the reader is conceived of in terms of
several receptive categories: mental vividness and desire
to know; sentimental situation; psychological disposition
and literary predilections; and finally, the mental and
physical space from which the cloistered reader or
"recogido en su albergue" approaches those episodes of his
Vida y hechos connecting with his picaresque adventures
and buffoon-like prodigies.

It is precisely this last type of reader for whom Estebanillo's narrative alleges a special function (Spadaccini, "La
picaresca y el lector"): as mediator of experiences that the
reader would not otherwise be able to obtain. The *pícaro-*
buffoon of the *Vida y hechos* projects himself as instrument and mediator of special kinds of knowledge.
Through his *Vida y hechos*, the reader gains access to certain social spaces which would otherwise have remained

unknown. The text makes it possible for the reader to know those who move in other social spheres, together with their languages and discourses, their motivations, worries, and *modus operandi*. If for this ideal reader the narrated prodigies of the *pícaro*-buffoon's life offer themselves as substitute for direct experience, it is perhaps for the sake of a more complete social perspective, even if the latter is never totalized (see Godzich and Spadaccini, "Experiencia y novela"). In this sense *Estebanillo González's* picaresque discourse incorporates aspects of Cervantes's critique of *Guzmán de Alfarache* (1599; 1604)—let us recall at this point that every attempt to totalize experience is put into question in *Don Quijote* (1605; 1615) and that, as far as the picaresque narratives are concerned, this critique is carried out explicitly in the *Coloquio de los perros* (1613).

In Estebanillo's *Vida y hechos* the proper name, the identity between author, narrator and main character is tantamount to what might be considered a rhetorical construct. Ultimately what stands out is a preoccupation for the narrative's internal truth, even while the narrator shows interest in constantly reaffirming the veracity of some historical happenings, especially the ones that refer to certain events, places and figures connected with episodes of the Thirty Years' War. His playful advice to the reader that his *Vida* is neither "feigned" (*fingida*) nor "fabulous" (*fabulosa*), nor "supposed" (*supuesta*), like the *Lives* of the other *pícaros*, but, rather, "truthful" ("*verdadera*"), functions as an orientational signal for the active receiver whose task is to build an imaginary world on the basis of the indications contained in the text. It is for this reason that throughout the narrative attention is called to the structural and ideological similarities and differences between the jester's *Vida y hechos* and those first-person picaresque narratives (some of them authentic bestsellers) that had caught the attention of readers for half a century. Moreover, while the allusions to those picaresque *Lives* are multiple, it is clear that other genres and models are also incorporated in Estebanillo's *Vida y hechos*: soldiers' *Lives*, the archetype of the buffoon, books of travel, lowly ballads, the *moria* tradition, Neo-Platonic poetry, Gongorist poetry, mural poetry, the folkloric tale, etc. That is, while masquerading as an authentic autobiography, Estebanillo's *Vida y hechos* is a hybrid text that widens the world of the *pícaro* and expands his spheres of operation; at the same time it is a text that manages to distance itself from those picaresque *Lives* that seek to totalize experience for readers.

Estebanillo's readers are not instructed or advised on how to read or interpret the various discourses that are incorporated in the *Vida y hechos*. The narrator limits himself to saying that jokes are mixed with truths. Those truths, however, are not defined in metaphysical terms. Rather they deal with the *pícaro*-buffoon's reflections on the dynamics of the war and the task of surviving in its midst. The recollected happenings of his *Vida y hechos* remind the implied reader (the "recogido en su albergue") that Estebanillo's function as narrator is not to preach about good and evil; that, while the reading of his *Vida y hechos* might be undertaken with the notion of gaining experience that would not be possible otherwise, this mediated experience is partial and, as such, requires a coherence attainable only within the sphere of critical, constructive reading (Todorov, "Reading as Construction"), one through which the reader transforms the universe evoked by the narrator. If it is true that the text itself intends to guides the reception of its individual parts and of the whole, it is never a question of an explicit attempt to totalize experience, as in *Guzmán de Alfarache's* case.

The best way to invent an identity through writing is to *say* that one is narrating one's own life. What bestows upon it an appearance of reality is not the story that is being narrated but the *act* of narrating it: "When I write my autobiography, even if I make an honest effort to stick to the truth, I sense well that it is my writing which gives consistency to my life."[17] In some ways Descartes's maxim *Cogito, ergo sum* could be paraphrased to apply to autobiographers: I write about myself, therefore I am.

While the processes described thus far have had a linguistic conception as a starting point, we would now like to suggest up to what point this process is valid from another field that questions the notion of the subject: psychoanalysis. Jorge E. Jinkis ("Una distinción tópica; el sujeto de la enunciación y el yo del discurso" 26) argues that "the I of the discourse names in the enunciated the subject of the enunciation. But what is this I of the discourse that psychoanalytic theory—the Freudian and the Lacanian— shows as not coinciding with the subject of the enunciation.... Said in another way, who speaks when someone speaks? And before that, why who speaks rather than what speaks?"[18] In asking this question psychoanalytic theory is carrying out a fracture between the "I" of the discourse and the subject of the enunciation which would radically change the presupposition upon which the autobiographical contract is settled, at least in the way we have been describing it here.

According to Jacques Lacan, once the linguistic structure is recognized in the unconscious, one should wonder about what kind of subject we can conceive for it:

> We can try, with methodological rigor, to set out from the strictly linguistic definition of the I as signifier, in which there is nothing but the "shifter" or indicative, which, in the subject of the statement, designates the subject in the sense that he is now speaking. That is to say, it designates the subject of the enunciation, but it does not signify it. This is apparent from the fact that every signifier of the subject of the enunciation may be lacking in the statement, not to mention the fact that there are those that differ from the I, and not only what is inadequately called the cases of the first person singular, even if one added its accommodation in the plural invocation, or even in the Self (Soi) of auto-suggestion.

Jinkis argues that with this statement Lacan asks himself: who is the I that says I? Thus revealing the place where the deception is produced:

> If we say that the I does not refer either to a concept or to an individual, but to discourse (in which it precisely designates the speaker), we are referring to the place where a double deception occurs and which is a condition for the appearance of truth: the dialogic situation, which is an unequivocal term in Lacan, and as far as it is possible to imagine from

everything that the liberal and empiricist tradition evokes in us. [...] This condition presupposes an I and an Other, or in other terms of discourse, an *I* and a *you*. [...] *Thus discourse presupposes this dialogic situation, asymmetric polarity, reversible, constitutive of the subject.*[19]

The difference between fiction and non-fiction is located in the pragmatic effect on the reader and is never an inner quality of the narrative itself. The ambiguity which is implied in the co-presence in the text of a grammatical "I," a (supposed) psychological "I," and a physical "I" cannot be dissolved through a key concept like the proper name, as Lejeune proposes. In effect, as Saraha wrote in the poem which opens this introductory essay, "[proper names] are only designations, denominations, conceptual terms of the usual appellations—simple names. There is not a real person behind them." The use of their existence as marks of authorship is only a *reading contract* imposed in every historical circumstance under different forms to be sure, but always present as contract. This contract tries to hide the fact that what is personal—the "I"—has access to language only if it dissolves itself in the impersonality of History as process and discourse. All text is, in this sense, (auto)biographical: it does not relate the inner life of anybody; it tells of one's inscription as absence in the stream of a discourse that does not belong to anyone. It is precisely this irreducible and radical difference (that is to say, this dialectical relationship) between reality and discourse about reality, between lived History and Language, which allows us to show the ideological character of artistic practices and to analyze their insertion in History as Discourse, where fiction and non-fiction have the same status because even if we think that its referent is exterior to Discourse we can never find it outside of Discourse. To that extent, we cannot escape autobiography.

* * * * *

The reader will no doubt notice that the essays included in this volume analyze in the same critical space, what traditionally has been called literature (Friedman, El Saffar and Talens), what used to be understood as non-fiction narrative (Mariscal, Dust, Levisi, Reed) and what attempts to establish a bridge between both (Zahareas).

Antonio Gómez-Moriana deals with the dialogic relationship between text and history, between narration and argumentation based on the analysis of a "functional" form of autobiography, the *curriculum vitae.* George Mariscal uses Francesillo de Zúñiga's *Crónica burlesca* to study the ways used by certain forms of textual subjectivity to become a kind of variant of autobiography even though their structures did not assume the rules accepted nowadays to define autobiography, history or memoirs. Patrick Dust establishes the possibility of a new approach to Santa Teresa's autobiography, in a productive dialog with deconstructive methodology.

Margarita Levisi and Helen H. Reed take up what is essentially the same question, how "History" becomes "story," but from different perspectives: Levisi focuses on common people (soldiers such as Jerónimo de Pasamonte, Alonso de Contreras, Miguel de Castro and others) while Reed deals with the autobiographical account of a politician who has fallen from grace from the height of power (Antonio Pérez). In both cases History, or the real foreground of the plot, is ultimately dissolved to allow the appearance of the inner world of the writer, who often looks more toward an understanding and an explanation of the self than toward an understanding of circumstantial reality.

Edward Friedman and Anthony N. Zahareas move toward the other direction: how "story" becomes "History." In both instances their approaches are anchored in the analysis of the tradition of picaresque narratives. Friedman tries to demonstrate how this displacement is historically and literally made, unifying in the same discourse of autobiographical impulse both confession (confessional literature) and the self-consciousness (and self-confidence) of the narrating subject. Zahareas shows how fiction (picaresque novels) and reality (autobiographies of social offenders) share the same conceptions and structures, and, consequently, may be analyzed mutually.

Ruth El Saffar examines the presence of the Other as a way to construct the narrative world from a fragmented "I." Dealing with Cervantes's work as a whole, El Saffar argues that it is possible to find in it signs of the feminine. Finally, Talens's essay attempts to develop a hypothesis for reading Cervantes's lyric discourse as a hidden and fragmented way of writing the biography of an "I" inscribed as absence and opacity. The Appendix that follows the last essay is a transcription, with English translation, of a *curriculum vitae* of Cervantes who not by chance, is the author most often quoted in these pages. Cervantes's writing anticipates many of the modern discussions on the theory and practice of autobiography.

NOTES

[1] "referido a un sujeto que manifiesta expresar sus opiniones, puntos de vista, referir una experiencia o unos acontecimientos respecto a sí mismo." (Lozano and Peña-Marín 93)

[2] Trans. Harriet de Onís. Woodbury, New York: Barron's Educational Series, 1959. xviii.
"Parescióme no tomalle por el medio, sino del principio, porque se tenga entera noticia de mi persona; y también porque consideren los que heredaron nobles estados cuán poco se les debe, pues Fortuna fue con ellos parcial, y cuánto más hicieron los que, siéndoles contraria, con fuerza y maña remando salieron a buen puerto." (Ed. Francisco Rico 10-11)

[3] Ernest Renan wrote that Goethe "chooses, as title of his Memoirs, *Truth and Poetry*, thereby showing that one cannot compose his own biography in the same way one would do a biography of others [for] what one says of oneself is always poetry [...] One writes of such things in order to transmit to others the world view that one carries in oneself." (Cited by Gusdorf 42)

4 "Récit rétrospectif en prose qu'une personne réelle fait de sa propre existence, lorsqu'elle met l'accent sur sa vie individuelle, en particulier sur l'histoire de sa personnalité." (14)

5 "As far as verses, properly speaking, my attitude was dictated by a very simple observation: while there exist thousands of 'autobiographies' [written] 'in prose,' one counts on the fingers of one hand autobiographies written in verse, if one understands by autobiography an account that sums up a life: Wordsworth, always cited for the *Prelude* (where the subtitle is 'An Autobiographical Poem'), Hugo with the *Contemplations*, Aragon with the *Roman inachevé*. Thereafter, it is true, I found some others, naive or sophisticated, but that does not go beyond the fingers of both hands." (27)

"Quant aux vers proprement dits, mon attitude était dictée par une constatation toute simple: alors qu'il existe des milliers d'autobiographies «en prose», on compte sur les doigts d'une main les autobiographies en vers, si l'on entend para «autobiographie» un récit qui récapitule une vie: Wordsworth, toujours cité pour le *Prélude* (dont le sous-titre est «An Autobiographical Poem»), Hugo avec *les Contemplations*, Aragon avec *le Roman inachevé* Depuis, il est vrai, j'en ai rencontré quelques autres, naïves ou sophistiquées, mais ça ne dépasse pas les doigts des deux mains."

6 In this case we cite from R. Carter's translation, "The Autobiographical Contract," *French Literary Theory Today*. Ed. Tzvetan Todorov. Cambridge: Cambridge University Press, 1982. 197.

7 See especially Michel Foucault, "What is an Author?" *Language, Counter-Memory, Practice*. Ed. Donald F. Bouchard. Ithaca: Cornell University Press, 1977. 113-138; Roland Barthes, "The Death of the Author," *The Rustle of Language*. Trans. Richard Howard. New York: Hill and Wang, Inc., 1986. 49-55; and, of course Benveniste and Lacan.

8 "the procedure sometimes appears in a fleeting way in some discourses which the narrator addresses the character that he was, be it to render him comfort if he is in a bad situation, or to preach to him or to repudiate him. From there to an account there is, to be sure, a distance but it is possible. This type of account would manifest clearly, on the level of the enunciation, the difference between the subject of the enunciation and the subject of the enunciated taken as a receiver of the account."

"le procédé apparaît parfois de manière fugitive dans des *discours* que le narrateur adresse au personnage qu'il fut, soit pour le réconforter s'il est en mauvaise posture, soit pour le sermonner ou le répudier. De là à un récit, il y a une distance, certes, mais la chose est possible. Ce type de récit manifesterait clairement, au niveau de l'énonciation, la différence du sujet de l'énonciation et du sujet de l'énoncé traité comme destinataire du récit." (*Le pacte* 17)

[9] "Que le «je» renvoie à l'énonciation, nul ne songe à le nier: mais l'énonciation n'est pas le terme dernier de la référence: elle pose à son tour un problème d'*identité*, que, dans le cas de la communication orale directe, nous résolvons instictivement à partir de données extra-linguistiques." (*Le pacte* 21)

[10] "a) Le pronom personnel «je» renvoie à l'énonciateur de l'instance de discours où figure le «je»; mais cet énonciateur est lui-même susceptible d'être désigné par un nom (qu'il s'agisse d'un nom commun déterminé de différentes manières ou d'un nom propre).
b) L'opposition *concept /pas de concept* prend son sens dans l'opposition du nom commun et du nom propre (non pas du nom commun et du pronom personnel.") (*Le pacte* 21)

[11] "C'est dans le *nom propre*, que personne et discours s'articulent avant même de s'articuler dans la première personne, comme le montre l'ordre d'acquisition du langage par les enfants." (*Le pacte* 22)

[12] "Dans les textes imprimés, toute l'énonciation est prise en charge par une personne qui a coutume de placer son *nom* sur la couverture du livre, et sur la page de garde, au-dessus ou au-dessous du titre du volume. C'est dans ce nom que se résume toute l'éxistence de ce qu'on appelle l'*auteur*: seule marque dans le texte d'un indubitable hors-texte, renvoyant à une personne réelle, qui demande ainsi qu'on lui attribue, en dernier ressort, la responsabilité de l'énonciation de tout le texte écrit. Dans beaucoup de cas, la présence de l'auteur dans le texte se réduit à ce seul nom. Mais la place assignée à ce nom est capitale: elle est liée, par une convention sociale, à l'engagement de responsabilité d'une *personne réelle*." (*Le pacte* 23)

[13] This is exactly what the autobiographical contract represents for Lejeune: "The autobiographical contract is the affirmation within the text of this identity [author=narrator=main character], referring in the last analysis to the name of the author on the cover."

"Le pacte autobiographique c'est la affirmation dans le texte de cette identité, renvoyant en dernier ressort au *nom* de l'auteur sur la couverture." (*Le pacte* 26)

14 "Ce seul fait exclut la possibilité de la fiction. Même si le récit est, historiquement, complètement faux, il sera de l'ordre du *mensonge* (qui est une catégorie «autobiographique» et non de la fiction.)" (*Le pacte* 30)

15 See, for example, *L'Autobiographie dans le Monde Hispanique.* (Actes du Colloque International de la Baume-lès-Aix, mai 1979). Aix-en-Provence: Univ. de Provence, 1980; and *L'autobiographie en Espagne* (Actes du IIe Colloque International de la Baume-lès-Aix, mai 1981), Aix-en-Provence: Univ. de Provence, 1982.

16 Bataillon discovered that the first edition was addressed to a very limited audience of nobles. See his "*Estebanillo González,* bouffon 'pour rire.'"

17 "Quand j'écris mon autobiographie, même si honnêtement je m'efforce de coller au vrai, je sens bien que c'est mon écriture qui donne consistance à ma 'vie.' " (Lejeune, *Mois aussi* 53)

18 "el yo del discurso nombra en el enunciado al sujeto de la enunciación. Pero ¿qué es este yo del discurso que la teoría psicoanalítica —la de Freud y Lacan— enseña que no coincide con el sujeto de la enunciación (…). Dicho de otra manera, cuando se habla ¿quién habla? Y antes aún ¿por qué quién habla y no qué habla?"

19 "Si decimos que el yo no remite a un concepto ni a un individuo, sino al discurso (en el que designa precisamente al hablante), estamos haciendo referencia al lugar donde se verifica un doble engaño y que es condición de aparición de la verdad: la situación de diálogo, término inequívoco en Lacan, y tan alejado como sea posible pensarlo de todo lo que en nosotros evoca la tradición liberal y empirista. Cuando preguntamos ¿quién habla?, siempre surge un yo que se precipita en una respuesta que permanece como pregunta y que lo constituye como *yo* . Siempre responde Otro. Esta condición supone un yo y un otro, o en términos de discurso, un *yo* y un *tú*. El *yo* y el *tú* mantienen una relación de oposición que no es idéntica ni simétrica, pero sí complementaria y reversible. *El discurso supone entonces esta situación de diálogo, polaridad asimétrica, reversible, constitutiva del sujeto.*" ("Una distinción tópica" 29-30)

WORKS CITED

Anonymous. *La vida de Lazarillo de Tormes y de sus fortunas y adversidades*. Ed. Francisco Rico. Madrid: Cátedra, 1987.

Anonymous. *La vida y hechos de Estebanillo González, hombre de buen humor, compuesto por él mesmo*. 2 vols. Eds. Nicholas Spadaccini and Anthony N. Zahareas. Madrid: Castalia, 1978.

Barthes, Roland. "An Introduction to the Structural Analysis of Narrative." *New Literary History*, 6 (Winter, 1975): 237-272.

Bataillon, Marcel. "*Estebanillo González*, bouffon 'pour rire'." *Studies in Spanish Literature of the Golden Age, presented to Edward M. Wilson*. Ed. R.O. Jones. London: Tamesis, 1973. 25-44.

Blanco Aguinaga, Carlos. "Cervantes y la picaresca. Notas sobre dos tipos de realismo." *N.R.F.H.*, XI (1957): 315-316.

Benveniste, Emile. *Problèmes de linguistique générale*. Paris: Editions Gallimard, 1966. English title: *Problems in General Linguistics*. Trans. Mary Elizabeth Meek. Coral Gables, Florida: Univ. of Miami Press, 1971.

Cervantes Saavedra, Miguel de. *Don Quijote de la Mancha*. 3 vols. Ed. Luis Murillo. Madrid: Castalia, 1978.

Derrida, Jacques. *Marges de la philosophie*. Paris: Minuit, 1972.

Eco, Umberto. *The Role of the Reader*. Bloomington: Indiana Univ. Press, 1979.

Genette, Gérard. *Figures III*. Paris: Seuil, 1972. Abridged English version: *Narrative Discourse. An Essay in Method*. Trans. Jane E. Lewin. Ithaca, N.Y.: Cornell Univ. Press, 1980.

Godzich, Wlad and Nicholas Spadaccini. "Experiencia y novela: del caballero al pícaro." *Homenaje a José Antonio Maravall*. Madrid: Centro de Investigaciones Sociológicas, 1985. 182-197.

Greimas, A.J and J. Courtés. *Semiotique. Dictionnaire raisonné de la théorie du langage*. Paris: Hachette, 1979.

Gusdorf, Georges. "Conditions and Limits of Autobiography." *Autobiography: Essays Theoretical and Critical*. Ed. and Trans. James Olney. Princeton: Princeton Univ. Press, 1980. 28-48.

Jinkis, Jorge E. "Una distinción tópica; el sujeto de la enunciación y el yo del discurso." *Cuadernos Sigmund Freud I: Temas de Jacques Lacan* (Mayo, 1971).

Lacan, Jacques. "Subversion of the Subject and Dialectic of Desire in the Freudian Unconscious." *Ecrits. A Selection.* Trans. Alan Sheridan. New York/London: Norton and Company, 1977. 292-325.

Lejeune, Philippe. *Le pacte autobiographique.* Paris: Seuil, 1975.

———. *Moi Aussi.* Paris: Seuil, 1986.

Lozano, Jorge, Cristina Peña-Marín and Gonzalo Abril. *Análisis del discurso.* Madrid: Cátedra, 1982.

Maravall, José Antonio. *Culture of the Baroque.* Trans. Terry Cochran. Minneapolis: Univ. of Minnesota Press, 1986.

———. *La literatura picaresca desde la historia social.* Madrid: Taurus, 1986.

Spadaccini, Nicholas. "La picaresca y el lector: La estrategia crítica del *Estebanillo González.*" *The Sixth Louisiana Conference on Hispanic Languages and Literatures.* New Orleans, Tulane Univ., February, 1985.

——— and Anthony N. Zahareas, Eds. *La vida y hechos de Estebanillo González, hombre de buen humor. Compuesto por él mesmo.* 2 vols. Madrid: Castalia, 1978.

Todorov, Tzvetan. "Reading as Construction." *The Reader in the Text. Essays on Audience Interpretation.* Eds. Susan R. Suleiman and Inge Crosman. Princeton: Princeton Univ. Press, 1980. 67-82.

CHAPTER 1:
NARRATION AND ARGUMENTATION
IN AUTOBIOGRAPHICAL DISCOURSE

Antonio Gómez-Moriana

(translated by James V. Romano)

Only recently, under the almost simultaneous impact of structuralism, semiotics and Russian formalism, have literary studies focused their attention on principles of textual composition as an organic, structured totality. This new orientation represented an attempt to go beyond the fetishism of the author as creative genius that nourished biographical research as well as historicism, the basis of the traditional search for "sources" and also of the study of the great ideological and social movements. Structuralism, in its violent reaction against any diachronic consideration, isolated the text as if it were dealing with an immanent and autotelic entity, removed from any spatial, temporal or social anchor. Thus, if traditional philology, marked by historicist positivism, closed the road to textual comprehension as a coherent and articulated totality, immanentist structuralism, by ignoring the tradition in which all use of word or pen is inscribed, closed the road to the comprehension of writing as transgression, or at least, as *dialog* with social convention.

The possible dialectical tension between system and event, tradition and act (of writing as well as reading), norm and use, "model" and "rupture," escaped immanentist structuralism, which was unable to account for the historical processes and changes (including those that affect systems and dynamic structures in their temporal forms of realization). With that, structuralism was equally incapacitated to account for the aesthetic effects that the dialectical tension between norm and transgression would produce in any work not limited to the purely mimetic reproduction of a model. Such is the case of irony, of parody, of the complete subversion through (ab)use of culturally marked elements (ritual discourse, for example), as well as for any process of signification based on the dialectic tension between that which the sign means by *itself* and that for which it is taken in a given, alienating use; or between the reserve of its use (sacred, taboo, etc.) and the demystifying profanation of itself; in sum, all use or abuse of what Bakhtin calls "the discourse of the Other."[1] The understanding of this "subversion" requires a two-fold study of the function of the sign: as system and as process. It is from this postulate that I believe I was able to explain in earlier works the text of *Lazarillo de Tormes*, as well as the rise of picaresque autobiography as a genre, parting from the "model" subverted in the confession of Lázaro de Tormes: the autobiographical confessions destined directly or indirectly for the inquisitorial tribunal and carried out by its (direct or indirect) orders.[2] I would venture to say that *Lazarillo* is to the subsequent picaresque what the aforementioned inquisitorial practices are to the *Lazarillo*: a transgressed discursive model. A simultaneously destructive and creative rupture (*Umbau*) thus gives way to a new model generating a whole series of texts, the so-called picaresque novel.

If I insist on the socio-aesthetic dimension of this rupture, it is to establish clearly that the introduction of this dimension is not simply a question of mere historicist pleasure, nor of a return to erudite positivism. More than the pleasure that erudition produces upon revealing the origin of something (a purely historicist pleasure that characterizes the traditional search for sources), the issue here is one of authentic liberation, as much in its effect inscribed in the text itself, as in its "archaeological" reconstruction vis-à-vis the other various discursive practices of that time and in that Spain, all elucidated by the literary investigator. The rupture within the text liberates the reader who is capable of recognizing the "model" put into play, which presumably is distinguishable by its pertaining to the memorizable repertory of everyday experience in the society-frame in which it is written. The anonymous author of the *Lazarillo* and the group of readers that bring together the conditions of its intelligibility as "dialogical space" establish in that way an authentic communication that should carry both writer and reader to the laughter which liberates one from oppression. If I may be permitted this autobiographical confession (in a work on autobiography), the reconstitution of the model and acknowledgement of its own subversion on the part of the studied text, frees the investigator from the ideological oppression of that mystifying culture of a past that was still present during the years of his childhood in Spain. And he hopes that, by communicating the results of his investigation, other victims of that ideological mystification are able to free themselves from its yoke. I believe there is something revolutionary in the text, and something culturally revolutionary—if I may be permitted the expression—in my study of it.

My thesis, then, proposes nothing other than a synthesis of diachrony and synchrony. This synthesis was already attempted by diachronic structuralism, though the results obtained by it fed a literary aestheticism closed to any dialog with the non-literary (and thus, to the socio-aesthetic dimension of this transgression or rupture). I have yet to situate my proposal with respect to this synthesis and its translation into two concepts as far apart in appearance as "narration" and "argumentation" (alerting at the same time against possible reductions of the concept of "model" to the sole model accepted in the recognized *literary* traditions). For that, before anything, we shall have to open the horizon in which the considerations made up to here are inscribed. Such a horizon has remained up to now limited to the paradigmatic and syntagmatic axes, that is, to the relations that the signs maintain between themselves, with that more or less constant tension that exists—especially in literature—between a system of potentialities and that of concrete realizations, what Charles Morris would designate as the "syntactic dimension" of semiosis. What I now propose is that we include the other relations that Morris postulated in his *Foundations of the Theory of Signs* with the dimensions of semiosis: the semantic dimension and the pragmatic one, indispensable complements of the syntactic dimension in any communicative process.

If the inclusion of the semantic dimension obliges us to revise our concept of "literature" (and of art in general) as an autonomous and autotelic entity (common denominator of the schools of diachronic structuralism that coincide in proclaiming their self-referentiality as specific to artistic and literary language), the inclusion of the pragmatic dimension will force us to take into consideration the socio-historical implications of *literary* praxes (including autobiography), at least as an "interdiscursive task." Thus, I oppose those who negate social risk with "Literature" in the name of some *aseitas,* or self-containment, presumably unaware of its continuous dialog with the external world. In other words, I propose that autobiography be studied as a "discourse" among "discourses" of the society that both produces and consumes it, including in the analysis of the autobiographical text the confluence of all those agents of communicative semiosis situated in a given time and society and participating in their circuits of verbal (and non-verbal) interaction.

The consideration of literature as part of the discursive practices of a given society, stripped of all transhistoricity and reduced to a condition of conventional and arbitrary social activity, should lead us to discover, like Jacques Dubois, that "literature does not exist, only specific practices that act in turn upon language and the imaginary" (11). It is this "working on language" that perhaps defines the specificity of literary discourse with respect to the other discursive practices of society that are less playful and, thus, more stable. Perhaps the social function of literature and its fundamental role in the collective imagination resides in the continual testing of its own models and those of the other social practices that Walter Moser calls the "testing of discourses" ("mise à l'essai des discours"). It was this conviction that led me to consider the "discursive model" of the *Lazarillo* instead of searching for historical referents to the characters or social sectors to which the satire is directed, and to break with the traditional framework of "literary models" in order to examine other discursive practices of the society in question. Thus, if by defining the social function of literature as one of "working on language" I concur with the consideration of poetic language as artifice (a consideration shared with New Criticism and the diverse "stylistic" schools of Europe, as with Russian Formalism and its different branches of recent decades), it is not for that reason that I concur with the conception of literary evolution common to them. In reality, the characterization of literary language as transgression is not new. There are rhetorical treatises from all ages that serve as inventories of linguistic anomalies arranged under categories such as "tropes" and "figures." But, even acknowledging the artifice and transgression of norms as basic components of the working of literature on language, I cannot share the consideration, generalized as it is, of the history of literature and its genres (autobiography among them) as the history of "construction," "deconstruction" and "reconstruction" of rhetorical artifices (always the same). Nor can I accept a consequence of this notion, that of the literary work as definable and analyzable simply as a "group of artifices," or the notion of the genres as "specific types" of such groups. The study of the autobiography here proposed cannot be limited to the identification of models in literary traditions that self-feed and interconnect historically, whether through the most faithful mimetic realizations or through the most radical break with them. The issue is one of establishing a dialectical action between the intrinsic and extrinsic in each text through the study of the stimuli of the various areas with which it dialogs. Hence there surfaces a need to establish equivalences and oppositions, as much internal as comparative, with the different textual organizations that situate it in the general text of the culture of which it forms a part, and which in turn forms part of it. The study of the text as *dialogical space*, using Kristeva's expression inspired by Bakhtin, is presented here as an authentic challenge to textual analysis, which will have to come to terms with how a text reads history and is inscribed in it. Furthermore, the literary text is not only a work based on a literary system, which evolves, nor is it solely based on the subsystem or genre to which it may pertain; the literary text works on language itself and on all the practices of interaction, both verbal and non-verbal, artistic and non-artistic, of the society in which it is produced. It is this that I call "interdiscursive working." Its privileged place is in literary practice, especially in the narrative, the genre of which I consider the autobiography a subgenre.

The inclusion of the autobiography in the narrative genre is not as evident as it may seem. By establishing two systems or "two different planes of utterance" ("history" and "discourse") that distribute the tenses of the French verb and, concurrently, the grammatical persons, Emile Benveniste expressly classifies autobiography as discourse, along with "correspondence, memoirs, plays, didactic works, in short, all the genres in which someone addresses himself to someone, proclaims himself as the speaker, and organizes what he says in the category of person" (209). Historical utterance, on the contrary, once defined by the three terms *"narration* of *past events,"* and presently reserved for written language, is now defined as

> the mode of utterance that excludes every "autobiographical" linguistic form. The historian will never say *I* or *you* or *now*, because he will never make use of the formal apparatus of discourse, which resides primarily in the relationship of the persons I : you. Hence we shall find only the forms of the "third person" in a historical narrative strictly followed. (206-207)

For Benveniste, the historical utterance, is characterized as existing in opposition to the autobiographical by the use of the "simple past" or "past definite" (*passé simple,* which Benveniste prefers to call by its Greek name *aorist*), always in third person. The imperfect and the pluperfect are equally historical tenses for Benveniste; the present, on the contrary, is excluded with the exception of a present that Benveniste refers to as "atemporal," as for example the so-called "present of definition."[3] It is this combination of tense and person that characterizes "history," whether it be the evocation of historical events themselves or the invention of a novelist. His statement in this regard is categorical:

> It can be stated as a fact that anyone who knows how to write and who undertakes the narration of past events spontaneously employs the aorist as the fundamental tense, whether he evokes these events as a historian or creates them as a novelist. (210)

On the contrary, the "autobiographical form par excellence" is for Benveniste "the perfect in the first person" (210). He explains that "the perfect creates a living connection between the past event and the present in which its evocation takes place" (210). Thus, if the historical utterance is characterized here as the *objective* presentation of *events,* (real or invented), without intervention from the narrator ("As a matter of fact, there is then no longer even a narrator.... No one speaks here; the events seem to narrate themselves"[4]), then discourse, on the contrary, and with it autobiography, is characterized "by contrast," by its pragmatic situation, by the indispensable presence of speakers, of subject-utterers that make use of word or pen in an attempt to influence in some way their interlocutor or audience. We arrive here at the now classic definition of discourse, as formulated by Benveniste: "every utterance assuming a speaker and a hearer, and in the speaker, the intention of influencing the other in some way" (209).

The distinction established by Benveniste between historical and discursive utterance has as a base the complementary distribution of tenses and persons in the French verb, a distribution that explicates via the establishment of two taxonomic morphosyntactic axes, in contrast to the traditional grammars that established the paradigms of French conjugation based exclusively on a morphological point of view. This distinction nevertheless has been received by critics as a universal one, despite the fact that such a complementary distribution of tense and person does not hold up in other languages. German, as English, uses only the imperfect, the same in written as in spoken language, for the basic reason that it does not know any other simple form of the past; Latin, as Spanish, employs the aorist (indefinite) in the first person, such that there is no temporal difference between narration in the third person and the first. The antonomastic example of the Latin aorist is precisely Caesar's well-known *Veni, vidi, vici*. It would be difficult to establish in this sentence the border between "history" and "autobiography" as Benveniste differentiates them. The epic preterite is known in all these languages, in each person, singular and plural. But the distinction is irrelevant from the point of view of modern narrative theories and speech act theory. Regardless of whether the utterance has the same grammatical subject or another (second or third person), the subject of the utterance, explicit or not in the text, is still a subject, individual or collective, that speaks in the first person, singular or plural (without the plural necessarily signifying multitude, given the use of the "majestic plural," the royal *we*). And there is no utterance without a subject who assumes it in an act of *parole*.[5] Thus, the difference between a discourse of "I" (or "we") about itself and a discourse about a second or third person (singular as well as plural) in which the speaker is equally "I" or "we," is a difference of objects and not one of subject-utterers. There is no doubt, then, that we are always dealing with a (first) person who guarantees the uttered as an instance of utterance, constituting himself/herself as a subject-utterer.[6] Hence I dare to include in the autobiographical genre the written autobiography (or dictated, as in the case of Ignacio de Loyola) in third person, a modality held dear by the Jesuits and customarily explained as a gesture of humility.[7] We note it as a break with the traditional model of the instructive spiritual autobiography, a break that becomes in turn a model for generating new texts.

The preceding considerations are not to be taken as an attempt to return to an individualistic subjectivism that affirms the position of the subject-utterer as the true organizing demiurge, *creator* of the autobiographical text, of biography and of "history" in general. If I speak of narrative discourse, regrouping its subgenres and characterizing it as uttered by an individual or collective subject that refers back to its past in order to explain its present, it is precisely to show that the autobiography functions in the double tension that frames all narration. As *discourse*, one must always understand autobiography as existing in front of a receiver/audience: at least, that explicit narrative to whom it is directed with the intention of "influencing it in some way." In its function as social convention, all discourse is inscribed in a social framework as well, with a logic that all "coherent" narration must respect, with norms that regulate the uses of the word (and genre), with the values recognized in acts, gestures and words: in sum, with the entire repertory of imperatives of behavior (ethic as well as linguistic) and aspirations (individual and collective) that all individuals unconsciously internalize from their most tender age and that constitute the parental and social super-ego instance. Furthermore, this double tension tends to be conflictive in the autobiography, in that the subject of it, by selecting and strategically ordering his narrative, is more or less conscious that it will be read by individuals or social groups of a quite different cognitive and affective nature. As I believe I have shown in previous works,[8] the *Lazarillo* demonstrates an extraordinary awareness on the part of its anonymous author of this reality that he reveals. If, on the one hand, he imitates faithfully a preconstructed and repetitive model as discursive officiality or ritual, on the other, he fills it with folkloric anecdotes (which the character shows as untrue of the supposed *vita*). Furthermore, he assures such coherence between the narrated "events" and the final resulting situation, which by the same effort that shows its fictionality, shows as well its verisimilitude. This verisimilitude is indispensable for audience persuasion (more than truth itself), for the well-organized discourse capable of the rhetorical seduction of the judges and listener that Plato would lament and that Gorgias would leave as a decisive example in the *laudatio* of Helen and in the discourse of the defense of Palamedes. This well-forged textual artifice is complemented further in the prologue with a denunciation of the double intentionality of these writings, exemplified by the action of the soldier who risks his life and with the sermon of the theological student (however much he may desire the deliverance of souls). The deeper reason for both these actions is, according to Lázaro, "the desire for praise," exemplified by the knight who was willing to let himself be swindled by a flattering buffoon. Thus there is in the *Lazarillo* a labor on language, on ritual discursive practices and on other media of interaction, verbal or nonverbal, active in its context, and which the text disarticulates. It is here where I see the way the *Lazarillo* reads history and inscribes itself in it. Other texts operate on a much lower level of consciousness, which does not mean they do not function according to the program already designed by traditional rhetoric in the selection of elements to transmit (*inventio*), its strategic ordering (*dispositio*) and its formulation in the "tone" most appropriate to its desired end (*elocutio*). I am sure that an analysis from this perspective of the autobiography of St. Teresa of Avila would open up the way to an understanding of more than mere "sophism" in such apparent naïveté. This "end," and the relevance of the means leading to it, is not the work of the individual who holds the pen. It is a question of socio-historical variables, moments that act as "stimuli" for that which all the rhetorical devices ever used are no more than parts of an "answer." The history of the autobiography should not be limited to the history of writing, nor to its mere classification as "models" or "rupture," as if each new wave were no more than the result of a rupture with the previous model. I would include those stimuli (sociohistorical variables) with which autobiographies dialog (consciously or unconsciously) in their argumentative discourse. In discursive narration this refers to the response to a stimulus: of functional (self)representations that obey a whole series of axiological postulates (and not merely the horizon of purely generic or literary expectations). Not always explicit in the text, these postulates must be discovered by their implicit presence in the text in which, without saying it, the narrator responds to meet his own needs.

An example of our everyday experience would be useful to better understand this individual-social dialog in which I inscribe the autobiographical narrative. At the same time, I believe that the example I shall bring into question will not lead us too far away from the topic, since—within its own limits—it may be considered as a (brief) form of (functional) autobiography. I refer to the *curriculum vitae*. In a world such as ours, framed by the division of labor, (super)specialization is an imperative in all sectors of life. Whoever responds to a job announcement, applying for a position probably defined in detail in the form of a want-ad or professional listing, will have to construct a *curriculum vitae* that responds as well as possible to the specialty described in the listing. This will be the criterion (more or less conscious) that the subject-utterer will put into play when he searches his memory to select the courses followed during his education and his pertinent professional activities. Other courses or activities might go unmentioned, and certainly so if they could be considered inappropriate or incongruous with the actual training required by the announced position. Furthermore, if the same individual in his search for work applied for two positions—nothing unusual in today's world—he would probably prepare not one curriculum, but several, in order to be able to respond to the specific requirements of each "external stimulus." Undoubtedly, the *curricula* will have much in common with each other, especially in the formal aspect of their presentation; but they will differ in other aspects, especially in content, in the personality described in his/her historical unfoldment, given that the applicant must respond in each case to a different function. It is in this dimension of functionality wherein lies the "truth" of a *curriculum vitae*. Through functionality we may read the stimulus-response tension, or in other words, the subject-utterer/society framework in which the text is inscribed. It would be an error, then, to analyze *curricula* in the absence of the texts describing the positions, as if one were dealing with autonomous and autotelic texts. This practice of ignoring the context of textual production is a direct extrapolation from principles of immanentist structuralism, including individualist psychology, with all the depth that, on the other hand, one may find in such (psycho)analysis. It will always be *partial*, since it will analyze the *it* without taking into account the super-ego. Furthermore, by analyzing the *it* one thinks he or she is analyzing the subjective individuality of the author, signalling the return to traditional biography mentioned earlier. To alleviate this lack in the *curriculum vitae*—of the autobiography and, if I may suggest, of all historiography—I propose that we investigate that other text that exists *within* the "actual" text, the one that is explicitly absent, but present in the *implicit* dialog that it generates. It is simply a matter of analyzing the text with all the understandings and suppositions, as well as all the informational assumptions with which it holds dialog. A *curriculum vitae*, an autobiography, will be presented to us as an incomplete syllogism, an enthymeme whose major premise (the supposition) will be the description of the vacant position—the horizon shared by the subject-utterer and his multiple audience, as much spatial and temporal as (especially) cognitive and axiological, in the case of an autobiography that is destined for publication and thus more widely diffused. The text of the *curriculum*—the autobiography—would be nothing more than the minor premise, and in its quality as such we should analyze the actualized verbal part. The context is considered here as an integral part of that whole, much larger and more complex than the sum of the phonemes, morphemes or lexemes that the subject-utterer emits or transcribes in the act of communication. The conclusion could be explicit or implicit, and it will be through it that we will be able to judge the accuracy or inaccuracy in the selection of the rhetorical means put into play by the subject-utterer. If this hypothesis is accepted,[9] the reader will agree that a *curriculum vitae*, an autobiography, is none other than an argument that responds to a specific variable as a stimulus. And that more than for the individual image (usually incomplete; often, deformed) of the subject that has word or pen, one will have to inquire into the *curriculum*'s (the autobiography's) social horizon of expectations in which it is inscribed. Clearly, this is not a new invention. I am simply going one step back to connect present narrative and discursive theories with the sophist models and classical oratory that Rome developed, as much in its juridical function (defense of the accused) and political role (technique of manipulation of the Senate and people), as a technique applicable to any other purpose. It is this functionality that changes when the Jesuits, for example, appropriate it for their theological arguments or for sacred oratory, just as when the modern world appropriates it for commercial purposes and massification of consumption, tastes and ideas to which we subscribe in our everyday life. It is through the observation of these functionalities and modes of argumentation that one must establish the history of the autobiographical models and their changes. In them, matter and form (or content and style) are united, individuality and sociality. The landmarks of the history of autobiography will thus come to be the landmarks of collective history, as testimonies not only of an individual, but of an epoch. It is here where we may find the reason for the predominance in certain ages of the spiritual autobiography, of that of soldiers, simultaneously with the picaresque as a counterpoint. In a subsequent age, we witness a process of secularization and change of feudal mentality for the bourgeois, producing a new autobiographical style, a new type of adventure and merit that coincide with the disappearance of the picaresque, at least in its progenitive tone, perhaps because that tone becomes the currently dominant style.

Returning to the *curriculum*, this time with a concrete text, we see immediately that the selection of the example was not completely innocent, but functional in preparation for the study of the Cervantes text about to be presented. Among the hundreds of *curricula* (authentic autobiographies at times, many preserved in Seville's *Archivo General de Indias*) soliciting positions in the Indies, we find that presented by Cervantes. We knew of this petition by Cervantes through his biographers' references, and also from its negative result. Perhaps it is thanks to this denial that we now have texts like the *Quijote* and the *Novelas ejemplares* What is certain is that this document counters, for example, the often-affirmed statement that Cervantes's father did whatever he could to obtain the ransom price during Cervantes's captivity in Algeria, after having spent his diminished fortune in the rescue of Miguel's brother Rodrigo de Cervantes, also prisoner in Algeria. There are curious names and facts in the adduced testimonies; yet, it is not the facts of Cervantes's life that attract my attention, but the silences and lacunas of the writer, since in them I believe one can discern an interesting criterion of selection that follows, without a doubt, the strategy that Cervantes considers the most propitious in order to obtain the position solicited. Like Ignacio de Loyola through Rivadeneira, Cervantes here presents himself through a *Relator*, Dr. Núñez, who offers an entire *curriculum* in which the services of Cervantes to "His Majesty" are highlighted,[10] especially as a soldier who has lost an arm at Lepanto and who had fought earlier in Italy, Goleta and Tunisia, as well as his long captivity in Algeria. The self-presentation is accompanied by a document from the Duke of Sesa and the response prepared by his father in 1578, incorporated in this curriculum with his new rubric dated Madrid, 29 May 1590. Its presentation is, nevertheless, somewhat later since it begins declaring that he "has served for the last 22 years; in the naval battle there, he lost a hand when he was shot with an arquebus." If 22 years have passed since the battle of Lepanto (7 October 1571), it would be 1593. At the time in which he composes this *curriculum*, Cervantes has known for some time then the success of his theater, with works such as *La destrucción de Numancia, Los tratos de Argel* and *La batalla naual*; he had brought a whole series of changes to the *comedia*, if we accept his own testimony in another *curriculum vitae*, that of Letters and not of Arms[11]; he published *La Galatea* in 1585; he contracted marriage with Catalina de Salazar y Palacios. None of this appears in this *curriculum*, just as in the other there is no mention of his life as a soldier. But while here we are dealing simply with the publication of his unstaged theatrical works, which explains why he speaks only of his activity in that area, in the solicitation of a position in the Indies it would seem more logical to find a more complete *curriculum*. Or would it not serve his majesties in sixteenth- and seventeenth-century Spain to author comedies or write novels or poetry? Very well, the response seems to be negative. At the very least Cervantes must not have considered his activities as a writer of fictional works relevant for obtaining a position in the Indies.

NOTES

[1] Cf. Mikhail Bakhtin/V.N. Volochinov, *Le marxisme et la philosophie du langage*. Paris: Les Editions de Minuit, 1977, especially the third part, Chapters 8 through 11.

[2] See my paper delivered at the Second International Symposium on "Autobiography in Spain" in *L'Autobiographie en Espagne. Actes du IIe Colloque International de La Baume-lès-Aix* (23-24-25 mai 1981. Aix-en-Provence: Univ. de Provence 1982, 69-94). *Poétique* published the French version of this paper in the special number *L'Autobiographie* (No. 56, nov. 1983). Other works of mine on the *Lazarillo* and the picaresque novel are included in *Lecture idéologique du Lazarillo de Tormes*, Montpellier: C.E.R.S., 1984 (Vol. 8 of the series *Co-textes*) and *La subversion du discours rituel*, Longueuil (Québec): Les Editions du Préambule 1985 (Collection *L'Univers des discours*).

[3] Compare Benveniste's complementary distribution of verb tenses with Harald Weinrich's, done at the same time. Weinrich distinguishes tenses of the commented world (*besprochene Welt*) and tenses of the narrated world (*erzählte Welt*). The most frequently used tenses in the register of the commented world are the present, future and compound past; in the register of the narrated world, the imperfect, simple past, pluperfect and conditional (*Tempus. Besprochene und erzählte Welt*, Stuttgart: Klett-Verlag, 1964). In a later work in which he returns to this topic ("Les temps et les personnes" in *Poétique* 39 [Sept. 1979]: 338-352), Weinrich again proposes this binary distribution, here as a possible basis for the literary distinction between the non-narrative and the narrative. Both history and autobiography enter into Weinrich's "narrative," though separated by Benveniste. It is this concept of narrative that determined the first component of the present

work's title (narration), though I added as the second component *argumentation* in order to insist at the same time on the discursive dimension of the autobiography. Note that we are dealing with two *dimensions* of the text and not a typological or generic distinction, as are the objects of both Benveniste and Weinrich. Better known here by the distinction established by Todorov in "Les catégories du récit littéraire" (in *Communications*, 8 [1966]: 125-151) between "reported events," which he calls "history" and "the way by which the narrator lets us know them," which Todorov calls "discourse." I believe that in effect all narration is argumentative, and on this axiom I base my thesis of the socio-historical conditioning that determines the changes of perspective in the selection and strategic ordering of the narrative material in all historical narration and in particular the autobiographical.

[4] Benveniste continues: "The fundamental tense is the aorist, which is the tense of the event outside the person of a narrator." (208)

[5] Oswald Ducrot insists on the need to admit that "utterances are produced, in other words, that there are moments when they do not yet exist and moments when they no longer exist." "What I need," Ducrot again insists, "is that one take into consideration among the historical facts the emergence of utterances at different points of time and space. The speech act itself is this emergence." In this way Ducrot introduces this collective volume of French expressions that reveal what he calls "a saying hidden behind what is said."

[6] Cf. Mieke Bal, *Teoría de la narrativa*, Madrid: Cátedra, 1985, esp. III, 2: "El narrador" (126-132). Bal distinguishes the following three dimensions in the narrative: *fable* (logical and chronological sequence of events), *history* (its presentation) and *text* (the narrator's work).

[7] Thus, for example, Frank Bowman, in comparing Ignacio de Loyola's *Relato* to Henry Suso's, who writes of his life in the third person calling himself "the Servant of Eternal Wisdom" (not unlike the popes referring to themselves as "servant of the servants of God"). On this form of autobiographical writing, see Philippe Lejeune's *Je est un autre*; on the various forms in which the autobiographical genre crystallizes, see Elizabeth Bruss's *Autobiographical Acts: The Changing Situation of a Literary Genre* (1976).

[8] See especially my "Procédés de véridiction dans le roman picaresque espagnol" in *Le vraisemblable et la fiction. Recherches sur le contrat de véridiction (Colloque de Montréal, 1974)*, Série Colloques, No. 2. Montreal: Univ. de Montréal, 1980, 12-25. For other works, see note 2.

[9] This hypothesis refers to the notion of rhetoric in its first stages, with the Greek Sophists, which would later give rise to the Latin oratorical

tracts and, again, in the new birth of the *ars dicendi* that becomes in Europe the Jesuit school of sacred oratory (but also of apologetic theology), and to the treatises of argumentation that proliferate in the sixteenth and seventeenth centuries, what Perelman calls *L'empire rhétorique.*" Perelman speaks of the "decline of rhetoric" towards the end of the sixteenth century as "due to the rise in bourgeois thought that widened the role of evidence, of the personal evidence of Protestantism, of the rational evidence of Cartesianism or of the sensory evidence of empiricism." (21).

[10] "Ynformacion de Miguel de Cerbantes de lo que ha seruido a su magestad y de lo que a hecho estando captiuo en Argel y por la certificacion que aqui presenta del duque de Sesa se vera como quando le captiuaron se le perdieron otras muchas ynformaciones fées y recados que tenia de lo que hauia seruido a su magestad" (Ramos 1 and 2, *Tira* 1 from *Archivo General de Indias, Patronato Real, legajo 253.* See transcription in the Appendix.)

[11] In the Prologue to the Reader of his edition of *Ocho comedias y ocho entremeses nuevos nunca representados* (Madrid: Viuda de Alonso Martín 1615), Cervantes writes: "in the theatres of Madrid *Los tratos de Argel* was put on, as well as *La destrucción de Numancia* and *La batalla naual*, where I dared to reduce the comedies to three days, from the original five; I showed, or better, I was the first to represent the imaginations and the hidden thoughts of the soul, bringing out moral figures in the theatre to the general and hearty applause of the listeners; I composed during that time up to twenty or thirty comedies, all of which were recited without the audience offering either cucumbers or other throwable objects: the plays ran their course without whistles, shouts or jeers. I had other things to work on, I left the pen and the comedies, and along came that monster of nature, Lope de Vega..." (Cervantes, *Comedias y entremeses*, Eds. Schevill y Bonilla San Martín, Vol. I, 7-8).

WORKS CITED

Bal, Mieke. *Teoría de la narrativa.* Madrid: Cátedra, 1985, esp. III, 2. "El narrador" (126-132).

Benveniste, Emile. *Problems in General Linguistics.* Trans. Mary Elizabeth Meek. Coral Gables: Univ. of Miami Press, 1971.

Dubois, Jacques. *L'Institution de la Littérature.* Brussels: Nathan-Labor, 1978.

Ducrot, Oswald. *Les mots du discours*. Paris: Les Editions de Minuit, 1980.

Kristeva, Julia. "Le mot, le dialogue et le roman." *Séméiotikè. Recherches pour une sémanalyse*. Paris: Les Editions du Seuil, 1969. 143-173.

Lejeune, Philippe. *Je est un autre*. Paris: Les Editions du Seuil, 1980.

Morris, C. W. "Foundations of the Theory of Signs." *International Encyclopedia of Unified Science*, I, 2. Chicago: Univ. of Chicago Press, 1938.

Moser, Walter. "La mise à l'essai des discours dans *L'Homme sans qualités* de Robert Musil." *Révue Canadienne de Littérature Comparée*, XII (1985): 12-45.

Perelman, C.W. *L'empire rhétorique. Rhétorique et argumentation*. Paris, 1977.

CHAPTER 2:
A CLOWN AT COURT: FRANCESILLO DE
ZUÑIGA'S *CRONICA BURLESCA*

George Mariscal

"Necesario y cosa razonable
es a los hombres buscar
maneras de vivir"

[It is reasonable and
necessary that men search
for ways to survive]
—F. de Zúñiga

The *Crónica burlesca del emperador Carlos V* by the
court *bufón* (clown-jester) Francesillo de Zúñiga (1490?-
1532) is clearly not an autobiography in any traditional
sense of the term. Given its title, the text would seem to be
more a mock-historical document representing a certain
moment of Charles V's reign and therefore more concerned with "external events" than an inner-looking narrative of a developing self. Yet, as some critics have noted,
this curious work, with its capricious selection of real occurrences sprinkled with autobiographical fragments, also

refuses to fall neatly into the category of historical writing. Where, then, are we to place this uncanny text by the former New Christian tailor who called himself the "chismógrafo oficial de la corte española" (official gossip-monger of the Spanish court)?

The premise of my essay is that the *Crónica* does not conform to modern notions of autobiography, history, or memoir because of the specific social and ideological context in which it was written. I will argue, however, that even though such a text does not fit any of the normative definitions of these genres, it may nonetheless foreground the ways in which certain forms of subjectivity were constituted in an earlier historical moment. For if, as recent criticism has taught us, autobiographical discourse is structured on the dialectical movement between a self and the world, the restricted yet symbiotic environment of the early modern court effectively precluded the kind of introspective project associated with modern autobiography, and in fact did not yet know a totalized and autonomous version of "self" as it has been theorized in Western culture for the past two hundred years. Given this, the so-called "retour sur soi" or reconstruction of the subject is in Zúñiga's text frozen in the non-dialectical act of a narrator who, although an outsider on one level, is in reality reproducing the ideology of the privileged class for whom he writes. The marginal character's assumed otherness in fact works to validate and confirm the boundaries of aristocratic consciousness itself.

It is important to remember, therefore, that in our analysis of all such cultural products of pre-capitalist social formations we must be wary of continuing to conceive of autobiography in nineteenth-century terms, that is, the product of bourgeois social relations. My references to subjectivity, then, are not to the transhistorical construct of philosophy or psychological discourse, but rather to the concrete positions which produce the subject within a specific cultural and material conjuncture. In view of this, generic classification according to modern categories becomes virtually impossible and is clearly a less important critical task than allowing the early modern text to speak on its own terms in so far as that is possible. This can only be achieved, I suggest, with a method both informed by history and interested in contextualization, thereby enabling us to delineate not only the objective conditions which determined the author's existence, but also the circumstances in which his text was produced and consumed.[1]

Born in the last decade of the fifteenth century, Francesillo de Zúñiga entered the imperial court as a servant of his provincial lord, the Duque de Béjar. We can be fairly certain that Zúñiga was not his original family name since, as was the case with most *conversos*, his true identity would have been discarded in favor of the adopted name of his protector or patron. In a like manner, the "Conde" which he often used when referring to himself was an example of the common practice of court clowns who adopted the title or even the complete name of the highest members of the nobility (the most famous case being the *hombre de placer* Don Juan de Austria, painted by Velázquez in the 1630's). Both of these strategies contributed to the assimilation of the non-aristocratic individual and in a figurative sense recreated him or her as a living parody of the dominant groups. At the same time, Francés's claim of being an Old Christian: "Our Lord watched over a poor prince named Pelayo, of the lineage of the noble Goths, from which I descend" (...guardó Nuestro Señor un Infante pobre, llamado Pelayo, de linaje de los reyes godos de donde yo desciendo [147]) would have undoubtedly caused a great deal of laughter in courtly circles, yet underlying such laughter was a profound uneasiness since many of those seeking royal favor laid claim to similar bogus genealogies. The practice of "dar perro muerto," or feigning noble ascendency, would become even more widespread in the next century and, in literature as in daily life, would be met not with laughter but with overt violence (cf. Francisco de Quevedo's *El Buscón*).

The *bufón*, then, is ironically positioned within the hierarchy of the court by names which do not signify a real identity but point beyond to the privileged class of which he is the distorted reflection. This kind of renaming, however, was merely one part of a context in which all language had a powerful exchange value. Castiglione would later categorize the various levels of courtly discourse, giving special emphasis to the pointed witticisms known as *detti* or *arguzie* which were the *truhán*'s stock in trade (*Il Cortegiano*, Libro II) and, as the following anecdote recounted in the *Crónica* demonstrates, clever language could often be "sold" for material gain: "The king entered Aragon and in the city of Catalayud was received with great pleasure and festivity; and passing through the streets the king carelessly had his mouth open; and a peasant approached him and said: 'Moses, close your mouth because the flies of this kingdom are mischievous.' And the king responded that he was amused and ordered that the peasant be given one hundred ducats since he was poor" (El Rey entró en Aragón y fue en la cibdad de Catalayud recibido con gran placer y alegría; y yendo por la calle el Rey iba descuidado, abierta la boca; y llegó a él un villano, y díjole: «Mosén, cierra la boca, porque las moscas deste reino son traviesas». Y el Rey le respondió que le placía... y el Rey le mandó dar, porque era pobre, cien ducados [77]).

While it is true that Francés would not have been rewarded as generously as was the witty peasant, it is also true that his well-being depended to a great extent on his ability to trade with language. In the pre-capitalist economy of the court, the *bufón* usually received little more than bread and wax as payment for his services. A preoccupation with word-play and clothing (Francés's other primary concern), therefore, reveals the real and symbolic value of what we, from our 20th-century vantage point, might mistakenly consider to be superficial externals. For the Renaissance courtier, however, these things were intimately bound up with subject-position and consciousness itself since the slightest attention afforded him by a superior could affect his place in the social hierarchy. Thus, we are repeatedly told of the favors bestowed on him from above: "the good Don Francisco was extravagant and when the emperor entered Cordoba he gave his crimson garment lined in white damask to this chronicler Don Francis" (...fue gastador este buen don Francisco [Pacheco], cuando el Emperador entró en Córdoba, su ropa de carmesí aforrada en damasco blanco dio a este coronista don Francés [97]) and of the rich wardrobe which marked his privileged position: "this author, the Count Don Francis, came out made up as a councilman with a flowing purple velvet cape lined in tan damask, which the city had given him. And if this author is taken at his word, in all the cities and villages in which His Majesty entered, they gave him such garments and even better ones" (...este abtor, el conde don Francés, salió al recibimiento hecho veinte y cuatro, con una ropa rozagante de terciopelo morado aforrada en damasco leonado, con que la cibdad le sirvió. Y si su voto deste abtor se tomara, en todas las cibdades y villas en que Su Majestad entró le dieran otras tales ropas y aun mejores) [139]. The point here is not that Francés was unusually preoccupied by fashion, but that each garment was a signifier for his status within the community surrounding the king.

The *bufón*'s primary activity of linguistically transforming (*motear*, *apodar*, or nicknaming) courtly reality, then, is both a service by which he earns his livelihood and a means to gain special favors from his superiors. We must not read such a practice, therefore, as the potentially subversive introduction of free-play into the power dynamics of the court nor as the liberating force of the carnivalesque since in fact it works to reinforce rigid social categories and conventions. A supplementary aspect of this commodification of language is the incessant reification of the human subject. Referring to himself, for example, Zúñiga writes: "this Don Francis, when armed, looked like the little man in the clock of San Martín de Valdeiglesias..." (Este don Francés parecía, armado, hombrecico del reloj de San Martín de Valdeiglesias...). By putting the language of daily life at the service of the privileged *estamentos* (for their entertainment and his own self-deprecation), the author reveals both his lack of a fully developed interiority and his complete identification with "official" ideologies. In view of this, Frances's role as court *decidor* only allows him to speak an essentialist language which forecloses the forms of subjectivity which have been traditionally associated with modern autobiographical discourse. The dynamics of courtly life required that the individual always situate himself in relation to others and define himself according to the division of labor in the court. What was of virtually no import (perhaps altogether inconceivable) was the representation of an interior consciousness in the process of development. Within the text itself this lack of interiority is figured forth by the decentering of the narrative voice which, in a series of strategic performances, moves along the textual surface by continually shifting from the feigned objectivity of the third-person ("this author," "this author-chronicler" [este abtor, este abtor coronista]) to the self-interest of the first-person, from the language of subservience to the use of the familiar "vos" in the presence of the king.

This kind of stylistic "break-up" of the speaking subject would be further elaborated in the great fictional autobiographies published in the seventeenth century, yet I want to stress that Francés is hardly a problematic hero on the novelistic model. To take only one example: while the protagonist-narrators of the classic picaresque novels struggle to conceal their social origins, Zúñiga seems eager to call attention to his own. Explaining the reasons why he was unable to accompany Charles V to Italy, he tells us: "a wound I received as a child, on the foreskin, still bothered me so that when nature calls I seem like a soul in Purgatory" (una herida que obe quando niño en el prepucio, me quedaron tales rreliquias que cuando es tiempo parezco ánima de Purgatorio) [171]. The reference to circumcision, an identifying sign of Jewish ancestry, is primarily meant to produce a comic effect within the anti-semitic and Old Christian context and by extension serves to reinforce the speaker's inferior status. The making public of such a private (and potentially alienating) trace further emphasizes Francés's willingness to identify with dominant cultural practice provided that it offers him refuge from the harsh realities of life outside the court. This, of course, should remind us of Lázaro de Tormes, Estebanillo González (another jester), and later literary heroes drawn from subordinate social groups. Despite their marginal status, each reveals a strong desire to reject any semblance of autonomy (and the introspective retreat from worldly affairs associated with a certain kind of autobiographical discourse, e.g. Montaigne) in favor of an adherence to collective values, even when those values expose the character to public derision.

In the early decades of the sixteenth century, however, the status of a *converso* did not yet present the more immediate dangers that it would in the decades to come. Francés's use of the word "primo" (cousin), for example, a word synonymous with New Christian, has a primarily humorous function as the author insinuates that he is not the only courtier with an "impure" lineage. In the parodic letter written to the Marqués de Pescara, who is addressed as "Unassailable Sir Cousin" (Inexpugnable señor primo), he writes: "I respect you so that I feel honored to be related to you. I thank God that in my lifetime I have seen someone of my lineage rise to such heights. You are so like your ancestors Melchizedek and Judas Maccabeus" (Tengo en tanto vuestra persona, que por honrado me tengo en que tengais deudo conmigo. A Dios doy muchas gracias que en mis días vea yo hombre de mi linaje valer tanto. Bien pareceis a vuestros antepasados Melquisedech y Júdas Macabeo) [*BAE* 36, 57]. The self-confidence of the aristocracy around Charles V would have certainly been unaffected by such remarks, and the assertion that the *bufón* somehow shared in the nobleman's genealogy would have merely reaffirmed the latter's sense of his own superiority.

Yet much of the humorous material based on Francés's *converso* status reveals a symbolic violence which both concretizes and reproduces the author's profound alienation. In the *Epistolario*, for example, he traces his "genealogy" for Charles V's *mayordomo mayor* so that a suitable coat of arms can be designed. Francés describes how his grandfather, exhausted from preparing a feast for King Melchizedek, had fallen asleep in the woods when suddenly:

a half-rabid boar, wounded, lept from the bushes and
approached where my grandfather slept, and the
boar, with a deadly rage, not knowing what he did,
ate my grandfather's foreskin, and because of this on
our ancestral arms, instead of a headpiece [foreskin]
there is a helmet for the road and a hood for the
street; so that these are the arms that your
excellency should put on the gold shield for me,
according to whatever works best for this device.

(un puerco montés medio rabioso, herido, se soltó de
la enramada y pasó por donde estaba este mi agüelo
adormido, y el puerco, con la rabia de la muerte, no
sabiendo lo que hacia, le comió el prepucio, y por esto
nos fue dado por armas que, en lugar de prepucio, de
camino trajésemos papahigo, y de rua muceta; así que
estas son las armas que vuestra señoría ha de poner en
la planzada del oro para mí, segun por este blason
mas claro paresce.) [*BAE* 36, 56]

The comic effect of the multiple puns on "foreskin" and
the suggestion of a phallic coat of arms is juxtaposed to the
violence of the scene itself, the wild boar in effect having
performed the circumcision. Once again, the identifying
mark of the New Christian sets the author apart, both
physically and socially, from his presumably Old Christian
audience.

The self-consciousness of this court *bufón*, as revealed
in the epigraph which begins my essay shows that on one
level the author was aware of his role-playing in so far as
he is able to locate the origins of his behavior in his own
socio-economic predicament (in a like manner, Estebanillo
González becomes a *bufón* "in order to rectify my naked-
ness" [por remediar mi desnudez]). Yet such signs of self-
awareness have little to do with the strategies of a Montaigne or a Cellini. Montaigne's project in particular,
founded on the rejection of social convention and traditional knowledge, was designed to realize a further interi-
orization of the subject and contributed to the on-going
project central to early modern thought of articulating the
myth of the autonomous subject.[2] Zúñiga's intention, on
the other hand, is not to construct a subjectivity born in

isolation, but rather to strategically position himself with regard to others in the courtly environment (including anyone reading or listening to his account).

Thus, practical concerns determined by everyday-life are what produce both Francés's behavior and his text. His self-deprecation and his subservient posture are the necessary and reasonable consequences of the very real desire to escape the insecurity of living outside the court and to survive what was often a hostile environment even within its confines: "The author did not dare to nickname these knights that travelled with the Count of Extremadura because he was informed that they delivered blows that took away one's speech" (Estos caballeros que iban con el Conde, de Estremadura, el abtor no los osó apodar, porque fue informado que daban espaldarazos que quitaban la habla) [123]. The threat of having "la habla quitada" would have been serious indeed for someone whose well-being depended to a great extent on speech, and in many ways the *Crónica* itself is a text still founded on orality. Unlike the "writing of the self" undertaken by later autobiographers, Francés's project is a kind of spoken representation that reproduces the structures of courtly conversation. The subject-positions articulated by such a linguistic economy, founded upon the opposition master/servant, were severely limited and while the potential for manipulating language was obviously very real, the system itself (i.e. those material conditions which generated discursive practices) was jealously maintained by the ruling elites. It is no surprise, then, that it was the *truhán*'s language that finally cost him his position and ultimately led to his violent death. In early 1529, as the Emperor prepared for a military expedition to Hungary, Francés angered his master by repeating once too often the phrase: "You are so predictable: You love those who do not love you and spurn those who want to serve you" (Bien acondicionado soys: que amáys a quien no os ama y alançáis de vos a los que os quieren seruir). Out of favor and no longer in the protected environment of the court, he would be stabbed to death in 1532 by a man who previously had been the target of his pointed remarks.

The *Crónica*, then, is not an example of the literature of becoming-in-the-world. The subject who speaks to us from this text is an entity firmly fixed by the ensemble of inter-relations that structure courtly life. Yet neither is this an example of conventional historical writing (nor even memoir as a sub-genre of history). On one level, as first noted by María Rosa Lida, it is a parody of Antonio de Guevara's *Marco Aurelio* (1528) in its imitation of Gue-vara's basic narrative plan. Here, I would argue, Zúñiga's text undoes Guevara's totalizing project (to reconcile a particular version of ancient thought with Christian reve-lation) because of its fragmented and random repre-sentation of historical events. In this sense, the *Crónica* confirms Bakhtin's account of the history of laughter in so far as it is a product of the transitional period of the 1520's and 30's in which written texts increasingly attack official medieval culture's seriousness (the *Crónica* and *Gargan-tua* [1534] are coetaneous texts). In Spain, however, this period was short-lived. The popular-festive tradition of representing important historical events and personages in a comic format, so skillfully adapted by Francesillo, had in Zúñiga's day already come under attack by contempo-rary traditional chroniclers such as Alonso de Santa Cruz and Guevara, and by the 17th century the satirical-histori-cal works of Quevedo and others would share very few of the narrative strategies we find in Zúñiga's text. (A de-tailed analysis of the immense ideological gaps separating the early and late decades of the so-called Golden Age as well as a discussion of the function of the historical subtext in the *Crónica* would be important steps towards a com-prehensive reading).

   In the final analysis, the author of the *Crónica* is less in-terested in recapturing the past than he is in influencing the present in the most limited of terms. This fact is cru-cial to our investigation of autobiographical variations; on more than one occasion, the narrator, by interjecting ad-vice or a personal complaint, undercuts the importance of external reality and forcefully privileges his own point of view. After a lengthy discussion of how Charles V had re-stored order to the Castilian cities (1522), for example,

Francés recalls the magnanimous nature of the Visigothic king, Bamba, and counsels: "So it is, Illustrious Emperor, if you recall these examples, it behooves you to pardon the Archbishop of Toledo and the Dukes of Béjar and Alba if one day they come to the Council presumptuous and full of their own importance. And besides, may God and Your Majesty forgive these knights who treat me unkindly" (Así que, esclarecido Emperador, si os acordiades destos ejemplos, conviene que perdones al arzobispo de Toledo, y al duque de Béjar, y Alba... si algún día vinieren al Consejo, muy presumiendo y por otra parte hinchados. Y demás desto, Dios y Vuestra Majestad perdone a estos caballeros quienes comigo lo hacen ruinmente) [99]. The insistence of the narrator's voice in its self-serving appeal to royal sympathy removes any claim to historical "objectivity" which might be made for this so-called chronicle, and forces us to reconsider it as a kind of record of how subjectivity was understood in the aristocratic context.

The reoccurring intrusion of the author's personal preoccupations is especially noticeable in the *Epistolario*, a series of humorous letters written to famous personages of the day. In a text addressed to the Emperor, Francés suddenly adopts a serious tone and makes a direct plea: "For the love of who you are, let me be heard" (Por amor de quien sois, sea yo oido...) for a pension of two thousand *ducados*: "because such a pension will rescue me from poverty and will grant authority to my person and estate" (porque la tal pension me podrá sacar de laceria, y mi persona y casa tener authoridad). It is with this text that we begin to understand the precarious situation in which Francés found himself (not unlike all minor courtiers) as we hear the complaints of a *bufón* to his master: "As for the rest, I must report that the Duke of Béjar does not look at me even if I pass right by him, the Lord Constable avoids me, the Marquis of Cenete threatens me, M. de Lasau has it in for me, and Sancho Bravo beats me. *Domine, adjuva me*. From the Pico gate where I remain as naked as the innocent of Laredo, ever watchful, awaiting good fortune. *Prince Don Francisco, your friend and ser-*

vant" (De lo demás, sé decir que el duque de Béjar no me mira, aunque pase por junto á él, y el Condestable me guiña, el marqués de Cenete me amenaza, musiur de Laxao me las jura, y Sancho Bravo me las pega. *Domine, adjuva me*. Del puerto del Pico, donde quedo desnudo como besugo de Laredo, el ojo abierto, esperando buena venta. - *El infante don Francés, vuestro amigo y criado*) [*BAE* 36, 62]. Few texts convey as vividly the anxiety which permeated this environment in which the slightest gesture could decide an individual's social status and identity.

Despite its realistic representation of a life at court, we may still need to ask whether the *Crónica burlesca* is not simply a jest-book, a form of courtly entertainment finally undeserving of critical attention. This in fact has been argued by some scholars including Márquez Villanueva.[3] Such a position, I would argue, ignores the serious function of courtly entertainment and especially the role played by the *bufón*, for according to certain medieval traditions the laughter provoked by the court clown was essential to the prince's well-being. The sixteenth-century edition of the Latin medical treatise, the *Tacuinum sanitatis* (1531), summarizes several major beliefs which had been held since the thirteenth century (many of which are echoed in the texts of Don Juan Manuel) concerning the curative powers of witty conversation, and we read for example that the prince who is properly entertained will have "his memory sharpened by the common talk and occurrences that swell up around him." This is not the place to recount the complex history of the idea of the "fool" which had given birth to Erasmus's folly and would culminate in the Shakespearean clown and the *gracioso* figure of the *comedia*. Suffice it to say that the court jester was always much more than a superfluous adornment.[4]

The *bufón*, then, is less an individual than a necessary function of the overall ensemble of social relations at court whose center is the king. Yet it is precisely because the jester is so closely associated with the source of courtly power (often having direct access to the king when others did not) that he must be taken seriously. A certain ambivalence surrounds the position of the *bufón* or *loco*, and in his instructions to his sixteen-year-old son Philip, Charles V writes: "and it would be well that you do not pay so much attention to buffoons, since you seem interested in them, nor permit them to silence you as they do" (y en quanto no hareys tanto caso de locos, como mostrays tener condyçion a ellos, ny permityreys que no cayan a vos tantos como cayan, no sera syno muy bien hecho). Later in the same text (written on the eve of the emperor's diplomatic journey to Italy in 1543), the future "rey prudente" is told "it is not wise to listen too much nor grant access nor give messages to buffoons" (no conuyene dar mucho credyto ny entrada ny mensajeryas a locos). That Charles felt the need to include specific advice relating to court "clowns" reveals the seriousness with which their role was treated. On this view, the *Crónica* is indeed a humorous text but to read it as nothing more than parody or topical humor would be to ignore its complex combination of narrative strategies as well as the "privileged" position of the *bufón*.

Despite the uncertainty in which he lived most of his life, it is clear that Francés could not have seriously considered or actively wished for an alternative social system. As I have been arguing, he enthusiastically endorses imperial polices to the point of self-ridicule, and his mocking of courtly behavior and the Spanish elites is never directed from an external point of view. Here, the internalization of hegemonic values is complete and the *bufón's* voice is that of someone always already defined and positioned by the powers-that-be. In his willing acceptance of his situation, Francés reminds us of Lázaro the wine-seller—contrary to certain schools of early modern thought, the basic instinct for self-preservation is far stronger than any sense of individual freedom. Thus, we can be fairly sure that this former tailor turned court clown would have had little use for the following kind of humanist teaching: "Who is it that, having some mechanical skill or talent, would not desire his proper and natural freedom with which he was born and would not want to be lord of his own house according to his will, to sleep, eat, work, and rest when he wanted rather than living by and obeying the will of another?"[5] (¿Quién es aquel que teniendo algún oficio o arte mecánica... que no quiera más con su propria y natural libertad con que nació, ser señor y quitar y poner en su casa conforme a su voluntad, dormir, comer, trabajar y holgar cuando querrá, antes a voluntad ajena vivir y obedecer?) Considering this, the choices made by Zúñiga the ex-tailor were his own although the alternatives available to him were surely far more limited than what we as twentieth-century readers might expect. The complete rejection of the patronage system, for example, and its reified and static positions for the subject would only come in a much later period—the moment of Rousseau, the Revolution, and the birth of modern autobiographical discourse. The *Crónica burlesca*, then, is not the record of a subject born in opposition to society; consequently, it defies contemporary definitions of autobiography.[6] Nevertheless it allows us to enter, as few texts can, into the reality of an individual and his experience of sixteenth-century aristocratic life. As Marx has taught us in the *German Ideology*, "the social history of men is never anything but the history of their individual development." This is to say that the imaginary split between self and society (a necessary heuristic device without which we could not discuss such problems) is in reality a dialectical relationship in which subjectivity and social conditions are twin moments of the same on-going process. Francesillo's individual existence, then, as it is figured within his various writings, is a representation of one aspect of the reality of Charles V's court during the first half of the sixteenth century (Although written from a different perspective and in a different historical moment, Antonio Pérez's *Relaciones* may be read in a similar way. See Helen H. Reed's essay in this volume). The *bufón*'s life was determined by especially rigid kinds of limitations and pressures, but it was not irrevocably predestined or programmed since even the most restricted social relations (in their temporal reproduction) are susceptible to individual acts or collective movements of contestation that ultimately lead to change.

   In conclusion, I would argue that the *Crónica* is an especially interesting text because it anticipates the kinds of problems we find in the more intensely obdurate context of seventeenth-century Spanish society. The constitution of the subject in early sixteenth century aristocratic culture and the attendant exclusion of non-aristocratic, non-theological qualities would become more general throughout the coming decades and would ultimately determine the identity of each and every social group. For the *bufón*, in particular, the situation was radically transformed: professional jesters such as Francés were now joined by the deformed and the mentally ill, many of whom were transported directly to the palace from the madhouse of Valladolid for the entertainment of the Spanish aristocracy. It is no wonder, therefore, that by the time Estebanillo González composes his "life story" the profession of court clown is adopted with a heavy heart and is associated with a profound melancholy.[7] On a more general level, the ideological "closing down" of the Peninsula from the 1550's on (particularly the attempt to monologize Castilian culture) created a situation inhospitable to forms of subjectivity being explored in the rest of Europe; the highly conventionalized society of "Baroque Spain" would be one in which the structures of Francés's peculiar existence became the norm. The cultural consequences of this repression would figure forth in the exaggerated characters of seventeenth-century literature: Quevedo's lyric speaker, Polifemo, Don Juan, and Don Quijote.

NOTES

[1] The primary material for this essay is drawn from Diane Pamp de Avalle-Arce's edition of the *Crónica burlesca del emperador Carlos V* (Barcelona: Editorial Crítica, 1981). All page numbers in parentheses refer to this text except those preceded by *BAE* which refer to Adolfo de Castro, ed., "Curiosidades bibliográficas," *Biblioteca de autores españoles*, 36 (Madrid: Rivadeneyra, 1855). The English translations are my own.

[2] Montaigne writes: "Have you been able to reflect on your life and control it? Then you have performed the greatest work of all... Our duty

is to compose our character, not to compose books, to win not battles and provinces, but order and tranquility in our conduct" ("On Experience"). A superior study of Montaigne's project is Richard L. Regosin, *The Matter of My Book: Montaigne's Essais as the Book of the Self* (Berkeley: University of California Press, 1977).

[3] See "Un aspect de la littérature du 'fou' en Espagne," *XIXe Colloque international d'études humanistes: L'Humanisme dans les lettres espagnoles* (Paris, 1979) 233-250.

[4] An interesting discussion of related matters (although not specifically focussed on the *bufón*) may be found in José Antonio Maravall, "Relaciones de dependencia e integración social: Criados, graciosos y pícaros," *I& L* 1.4 (1977): 3-32.

[5] Cristóforo Gnósofo, pseud., *El Crótalon*, ed. Augusto Cortina (Buenos Aires: Espasa-Calpe, 1942) 271. The humanist ideologies which inform the *Crótalon* (1553?) produce a harsh critique of the kind of life for which Francés opted:

I do not now wish to speak of those whom the common people call *truhanes* and *chocarreros* whose profession it is to flatter in order to gain some petty reward. These types are madmen, fools, idiots... Nature left them among the dregs and waste of the men she created... Thus for them it is not abuse nor an insult if, affronted and reviled by their masters, they suffer senselessly, as long as they receive their miserable pay.

Con solos aquéllos no quiero al presente hablar que el vulgo llama truhanes, chocarreros, que tienen por oficio lisonjear para sacar el precio miserable. Que estos tales son locos, necios, bobos... Y ansí, pues, ella [la Naturaleza] los dejó por la hez y escoria de hombres que crió ... Y ansí ellos, por esta causa, no les es alguna culpa, ni injuria si, afrontados y vituperados de sus señores, sufren sin sentir, con tal que les paguen su vilísimo jornal y interés. [262]

The author's severity here originates in the belief that a life of courtly service is despicable precisely because it surrenders the subject's free will to the control of others. This attitude, of course, has little to do with the one with which Quevedo condemns to hell "los bufones, truhanes y juglares chocarreros" in the "Sueño del infierno."

[6] The fact that Francesillo de Zúñiga was the only "loco" to produce a written artifact of his experience makes the *Crónica* an important historical document despite its refusal to fit neatly into normative generic categories. Because of the wealth of material contained in such marginal texts, current critical practice would do well to reconsider the strict differentiations between these three primary modes of narration:

autobiography, memoir, history. Such a reformulation is being theorized, for example, in the work of Prof. Alda Blanco of the University of Wisconsin. I would like to thank Prof. Blanco for her assistance in the preparation of this essay.

[7] On Estebanillo's sense of "el servicio vil de un bufón," see Nicholas Spadaccini and Anthony N. Zahareas, "Introducción," *La vida y hechos de Estebanillo González* (2 vols., Madrid: Castalia, 1978) especially 40-48. The deep-seated sadness which permeates Estebanillo's account is virtually non-existent in that of Zúñiga.

CHAPTER 3:
A METHODOLOGICAL PROLEGOMENON
TO A POST-MODERNIST READING
OF SANTA TERESA'S AUTOBIOGRAPHY

Patrick Dust

There can be little doubt that the literary critical enterprise today has come to be characterized by a certain awkwardness. As recently as only twenty-five years ago, a critic
could approach the subject matter with tremendous confidence, choose from several methods, all of which assumed the unquestioned value of literature, and proceed
to demonstrate how the work gave expression to universal human problems in a language that was as artful as it
was beautiful. Aesthetic form and philosophical vision
were viewed as mutually reinforcing, and the critic's job
consisted, indisputably, in explicating a work that inspired
admiration and awe. Today, all that has changed. Literary
criticism has entered a crisis of foundations which has left
no sacred assumptions untouched, and no traditional
views intact. In the sixties, Structuralism succeeded in
stripping the work of its extra-literary reference, and, ap-

ing the natural sciences, reduced it to a series of linguistic transformations which, although subtle and complex, could nevertheless be brought into the cold light of rational analysis and thus "explained." In the end literary works were defined as merely language about language, and the divorce from reality was established as absolute. With Structuralism the groundwork was laid for the final assault on traditionally cherished notions about literature. Subsequently, the philosophy known as Deconstruction could move in, as it were, for the kill, completing the destruction of conventional "understanding," and replacing it with a skepticism that has turned out to be as absolute and dogmatic as the logocentrism and aestheticism it had set out to eliminate. The history of this complex development cannot be studied in detail here.[1] The end result, however, the unprecedented awkwardness or crisis mentioned above, should certainly be taken into account when one attempts to embark upon a serious study of Santa Teresa's autobiography. If progress is at all possible in the field of literary studies—and I believe it is—, it must be possible in the very face of the most radical and stubborn challenges to its legitimacy. Consequently, the present paper proposes to tackle the difficult question of the theoretical and philosophical underpinning that would support a post-modernist, that is, a post-deconstructionist, reading of Teresa's *Vida*. It should be clear that this paper is not that study itself, but rather a struggle with more preliminary issues—hence the title. The working through or clarification of these issues should then constitute the indispensable foundation for an appropriate reading of Teresa's autobiography in the eighties.

There will be three parts in this prolegomenon: the first is a dialogue between two people who have read the *Vida* and fall into a chance conversation while on a train. One of them is a Catholic nun and the other is a graduate student who has recently been exposed to the deconstructionist approach at a university. The second part consists of an extended commentary on the issues raised in the dialogue. If I am successful, this will lead to a kind of methodological plateau in part three, which should culminate in the creation of a solid foundation for a more detailed study of Teresa's autobiography. The present pages, it should therefore be clear, have a limited goal: they are content to try to formulate the theoretical philosophical justification for that future study.

I.

—Hello sister. Do you mind if I ask what you're reading?

—Why not at all. It's the autobiography of Saint Teresa of Avila. She was a Spanish mystic who lived in the sixteenth century.

—Really! What a coincidence! As it turns out I've been reading the same text myself for one of my professors and I find it simply fascinating. The whole problem of writing and of autobiography as genre emerges there in a dramatic way.

—Oh. I'm sure that must be very interesting. I confess that my reading of it is not very sophisticated or academic. You see, as a Catholic nun I read the *Life* for spiritual guidance in my vocation. I feel a special bond with Teresa since we share the same goals and live what is basically the same story.

—What story is that?

—Why, the story of the soul's quest for salvation, of course. Her description of the four stages of prayer, if practiced with diligence and humility, can have a tremendous practical impact on our lives.

—I see. Tell me, sister, have you thought much about what happens when someone writes an autobiography?

—Well, I confess I have thought about it some. I guess I would say that it's as if my own being merges with Teresa's at some very deep level. The truth of her life somehow becomes one with the truth of my own life in a spiritual sort of way. One of my confessors, when we talked about this, spoke of a special experience of belongingness that had a German name. I think it was *zugehorigkeit* or something like that. He's a very learned man. But more importantly, he's a very good man who also enjoys reading about Teresa's life... Why are you smiling?

—I'm just a little amazed, that's all. The perspective we get at the university is certainly different from the one you just described. We learn there that the fictional self in autobiography can never coincide with the real life of the person who wrote. Indeed, as a genre, autobiography contains a unique contradiction: while it insists that it tells about a real life, in fact it is a literary text which inevitably constructs a fiction. It's kind of like a square circle, pretending to be history while asserting itself as poetry and pretending to be poetry while asserting itself as history. And since "to write" in a literary sense is ultimately an intransitive verb, it tells us nothing whatsoever about reality. It's too busy constructing an anti-reality called fiction. According to a French *savant* named Jacques Derrida, the "I" of written discourse never signifies the author's self-presence, but only her absence from being present to herself or others. Saint Teresa's autobiography, then, has nothing to do with truth. It is simply a text with strategies which create and then deconstruct the illusion of truth or of a real life. My professor would say that your relation to the text is an example of an extreme but understandable naïveté, and that ultimately you've been taken in sister.

—Is that the kind of thing they teach you in universities? I can't pretend to have understood everything you've said. But I do think I got the gist of it, and it sounds to me as if your professor's sophistication got the best of him. Those ideas are diabolical, and I must say that I think he is the one who has been taken in.

—Well, the train is coming into the station. It won't stop for long. Excuse me. I've got to get my luggage from the rack. I've enjoyed our conversation. I hope the rest of your trip goes well.

—May God be with you my son.

II.

A number of crucial questions emerge in the course of this brief dialogue. What exactly is an autobiographical text? How can we conceptualize its relation to reality? What are naïveté and sophistication? Is there such a thing as a hypersophistication which, in seeking to escape naïveté, destroys the original knowledge sought? And finally, and of course most importantly, just who has been "taken in" here?

One way to get out of this dilemma is to say that there are two different but equally valid ways of reading, each one serving a different purpose. The nun reads the *Vida* as a religious document and finds that it provides edification and spiritual leaven for an ethical drama involving her soul and a hostile world. The graduate student, on the other hand, reads the story of Teresa's life exclusively as a literary artifact. For him it is a work that is basically self-referential and thus bears no relationship to reality beyond the artistic transformation of words into a text.

The difficulty with such a solution is that there exist many literary critics who are comfortable adopting and defending an attitude toward the text which is not very different from the attitude of the nun in the dialogue. I am not alluding to any use of autobiography as a weapon in a battle against the devil, but rather to the underlying assumption—and there is no belief more powerful than the one taken for granted or assumed—that the words of an autobiography succeed in capturing and conveying the real life drama of its author. This, in fact, is the long-standing, traditional, and even hallowed view, according to which the form of a work makes its content transparent or "expresses" it. In this framework, art is clearly subordinated to and serves ideology. Or stated more programatically, *literature contains an undeniable power of reference which re-presents reality to the reader transformed and filled with meaning.* There is no philosophical presupposition, no belief or assumption that is more potent nor influential in the traditional view than this one. It constitutes, so to speak, the most intimate core of an attitude that has justified and given purpose to literary criticism probably from its beginnings.

An eloquent restatement of this view has recently been elaborated by Barret J. Mandel in an article he significantly titles "Full of Life Now." There he explicitly maintains and defends such conventional premises as the following: autobiography "transcends one's memories, petty lies, [and] grand deceptions;" in it "language creates illusions that tell the truth;" and finally, "the author... is always present in autobiography" ("Full of Life Now" *Autobiography* 63-64). Moreover, Mandel does not hesitate to adopt a position before the text that coincides rather closely with that of our nun. He places a central emphasis on the possibility of sharing the real life of the author, who "springs open a door and gives me a glance into his or her deepest reality, at the same time casting my mind into a state of reverie or speculation... I plummet deep into my own veiled assumptions, feelings, and self-meaning" (*Autobiography* 69). The example Mandel chooses in order to illustrate this momentous merging of his own self with that of the autobiographer is the moment in Teresa's *Vida* when she describes her reaction on reading the garden scene in St. Augustine's *Confessions*. For in that instant, Teresa believes that she re-experiences the Church Father's conversion as a powerful mystery that has become inseparable from her own conversion: "When I began to read the *Confessions*, I thought I saw myself there described, and began to recommend myself greatly to this glorious Saint. When I came to his conversion, and read how he heard that voice in the garden, it seemed to me nothing less than that our Lord had uttered it for me: I felt so in my heart, I remained for some time lost in tears, in great inward affliction and distress" ("Como comencé a leer las Confesiones, pareceme me va yo allí: comencé a encomendarme mucho a este glorioso oyó aquella voz en el Huerto, no me parece sino que el Señor me la dió a mí, segun sintió mi corazón: estuve por gran rato que toda me deshacía en lágrimas, y entre mí mesma con gran afleción y fatiga" [*Autobiography* 69]). Mandel—and this is what is important here—accepts the truth of this scene at face value and attributes to it a paradigmatic value. According to him, Augustine's voice speaks not only *to* Teresa, but most importantly, *in* her; and we are given to understand as well that the voices of both saints somehow manage to resonate yet in Mandel today, creating, in his words, "a moment of transcendence" ("Full of Life Now" *Autobiography* 69).

And exactly how is this communion of lives, this "transcendence" possible? Mandel provides the following explanation: "because their (and our) reality is largely rooted in the shared assumptions of our culture, the written autobiography becomes a formal mode of maintaining the reality of reality. The autobiographer discloses the truth and at the same time fixes it by making it, paradoxically, more real, truer. One's 'life' exists only in one's faith that what one assumes to be real actually is real" ("Full of Life Now" *Autobiography* 72). Only by an act of faith, then, by the acceptance of an assumption that is at bottom paradoxical, can one come to grasp the essence of autobiography. What lies at the very heart of the phenomenon is a prior and unquestioned belief about the possibility of a communion of lives realized and implemented by the written word. This is the philosophical, or some might prefer to say, the religious foundation on which the traditional definition of autobiography rests (See Gusdorf and Olney).[2]

As one might well expect, the deconstructionists approach the traditional view with an attitude of unmitigated scorn. Focusing on its fundamental circularity and on its naïve equation of aesthetic illusion with reality, they are convinced that those critics, like the nun in our dialogue, have been seriously "taken in." The so-called referential power of the text, one that has been accorded a reverential status, can and ultimately *must* be denied, since it fails to see that the essence of literature is fiction. The basis, in other words, for the deconstructionist critique is the stubborn conviction that literature constantly deconstructs or annihilates reality. Writing, from the outset and irremediably, is defined as an act of alienation.

Notwithstanding the mystification concerning "the shared assumptions of our culture," and the presumed communion of souls engendered by the aesthetic qualities, the very condition for the appearance of autobiography as fiction is the absolute destruction of the real.[3]

A good example of these presuppositions applied to the autobiographical genre is an article by Louis A. Renza titled "The Veto of the Imagination: A Theory of Autobiography." The contrast with the premises that Mandel defended earlier could hardly be more dramatic. Whereas the latter affirmed that the genre transcends mere memories and petty deceptions, and that the author is always present in it, Renza insists that autobiography *qua* autobiography is characterized by a "split intentionality," that it contains within itself "suicidal implications," and that its author is *never* present in the written word (*Autobiography* 268-295). Furthermore, Renza, like his traditional counterpart, also has occasion to apply his ideas to the example of Santa Teresa's *Vida*, and once again the result is a revealing contrast. Renza prefers in his analysis to transpose the conflict between literature and life into a drama of a "self-referential privacy" on the one hand and a failed attempt to make that privacy public on the other. Since Teresa writes in obedience to a mandate of the Church, the latter's authority forces her to submerge or hide her intimacy "behind the verbal persona of her life."[4] This repression of her private experience, however, works to her advantage, for in the last analysis it fulfills a second desire which was hidden and in conflict with the first one of self-revelation. It allows the saint to offer up to God in a project of Christian self-abnegation "the untouched because unsignified virginity of her being." Teresa therefore can be said to have cloistered herself in language "by silently writing in reverse— toward herself alone...." Renza does not hesitate then to relate this complex discovery about Teresa's drama to autobiography in general, declaring that there the author "explicitly testifies or 'confesses' to his own separation both from his written 'I' as he writes and from the intersubjective imperatives incurred by this act of writing." The result is the conclusion—and what is ultimately also the point of departure—in every deconstructionist analysis: the true experience of the author is subverted by the presentation of the false writing self; reality is relentlessly deconstructed by fiction. The autobiographer's attempt to create a written account that is "full of life now" (Mandel) is doomed to failure from the outset by the "veto of the imagination" (Renza).

That all of this is highly ingenious and even creative is undeniable. The freshness of the perspective along with the possibilities it generates would seem to be a sufficient guarantee of its validity. The real question, however, is whether or not it is, in the nun's phrase, "diabolical," that is, whether it contains a truth that commands our respect, or whether it arbitrarily invents logical conclusions that are merely imaginary rather than truly imaginative. This question, the key distinction just suggested, and the implications that accompany both, must be recognized as the central problem requiring discussion and clarification in the next part of this study.

III.

At this point we have reached a kind of plateau. But it also appears to be an impasse which confronts us with two antithetical and mutually exclusive alternatives for interpretation. *Either* we choose an overdetermined skepticism that ruthlessly decontextualizes, holds that all representation is misrepresentation, that operates in a denial mode with an atemporal text, and which culminates in a stubborn refusal of understanding. *Or* we choose an undetermined naïveté that is rooted in the affirmation of a quasi-miraculous participation in the life or history of the author, and which culminates in the ratification of a truth that was never seriously questioned from the beginning. The deconstructionist approach makes it impossible to avoid failure, while the traditionalist methodology seems to predetermine and guarantee success. Is there any way out of this impasse?

There is a way out, but in order to find it we must make a detour. We must draw back from the concern with

Teresa's autobiography in an attempt to gain a broader perspective. A look at the evolution of literary criticism in this century and, more importantly, an interpretation of the current crisis in the discipline should provide that needed perspective. Then it will be possible to return to Teresa's *Vida* and to make valid suggestions for a post-deconstructionist reading of it.

First of all, it is necessary to recognize that Deconstruction is the most extreme expression of the movement in our time that has come to be known as "Modernism." The latter phenomenon is characterized by a total disillusionment with all the ideals the world has to offer. Both classical solutions from the past and modern attempts at answers in the present are portrayed in that literature as cruel fictions which turn man into a victim, a freak of the universe, and a fool. Although this may sound like an indictment, it is meant to be an accurate description of a singularly pessimistic world-vision. By it's very nature, then, Modernism is radically subversive and iconoclastic (See *Modernism* and Goodheart *The Failure of Criticism*). The deconstructionist version of this *Zeitgeist* expresses the above attitudes in what may be thought of as their most pure forms: they appear so potent precisely because they are so concentrated.

Within literary criticism Deconstruction set out to undermine the foundational assumption concerning transcendence that traditionalists had refused to doubt. This is the conviction, mentioned earlier in these pages, that "literature contains an undeniable power of reference which re-presents reality to the reader transformed and filled with meaning." Because this sacred assumption had remained unchallenged, traditional critics—whether of an ideological or formalist persuasion, whether Humanists, Marxists, Russian formalists or New Critics—were operating from within a naïve set of preconceptions. Deconstruction thus emerged as a critique and a denial, with the avowed task of a radical demystification. And as such—at least to many—it seemed to contain the promise of a higher and better truth which might correct the error in which critics were unwittingly immersed. Furthermore, it is also important to emphasize the fact that De-

construction is committed throughout its course to a
stubbornly rational mode of analysis. Indeed, it self-consciously employs reason as its favorite weapon in the war
against false ideals.

Ultimately of course, the idea that critique can fore-
shadow a better truth is an Enlightenment notion, so it
turns out to be a mystified way of looking at demystification, one more ideal that has to be attacked and destroyed.
Deconstruction takes a crucial step beyond this conventional and logocentric notion. In the end its relentless rationality pursues an entirely irrational result: it relativizes
all perspectives without exception and seeks to abolish the
very notion of truth itself.[5] No wonder the initial reaction
among many critics was so negative! People are never
pleased to have their most precious convictions about self
and reality so radically challenged, and to see them wan-
tonly reduced to absurd proportions. But the result of all
this is that the essence of Deconstruction can now be isolated and seen for what it is: *an attempted liberation of the
imagination from the oppressive weight of reality*. It sin-
glemindedly promotes an annihilation of reality, and it
tries to set up in its place a completely unfettered
imagination, one that floats freely, unanchored in anything but its own playful activity.

At the same time, however, it must also be emphasized
that this secular apology for imagination has nothing
whatsoever to do with Romanticism. The imagination
there, in Coleridge, Schelling, or Wordsworth, for example, was glorified precisely because it was conceived as the
highest and most powerful form of transcendence.
Deconstruction as an extreme version of Modernism is a
violent assault upon that very notion. The imagination
the deconstructionist extolls is one that is not full but
empty; it is fundamentally non-transcendental and
meaningless.[6]

But why this tremendous and all-consuming will to
absurdity? Where does it come from and why has it struck
a responsive chord—as indeed it has—in a surprising
number of literary critics today? It is not an adequate form
of explanation to take refuge in the cliche about it merely
being a fad. To find an answer to these questions we need

momentarily to expand our vision and look more closely at the human condition.

Above all, we need to focus clearly on the decisive shift that has transpired in man's perception of himself and the world. He began by taking material fact and his own life as the "real," and he ends by redefining the latter as writing, culture, and fiction. There has been, in other words, a momentous transition within man's being from the realm of matter and history on the one hand to the improbable dimension of poetry on the other. It is worth a pause to consider exactly what this means. It is, of course, simply the development of man as a conscious creature, and as such a phenomenon usually taken for granted. But the evolutionary event that made that development possible invites sustained and careful scrutiny. For that capacity for consciousness, that distance from the nature in which man is at once immersed and constantly in the process of leaving behind, produces what is surely the strangest of all entities in the universe: the human imagination. The important thing to see here is that from that moment on, the relation between the "real" (all that was pre-conscious or pre-imagined) and   imagination (all thought and fantasy) becomes *the central drama of man's existence.* From that point on man is involved in an ongoing and never completed struggle to reconcile the very different claims that each makes upon him continuously during his life. In what amounts to an evolutionary watershed, brute existence is transformed and becomes distinctively "human" (Ortega y Gasset 617-624).

The relevance of all this for our understanding of the crisis in contemporary literary criticism should begin to become apparent now. And it can be summed up in a single observation: the bitter war over the status of real life and fiction that is being waged by traditional and deconstructionist critics is fundamentally an intellectual manifestation in our time of that deeper conflict within the human condition. It is rooted ultimately in the universal conflict between reality and imagination that always constitutes man *qua* man. In the late twentieth century, the dispute over methods is simply literary criticism's way of turning out to be human.

Perhaps some speculative observations are in order at just this point. In life, if not in logic, reality and imagination are not antithetical and mutually exclusive. Only a naïve rationality could confuse the law of the excluded middle with the vagaries and paradoxes of human existence. In the latter reality and imagination, like other apparent "opposites"—naïveté and skepticism, affirmation and critique, memory and fantasy, tradition and novelty—coexist in what is either a dialectical or a complementary relationship. I will go even further and suggest that reality and imagination always interpenetrate and constitute one another in an ongoing, dynamic process in which mind and matter, animal nature and human culture fuse and blend indissolubly from beginning to end, with now one, now the other predominating. To place them in mortal combat with one another is to use reason—and a half-blind reason at that—to create a false opposition. Deconstruction would appear to be the victim of just such an imaginary drama, and its apotheosis of a non-transcendental imagination, one that is cut off from and absolutely irreconcilable with all that is not itself, represents the kind of imbalance we usually associate with illness. Because Deconstruction invariably isolates the text from its natural context, because it severs imagination, fiction and poetry from history and real life forever, it begins to take on the appearance of an error and an aberration. Another way to make the same point is the following. To the question "Should human imagination be grounded in anything other than itself?" the deconstructionist vehemently answers "Never!" I am suggesting that it does not really have a choice, but that it can pretend to have one, thereby dehumanizing itself as a kind of metaphysical disequilibrium in the midst of the surrounding humanity. Perhaps the nun of our dialogue was right earlier when she branded the professor's ideas as "diabolical." In the perspective just presented it is clear that there does exist a hypersophistication which, in seeking to overcome naïveté through a complicated use of reason, ultimately succumbs to a more complex and dangerous form of what it wanted to avoid. Deconstruction is thus the most intellectualized form of naïveté invented by the twentieth century.

It should be evident that it is not imagination *per se* that is being condemned here, but the *absolutization* of the imaginary as an end in itself. An important distinction might be useful at this point between the "imaginative" and the "imaginary." The former may be seen as a capacity for imagining that always retains some fruitful relation to the given, to all that is not merely its own ethereal invention. The "imaginary," in sharp contrast, represents a loss of contact with reality and hence a loss of man's humanity as this has been defined above. The difference between Thomas Jefferson, who imagined the possibility of the United States of America, and a psychotic who imagines that his father is Jesus Christ can serve as an illustration. The first is sane not because he turned out to be right, but because he worked stubbornly to make that fantasy a part of the reality that preceded it and continued to envelope it after its birth. He pragmatically took reality into account in his efforts to realize his dream. The psychotic, on the other hand, not unlike the Deconstructionist, prefers to sever all ties with the real; he denies its existence and remakes his own "reality" with a perverse and perverting imagination. Jefferson is not only "imaginative," but he is rightly considered a hero. In contrast, the poor psychotic is the victim of a misguided will to supplant the real with the "imaginary." The real culprit here, when all is said and done, is a deliberate isolation of fantasy from reality, a radical decontextualization at a fundamentally ontological level.[7] Now it is worth remembering that much of Western Literature from the Greeks to the present is a meditation on the catastrophe that results when the *hubris* of man cuts him off from reality—defined variously as nature, the gods, God, and today History—and plunges him into a solitude that is solipsistic and devoid of meaning. Deconstruction seems ignorant of this lesson, but the broader spectrum of literary criticism in the twentieth century need not be.

The place we have reached in our plateau is no longer an impasse. Deconstruction has emerged in this analysis as a gigantic imbalance appealing to a deep but partial predisposition in man. It has been exposed as a subtle, even powerful invitation to professors and their students—like the graduate student in our dialogue—to be, bluntly put, "taken in." But it is an invitation that fortunately can be declined, because worthy methodological alternatives are available in the post modernist age that we are entering. Before going on, however, we need to apply the interpretative framework of reality and imagination to autobiography as genre. Such an application will produce a surprising result.

What is it that makes autobiography unique? Our graduate student summed it up succinctly when he told the nun that "it's a kind of square circle, pretending to be history while asserting itself as poetry, and pretending to be poetry while asserting itself as history." Autobiography thus appears as a double pretense and has about it the aura of an impossibility. This complex status is not secondary or accidental. On the contrary, it is *the* defining characteristic of the genre, separating it from pure history at one pole and from pure fiction at the other. Autobiography, in other words, makes the—from the logical point of view—extravagant claim that it is fundamentally real and unreal, factual and fictional at the same time. A brief comparison might help make clear what this means. Autobiography may, in a non-trivial sense, be thought of as the proverbial glass of water that the optimist sees as half-full and the pessimist sees as half-empty. (It is hardly necessary to insist which of these viewers is the traditionalist and which is the deconstructionist.) In the last analysis, however, neither is correct because each fails to grasp the larger whole, which is a more complex vision that affirms that the glass is *both* half-full *and* half empty. In an analogous fashion, autobiography accomplishes a similar feat when it insists that it is two different things at once, that it is both reality *and* imagination.

The fascinating paradox that lies at the heart of the genre has created a dilemma for some critics, who have exhibited a tendency to focus on only one of these dimensions at the expense of the other. Thus Barret Mandel, in the article cited earlier, tries to fend off the deconstructionist rot and to defend his own view of autobiography as a real participation in a real life by insisting on "the simple truth that autobiography is not fiction"

(*Autobiography* 62). And conversely, Louis Renza, like any good—that is, disillusioned—modernist, insists that the so called truth of the real life is invariably swallowed up by an insatiable fiction. Both of these critics see a partial and important truth, but because neither sees the totality, that paradoxical fusion of the real and the imagined, their respective theories remain unnecessarily one-sided. Autobiography is certainly not as empty as the deconstructionist would have us believe it is. And it does not appear to be as "full of life" as Mandel would like to think. Yet, if it can manage to convey *some* truth, why not more? Could it turn out to be more full than even this analysis suggests?

At this time we have reached a kind of unexpected peak within our plateau. And from the vantage point it offers, we can now see a conclusion that was denied to us before: the same combination of forces that animates the autobiographical project also founds or constitutes the human condition. Fundamentally it too is a paradoxical coexistence and interpenetration of what at the surface appear to be logical opposites. It too is a double pretense with the aura of a metaphysical improbability. The result sounds like a cliche, but it is an important cliche which deconstructionists mistakenly thought they had undermined, and which in the course of this study we have tried to provide with a new philosophical and theoretical substance. It is an old maxim that can come alive again today, when we are approaching the threshold of a postmodernist age, and that states simply that "autobiography portrays a life."

We know that the autobiographer sets out to capture a life in words, or stated more carefully, that she seeks to reproduce the deepest and truest experience of what it has meant for her *to be human* in a particular place and time. And we also know from the previous pages that being human means that one is a kind of clearing within being for a convergence of contradictory forces, a dramatic tension between imagination and reality. Hence the remarkable and now warranted conclusion that *autobiography coincides in its own being with the deepest being of man.* Autobiography portrays a life because it dramatizes in its

own artistic and philosophical depths the complex substance of human life. At the level of its own inner logic it
performs a successful and extraordinary mimesis.

The irony of this situation is that the fate of autobiography has been somewhat sad. Until quite recently, it was
maligned, ignored, and underestimated. But in fact, as our
analysis suggests, it has always contained within itself a
unique potential for reproducing the human drama with
a comprehensive fidelity that is uncommon in the other
more studied genres.

Furthermore, in rehabilitating that crucial theoretical
premise—"autobiography portrays a life"—it should be
equally clear that we are infusing new life into at least the
first part of the traditionalist assumption concerning transcendence. It boldly stated that "literature contains an undeniable power of reference which re-presents reality to
the reader transformed and filled with meaning." That
the autobiographical word does contain a referential
power which returns reality to the reader seems undeniable after the above pages. That it re-presents a reality that
is "transformed and filled with meaning" is, on the other
hand, a separate and more complex metaphysical problem. To deal with that problem would require an even
more ambitious excavation into the breadth and power of
human imagination, and would involve far-reaching
speculation concerning philosophical and religious views.
It is clearly an enterprise that goes beyond the boundaries
of the present study. But that imaginative project is no
less relevant and significant in the reconstruction of the
foundations of literary criticism in our time.

Ultimately of course, we desperately need a criticism
that is comprehensive in scope, balanced in its vision, and
sound in its methods and techniques. And this, in turn,
must be firmly grounded in a mature and philosophically
confident humanism, which can reestablish the vision of
realistic ideals without which any society is doomed. After
a ruthless dissection of all literature, Deconstruction, true
to its modernist origins, triumphantly proclaimed the
death of autobiography. Deconstruction may justly be seen
as a bizarre penchant for writing obituaries. As unwilling
heirs to an age in which hyperskepticism and hyperso-

phistication run rampant—especially in the pride of our civilization, the university—, we have declined the invitation of the "imaginary" and attempted to resurrect the unique powers of autobiography. In an effort to remain simply "human," we have been obliged by the modern crisis to try to lay to rest an influential trend in criticism and to rehabilitate an entire literary genre. Nothing less than this formidable enterprise has been necessary in order to forge an adequate foundation for the study of Santa Teresa's *Vida*. The reader will judge the relative success or failure of this enterprise. But it should be evident that the value of some activities lies as much in the attempt as in their partial realization.

Attempts, realizations, successes, failures. At the end of this study, as always, we come back to perennial themes of the human condition: the place of fantasy in life, the *hubris* of exaggeration, the search for balance, and of course, a certain inevitable humility before the mystery we never cease to be. This in fact, may be the greatest lesson that autobiography has to teach us, and as such, the most appropriate conclusion to this prolegomenon for a post-modernist reading of Teresa's life. Is a participation through the medium of words really possible across time and in spite of tremendous differences in sex, creeds, circumstances, and so many other accidents of birth? Can we actually presume to share in Teresa's wonder and perplexity at being "human" in a place called Spain during the Renaissance? I confess that I like to imagine—hopefully in a somewhat "imaginative" way—that she hears these strange questions addressed to her from a faraway, illusionless society, and that she responds affirmatively, inviting us to descend in the pages of her autobiography "a las mesmas vivas aguas de la vida."

NOTES

[1] For a brief but provocative examination that respects the full diversity of this development, see Hayden White's "The Absurdist Movement in Contemporary Literary Criticism," in *Directions for Criticism:*

Structuralism and its Alternatives, eds. Murray Krieger and L. S. Dembo, Madison: Univ. of Wisconsin Press, 1977, 85-110.

[2] Gusdorf develops what is basically a Hegelian perspective, while Olney defends a variation on an equally idealist position. I also need to mention that I am indebted to Mandel and Renza for some of the ideas that appear in the dialogue between the nun and the graduate student.

[3] One senses the presence of Sartre's work on phenomenology of the imagination here. Frank Lentricchia has commented perceptively on Paul de Man's deconstructionist transposition of the existentialist's notion of "bad faith" into textual terms. See Lentricchia's *After the New Criticism*, Chicago: Univ. of Chicago Press, 1980, 285-287.

[4] The passage Renza cites is from the E. Allison Peers translation of Teresa's *Life*: "I wish I had also been allowed to describe clearly and in full detail my grave sins and wicked life...[But] I have been subjected to severe restrictions [by my confessors] in the matter." St. Teresa, *The Complete Works of St. Teresa*, 3 vols. London, 1946, 1:9.

[5] Hayden White nicely paraphrases and clarifies Derrida's thought on precisely this point: "There is no 'perception' by which 'reality' can be distinguished from its various linguistic fiturations and the relative truth-content of competing figurations discerned...There is only figuration, hence no privileged position from within language by which language can be called into question. Being, itself, is absurd. Therefore there is no 'meaning,' only the ghostly ballet of alternative 'meaning' which various modes of figuration provide." "The Absurdist Movement in Contemporary Literary Criticism" 109.

[6] With good reason René Wellek has perceptively suggested a similarity between Deconstruction and Dadaism. Cf. "A Historical Perspective: Literary Criticism," in *What Is Criticism*, ed. Paul Hernadi, Bloomington: Indiana Univ. Press, 1981, 317. Indeed, a very similar need to shock combined with a penchant for the bizarre do seem to be at the root of this thought.

[7] Alfred North Whitehead, with his accustomed sagacity, remarks: "Connectedness is of the essence of all things of all types... Abstraction from connectedness involves the omission of an essential factor in the fact considered. No fact is merely itself. The penetration of literature and art at their height arises from our dumb sense that we have passed beyond mythology; namely, beyond the myth of isolation. And again: "in every consideration of a single fact there is the suppressed presupposition of the environmental coordination requisite for its existence." *Modes of Thought*, New York: The Free Press, 1966, p. 9.

WORKS CITED

Goodheart, Eugene. *The Failure of Criticism.* Cambridge, London: Harvard Univ. Press, 1978.

Gusdorf, Georges. "Conditions and Limits of Autobiography." *Autobiography: Essays Theoretical and Critical.* Ed. and Trans. James Olney. Princeton: Princeton Univ. Press, 1980. 28-48.

Lentricchia, Frank. *After the New Criticism.* Chicago: Univ. of Chicago Press, 1980. 285-287.

Mandel, Barret J. "Full of Life Now." *Autobiography: Essays Theoretical and Critical.* Ed. James Olney. Princeton: Princeton Univ. Press, 1980. 49-72.

Modernism 1890-1930. Eds. Malcolm Bradbury and James McFarlane. New Jersey: Humanities Press, 1978.

Olney, James. "Some Versions of Memory. Some Versions of Bios: The Ontology of Autobiography." *Autobiography.* 236-267.

Ortega y Gasset, José. "El mito del hombre allende la técnica." *Obras Completas IX.* Madrid: Revista de Occidente, 1983. 617-624.

St. Teresa. *The Complete Works of St. Teresa.* Trans. E. Allison Press, 3 vols. London, 1946. 1:9.

Welleck, René. "A Historical Perspective: Literary Criticism." *What Is Criticism.* Ed. Paul Hernadi. Bloomington: Indiana Univ. Press, 1981. 317.

White, Hayden. "The Absurdist Movement in Contemporary Literary Criticism." *Directions for Criticism: Structuralism and its Alternatives.* Eds. Murray Krieger and L.S. Dembo. Madison: Univ. of Wisconsin Press, 1977. 85-110.

Whitehead, Alfred North. *Modes of Thought.* New York: The Free Press, 1966.

CHAPTER 4:
GOLDEN AGE AUTOBIOGRAPHY:
THE SOLDIERS

Margarita Levisi

Despite the fact that autobiography has been written since Antiquity, only recently, and to a great extent owing to seminal works by Misch, Gusdorf and Lejeune among others, has it begun to be seriously studied.[1] The narration of one's life has always varied widely in kind or nature and its study can be focused on from the angle of history, psychology or psychoanalysis, from that of cultural history and naturally, from that of literature, in which the autobiography is related to fiction in the first person and even to lyric poetry. For these reasons, research in the theory of autobiography has also approached the problem from very diverse angles. Among these, the formalist and linguistic theories of recent years acquire a special importance because, in addition to focusing on the very nature of autobiography, they also aid in its differentiation from related genres such as memoir, self-portrait or intimate di-

ary. In this sense, Lejeune's works have been very useful
in creating an immediate and intense dialogue, particularly among those who have reproached him for not having born sufficiently in mind the problems inherent to literary history. Although Lejeune partially modified his
first and apparently excessive dogmatic position in later
studies,[2] his work has had the virtue of attracting critical
attention to the genre in an international arena, and the
ensuing critical response has been immediate. In as much
as concerns the Hispanic world, the traces of Lejeune's
studies are to be observed in the whole of critical works
that have begun to fill the void in an evident lack of studies on Spanish autobiography, and can also be seen in a
most evident manner in the two Baume-lès-Aix
International Conferences held in Provence in 1979 and
1981.[3]

I believe that in order to be solidly developed, a critical
theory must begin with consideration of individual texts
from a given period since any writer produces his work
within a system of intertexts and cultural values of a
specifically temporal nature. In as much as this relates to
the Spanish Golden Age, the works of an autobiographical
nature can tentatively be divided into two large groups: in
the first we find those written by the religious, generally to
present or justify the stages or facets of their own spiritual
life—an area still in need of critical attention. In the second group we find the narrations of the laity who, for one
reason or another, must or desire to give an account of the
events of a life whose fortunes provide the author with
raw material and anticipate the interest of a possible
reader.

When we attempt to apply Lejeune's theoretical proposals to these works, we immediately observe that although we are confronted with the retrospective narrations of real people who relate in prose the history of their
own existence, what is lacking is the stress on the history
of their personality as required by the French critic's definition.[4] Even in the case of the religious, a preliminary
observation tends to indicate that the consideration of the
inner self is subjected to normative categories stipulated a
priori by a theological system. There is no gratuitous self-

observation but rather a desire to demonstrate that a higher power has favored them with grace.

The autobiographies written by Spanish laity of the sixteenth and seventeenth centuries focus on the progression of the inner world to an even lesser degree than those by religious writers as Lejeune requires, and as occurs starting with Rousseau's *Confessions* in which there is an explicit wish to expose the most intimate recesses of the inner self to the reader. If we refer solely to those Spanish texts apparently uncontaminated by fiction, what we find are narrations of personal facts in which the recounting of external events is stressed. However, after completing our readings we can not avoid the impression that these individuals have somehow projected a consciousness of the progress of their own "I," which is manifested indirectly by means of strategies that vary from case to case. Nonetheless, as Starobinski states, "Every autobiography— even when it limits itself to pure narrative—is a self-interpretation."[5] Circumstances relative to the cultural world or literary context, require that means other than direct expository form be utilized to communicate what constitutes a fundamental aspect of the autobiographical genre, that is, the interpretation of one's own "I" or the inner processes that sustain it. It is essential that we recognize that the autobiographical pact between an author and an implied reader proposed by Lejeune can only be fully realized among contemporaries, and that it cannot be established across the centuries without varying certain rules, all of which imply critical flexibility and the intervention of historical factors which might allow for the text's insertion within the literary and social parameters of a given moment.[6]

Considering that an abundant production of "Life stories" or "Memoirs" exists among the Spanish soldiers of the latter third of the sixteenth and the early part of the seventeenth centuries, I have chosen three in order to illustrate previously indicated points: the *Life* of Jerónimo de Pasamonte, that of Alonso de Contreras and that of Miguel de Castro. All three of them lived very similar lives in almost identical environments, and although they had no literary pretensions of any kind, at a certain point they decided to relate their adventures in written form. They all shared a social, historical and geographical milieu with Cervantes who, although he never wrote an autobiography, did speak about himself on multiple occasions. After briefly discussing each of these *Lives*, I shall indicate the strategies they make use of in order to speak indirectly about the evolution of their own personality and Cervantes's works will be used for corroboration.[7]

Jerónimo de Pasamonte presents a curious case. His autobiography, apparently finished in 1605, narrates a pathetic story: a solitary and sickly childhood and an unfulfilled desire to enter the convent characterize his early years. He enlists in the army as an adolescent, fights in the battle of Lepanto, later falls prisoner to the Turks and spends eighteen terrible years as a galley slave. The narration of the years of captivity is a report of continuous privations and terror at his captors' world whose functioning he never fully seems to comprehend. There are also frustrated attempts at flight followed by cruel reprisals. His only relief is a stubborn adherence to prayer. He is ransomed and returns to a homeland where frustration and poverty await him. He mentions having violently attacked some relatives whom he believes are persecuting him. There follow new attempts to enter into religious life, but in the end he marries in Naples. Illnesses and problems of all kinds befall him and he begins to suspect that his parents-in-law and other individuals are witches who are casting all sorts of evil spells on him because he refuses to yield to their ill intentions. He writes of visions of demons who tempt him, others who persecute him, and claims to have heard voices urging him either to resist or to give in, all of which drive him to despair and even to an attempted suicide. At this point in the narration he declares his express objective for writing his story: to demonstrate through his own experience the existence and evil doings of witches and demons. He proposes a remedy, that is to bring down upon them the entire weight of the Church through its power of excommunication. He affirms that his authority is derived as much from the blood he shed in Moslem lands as from the fact of having always remained faithful to religious practices, and he declares that just as he has related his outward life, now it is time to reveal his inner life. In what constitutes a second autobiography he begins to re-tell his story from childhood on, this time focusing only on the favors received from God as well as the oral prayers and acts of devotion practiced throughout the course of his life until the time of writing. He transcribes these prayers with great care, mentioning the needs he wishes God to fulfill by reciting them. Finally he attempts to support with rather confused theological and scriptural bases what constitutes the motive of his narration: to show why the Church should excommunicate those who are in contact with evil spirits.[8]

What one first observes in Pasamonte's account of his religious practices is the absence of the essential current of love that characterizes the relationship between the truly religious soul and his God. In Pasamonte's prayers there is a noticeable and constant anxiety: to him, prayers are a means to placate a demanding and threatening deity. This is not something that Pasamonte explicitly manifests or even comprehends, but rather is revealed by the content of his narrative episodes and in the minutely intense detailing of his rituals. As seen from the reader's angle, this narration is undermined by a series of obvious contradictions which have led the few critics who deal with this work to consider its author a fool or, worse yet, a liar seeking to obtain economic aid from the Church by displaying false saintliness. Nonetheless, it is important to note that objective truth, which the reader can glimpse many times throughout the narration, is one thing, but the truth as Pasamonte understands it could be quite different. In order to find coherence in this text and to understand the reason of the unusual double autobiography, it is helpful to consider Pasamonte's narrative in light of recent psychoanalytic conclusions concerning the trauma that affects some survivors of contemporary concentration camps.[9] Pasamonte had a very sad childhood, fell captive in early adolescence and, not only according to his own story but also from historical accounts, slaves' living conditions were such that severe trauma could ensue.[10] The psychological consequences of that type of mistreatment are documented in medical literature and include depression, fits of anger, aggressiveness, suicidal intentions, mania of persecution, obsessive rituals charged with anxiety, desire for vengeance (the excommunication Pasamonte proposes against his presumed persecutors can be nothing else), physical problems, and also a sort of schizophrenic dissociation of the "I" between inner and outer world. When this is transferred to Pasamonte's text it explains the story's contradictions between appearances of sanctity and violence, and also the strange format of the discourse with its double autobiography, as if the components of his own identity were split and separate from each other. Seen in this manner, Pasamonte's writing is not that of a liar but the utterances of a sick man whose psychological imbalance leaves its traces in his discourse.

In terms of genre, the final chapters of Pasamonte's inner autobiography in which only prayers or pious activities are mentioned constitutes, from the narrator's point of view, a long introspective discourse. But the truth is that he reveals his inner world's content to the reader not by explicit declarative formulas, which are essentially forms of activity, but rather by mentioning the intentions of the prayers he is reciting. We can thus notice a series of emotions that were never made explicit in the narration: gratitude to benefactors, fear of sickness, love for his children, uncertainties due to economic problems, desire for revenge and fury at those he considers his enemies. And however aberrant it may seem to us, it must be emphasized that Pasamonte at the time of writing has discovered the meaning of his own trajectory, that is, to facilitate the triumph of Christianity over the forces of evil. That discovery is in turn the point of origin of the autobiographical act carried out in order to disclose what he has understood as his mission on earth.

But, as was already pointed out, it is important to note that even when he speaks of his inner world, Pasamonte does not conceive of introspection in modern terms: for him it means enumerating or transcribing oral prayers whose repetition, in the final analysis, is nothing but a form of physical and mental activity. Pasamonte, like many of his contemporaries, sees himself in action, be it internal or external, and he cannot conceive of self reflection, as we understand it today, of any possible interest to an eventual reader.

Alonso de Contreras: The *Life* of this soldier is perhaps the most fascinating of the autobiographies of Golden Age soldiers, as attested to by the presence of translations and modern editions. Contreras wrote the longest part of his story in 1630, but there are two briefer additions, one concluded in 1633 and the other probably in 1641. Although he wrote other documents of a practical nature, he was certainly not a professional writer and his connection with the literary world is limited to his friendship with Lope de Vega who dedicated a comedy to him.[11] It is not clear to whom this *Life* was addressed or what its purpose was. There are indications that it could have been destined to recall for the Count of Monterrey, one of Contreras's protectors, the extent and excellence of his deeds, just as a military account of activities would have done in a more condensed form.

Contreras relates a life full of vicissitudes: he runs away from home at fourteen, arrives at Naples and from that point on he is constantly crisscrossing the Mediterranean first as a sailor and later as a Captain of one of the Order of Malta's ships. Upon his return to Spain, he serves in the Spanish army for a while, but irritated because Philip III does not compensate him as he considers just, he leaves for Moncayo to become a hermit. Driven out by the authorities who accused him of being king of the Moriscos, he manages to escape and to demonstrate his innocence and is given different missions by the army. There follows a series of adventures that take the protagonist to Portugal, Flanders, Naples, Puerto Rico, again to North Africa and Spain. Needless to say he is constantly faced with victory and defeat, treason, love and adventures of every sort. He ends up in Rome at the age of forty-eight in the service of the Count of Monterrey who helps him obtain the title of Knight of the Order of Malta. The two last segments of his autobiography give an account of his Italian trajectory, his disagreements and later reconciliation with the Count of Monterrey, and additional honors bestowed on him by the Order of Malta.

The unquestionable importance of this text lies in the fact that Contreras's life is in itself extremely interesting and he narrates it in a lively, concise style. He does not describe, he only states the facts with a notable economy of expression, and utilizes dialogue with admirable ability. His story is truly fascinating, but of himself, or his inner world, Contreras tells us nothing. Thus we are confronted head on with the problem of the autobiographical genre in this period: if this soldier only narrates adventures without the slightest allusion to his inner self or its development, how can we justify the inclusion of his *Life* in a genre whose defining characteristic is precisely that of revealing the individual's evolution?

Narrating one's own life always implies memory and selection: among the multiple episodes of a human trajectory, only those which the writer considers pertinent to exposing his self-image are chosen for the telling. Bearing in mind that observation, what we first notice in Contreras's *Life* is that he gives an account of a gradual progress from the initial poverty that forced him to leave home up until the time of writing, in which he is an honored member of the Order of Malta. Throughout the text, Contreras mentions the names or nicknames, the military ranks and titles he earns as a consequence of his activities. He points out how each successfully completed mission earns him another assignment more dangerous than the one before. While he also notes his defeats, they are viewed solely as obstacles he has overcame: once success is gained, his personal worth is again manifested and recognized by others. For Contreras, his own trajectory has been a series of challenges to his strength, wit, ability or valor. The fact that he surmounted them all reveals a very positive self image. He also mentions the behavior of others in his regard: women offer themselves to him, high authorities of many institutions select him to carry out particularly dangerous tasks, and demonstrate in many tangible ways just how much they value his participation in their plans. Even the great Lope de Vega, with whom he had never spoken before, stops him on the street and offers him shelter in his own home during one of Contreras's periods of economic difficulty. There are also mentions or short descriptions of the progressive improvement of his own attire: in a narration dedicated almost totally to an account of actions, these brief allusions to improved outward appearance are obvious signs of satisfaction. These episodes or circumstances are stated without comment, but the implications are clear to the reader: without ever saying it, Contreras reviews his life and sees himself as a success. He is fully aware of his own worth and sees his improvement in both honors and wealth as something that deserves to be brought to others' attention.

But perhaps it is in the abundantly utilized direct or indirect dialogue where the mental position of one or more participants in a given situation can be observed best. Contreras, perhaps indirectly influenced by Lope, or possibly due to an innate inclination towards verbal economy, lays out the facts using the same techniques that were common in that period's comedies. In fact, many of the episodes of this autobiography could be considered as miniature plays, clearly divided in parts and with characters whose motivations or sentiments become transparent by what is said or by the manner and context in which it is said. Through the dialogues we gather specific details of what is happening and where, the participants' social status, their moods and desires. When Contreras re-creates his own speeches, the words he chooses in formulating his discourse are an expression of the inner life of his former self. Thus, dialogue is an instrument of self-revelation, and given the lack of secondary or explanatory details, the reader must interpret it in terms of the cultural parameters of the historical period. For example, Contreras, as a character appears using in his dialogues the expletives and oaths which characterize the lexicon of soldiers during the Golden Age. From this we infer that Contreras, the man, feels perfectly integrated within this social group without his ever having to tell us so directly. Obviously, since he is the main character, he is the center of our attention and in order to evaluate his state of mind it is important to balance the dialogues with the facts previously stated. On one occasion, Contreras is not satisfied with the results of his audience with King Philip III. He states that during the night he decided to abandon the court and become a hermit. He immediately heads for the mountains and when someone asks him where is he going, he answers: "To serve another King, for I am tired." He never states what he felt when Philip denied his petition, but his radical action and his answer reveal his fury: as far as he is concerned, Philip III has been dethroned and replaced by a superior authority. Obviously many other reasons could have been present for Contreras's quick retreat from the court, some quite less pious than the one given in his answer, but the fact remains that through the dialogue we can infer the individual's inner reaction, which is never revealed in the text.

Contreras's *Life* is an example of the strategies that can be used in an age uninterested in the revelation of inner processes in order to present indirectly one's inner world and its progress. Seen in this light, Contreras's text is not an adventurer's book but a full, although reticent, autobiographical work, even in light of modern theories of genre.

Miguel de Castro: His *Life* must have been written while still a young man, circa 1611, probably as a confession of his failings made before some noble who, on pardoning him, could aid in his advancement. This soldier does not have great feats to tell and the text has very limited literary value.[12] However it is interesting as a document illustrative of daily life and gives an account of Neapolitan court events, both great and small, to which Castro was a witness. But Castro's autobiography, owing precisely to the author's scant literary skills, represents another strategy of self revelation that can be added to those already observed.

Like so many others, Castro enlists in the army as a youth, goes to Italy, participates in some military encounters in the Mediterranean, and is chosen as the servant of a Spanish captain with whom he remains in Naples. There Castro develops a passion of disastrous consequences for a courtesan. In order to be with her, many nights he escapes the home of his master from whom he also steals delicacies and to whom he constantly lies. He is admonished and punished many times as his misdeeds are discovered, but all this is not sufficient to separate him from his beloved. Not even when he takes service with the Count of Benavente, the Spanish Viceroy, do his escapades stop. This time, however, the consequences are much more serious because, Castro, in order to be with his lover, abandons the Viceroy without notice, and in so doing, permanently terminates his career as a nobleman's valet. When the love affair ends, Castro stays briefly in the service of some knights of the Order of Malta with whom he travels to Sicily. After recounting a few more events, the manuscript is interrupted. On recalling his past, Castro vacillates between repentance for having sinned against the laws of God and anguish for having lost the opportunity of advancement in his career. It is difficult to decide which of the two emotions prevails.

Although Castro's normal prose is incorrect, full of Italianisms and has a pronounced oral formulation, he was undoubtedly familiar with literary works. There are certain similarities between episodes of his *Life* and others from *Guzmán de Alfarache* and *Lazarillo de Tormes*. Even so, these similarities seem to be more a coincidence of circumstances than purposeful imitation. But Castro must have been familiar with that period's poetry not only because he claims to have composed poems for his beloved, but also because he uses a pseudo-poetic or more elaborate style to treat themes of an amorous nature or for reflection on his own moral or spiritual state, while for the exposition of normal occurrences and circumstances his prose is simple, incorrect and as noted previously, almost oral. Unfortunately, when Castro employs poetic language, his discourse does not improve because he includes indiscriminately all manner of learned, erudite or complex rhetorical devices, distorted mythological allusions, set phrases, worn or absurd comparisons and in general, a plainly worn Petrarchan lexicon. Although the greater part of the narration refers to common events and although his incursions into the lyric world do not abound, it is important to note the use of two different linguistic registers whose usage varies according to theme, a recourse also quite normal in spoken language

In the case of incidental writers such as Castro, their aesthetic failure matters little. What counts is the existence of two linguistic levels and the adoption of the one which—in his judgement—possesses greater prestige for certain fixed occasions. This clearly documents the consciousness and the need to express different levels of his inner self. If the autobiographic genre is dependent on self-knowledge and its written revelation, then the literary language and customs of a given historical moment must in turn provide an adequate means for so doing. When these are insufficient, the writer must find substitutes wherever he is able. In addition to his adventures, Castro gives an account of his amorous problems or his moments of repentance and finds no other instrument than that of the language of lyric poetry, traditionally used for these ends by pens much abler than his. Poetic language, as unsure and as mistaken as his use of it may be, is the only instrument within Castro's reach for the manifestation and implicit ranking of his inner world's alternatives.

The points previously made, viewed from a social angle, illustrate Castro's personal situation. By birth and education, he belongs to a socioeconomic class well below that of the nobility and in his free moments he can only socialize with other servants whose adventures are those of picaroons. But he also coexists with the Viceroy and his role as a valet obliges him to serve his master in the most personal tasks of daily life, thus creating the appearance of an intimacy that will never be reflected in social acceptance, even if it could yield economic gains. His written language reflects this coexistence without integration. The close proximity of the social strata's living arrangements imposes on the inferior two very diverse roles and seems to leave a clear imprint on his literary production. This can explain why Castro expresses events he considers commonplace in a much less elaborate register than the one he uses to disclose his amorous sentiments or his moral reflections. He intuitively assesses these as the noblest or worthiest aspects of his identity and lends them dignity by disclosing them in the code of a higher or more educated class than his own. This also implies the best demonstration that primitive autobiography, even at the hand of someone who lacks literary skills, manages to express indirectly one of the genre's essential elements: the focus on the self. Castro, a man of little education and even less fortune, presents his self concept when he bestows on the language used for the expression of his inner processes what he considers a greater dignity.

Miguel de Cervantes: While autobiography perhaps responds to an atemporal human need, in the Spanish Golden Age there is clearly no set formula for speaking about one's self. Even though autobiography is not yet a well defined genre, the literary and cultural forces, the conscious and unconscious models of the period act uniformly on the writings of a homogeneous group of individuals: the soldiers. Among the latter is Cervantes, whose methods could be prudently utilized as corroborating evidence in the formulation of conclusions pertaining to the soldiers' autobiographical techniques. The fact that the temporal trajectory and external circumstances of all these men have remarkable similarities allows for a common social and referential field. Neither the artistic difference that separates Cervantes from the previously mentioned soldiers nor the need for further research in his autobiographical techniques should detract from the use of his works for these purposes.

Cervantes never wrote an autobiography, but he allowed many facts about his life to appear in his work.[13] Moreover, many of his characters use an autobiographical formula within his works of fiction in order to recount their personal trajectory to other characters. And lastly, as on so many occasions, we can count on his critical reflections to deduce his theoretical ideas with regard to self-revelation.

Though Cervantes speaks of himself in many of his *Prologues*, it is in the *Journey to Parnassus* where his techniques of self-revelation can best be noted. Even though the mythological nature of the work would never allow it to be considered an autobiography, from the beginning we identify Cervantes as author-narrator-character since he attributes to himself works and deeds well known by all and since the fictional interlocutors within the text refer to him by his true name. In chapter IV, Cervantes speaks of himself rather extensively, and limits his self-presentation to that of an author whose literary production in terms of quality should have assured him a place among the poets of Parnassus, if it had not been for the envy of others who have also caused him to be left a pauper. He alludes very briefly to his moral qualities, but it is important to note that of the twenty-three tercets dedicated by Cervantes the character to talk about himself, more than eighteen recall with undisguised satisfaction the books he created. But while the enumeration of his publications is recited in the first person by Cervantes the character, the glorification of his heroic conduct as a soldier is confided to another character. Therefore one notes that when Cervantes adopts narrative modes akin to autobiography, his interest is not concentrated on the presentation of his inner processes, even though the tone or the content might presuppose them. What he mentions is the world of his activities, be they arms or letters, and he points out directly or indirectly the scant economic success they have brought him.

In a different context, when a character in his works tells of his or her past life before an audience composed of other characters, in other words, when within a work of fiction there occurs what could be called an autobiographical narration, the greater part of the discourse is given over to the mention of actions, while the consideration of sentiments or elaborations on the inner self are very few. In *Don Quijote* (I, 39-41) the story of the captive Ruy Pérez de Biedma is a good example. The detailing of sentiments inspired by his love for Zoraida, or the presentation of his inner trajectory before a group of characters who wish to know the reason for his attire and his accompanying a Moorish girl would have been impertinent and unnecessary. In this way we see the logic in the selection of narrative materials in a fictional autobiography whose validity can be extended to and act on the soldiers' narrations previously considered. Just as the Captive, they assume and respond to an interest in action that exists among the receivers or implied receivers of their work, and this is what they offer. When Berganza in the *Dialogue of the Dogs* reflects on his experiences, he does so in order to find in them a universal moral value not an individual one or one of self-knowledge, even though the narration of his life will ultimately produce the discovery of his "true" identity. His is a story that fluctuates between the formal boundaries of the picaresque and the autobiography, in order to give the latter a universal ethical value just as the period requires.

From our modern perspective, the tension between two similar narrative formats, the picaresque and autobiography, is observed very clearly in the episode of Ginés de Pasamonte in the *Quijote* (I, 22) where once again we note Cervantine critical reflection. Paradoxically, the *Life* written by Ginés is never revealed and we must content ourselves with hypothetical conjectures about format, content and purpose as deduced from his dialogue with other characters. It has become a tradition to note in this passage the author's position on the picaresque, however it is also legitimate to consider it as an observation of the formal characteristics of the narration we now call autobiographic. Ginés is, within the story, a real individual, and as such, is granted the authority to present that which the author, Cervantes, considers the essential characteristics of self-referential narration as they are conceived at that time. These would be: 1) the identity of author, narrator and character, as can be deduced from the initial dialogue between Ginés, the guard and Don Quijote, 2) the narration of "true" events that, for this very reason, are better than those of Lazarillo which are not; 3) the aesthetic level of his narration that tells "truths so elegant and so witty" that they can not be surpassed by any fiction. Where form is concerned, the essential characteristics would be: 4) the chronological progression of the narration of events ("from my birth until the last time they threw me into the galley" says Ginés); 5) an open end, since he is still obviously alive. With respect to content, we can deduce that the hypothetical readers of this hypothetical story of an individual famous for his villainy can only expect gallows adventures, the origin of Ginés's present fame, and not reflections on his "I." The unrepentant Ginés seems ill-inclined to offer this sort of material, though there is self recognition when he states that his intelligence did not bring him success, as usually happens to all men. We also note that for Ginés the writing of his story has an eminently practical value because it provided him with money when he pawned it.

If we compare the content of Cervantine reflection on the theme of autobiography with the practice of the soldiers previously considered, we note that the greatest difference lies in the fact that Cervantes notes the product's aesthetic importance, a point that does not interest the soldiers. It is not surprising that Cervantes's professional interest leads him to take note of an aspect of autobiography that will not become completely clear until almost two centuries later with Rousseau, and thus allow the appearance of autobiography as a full-fledged literary genre. The soldiers did not touch on the theme of literary elegance, and if they did it was only to lessen its importance. Instead, they insist on the truth in their narrated events, or the usefulness their narrations may have for others.

After this overview, certain conclusions about the autobiographies of these Golden Age soldiers should be drawn. If Cervantes represents the dawn of artistic consciousness in a genre that has not yet formalized its rules, the writings of individuals such as Pasamonte, Contreras or Castro exemplify a prior state of the problem that is delimited by social sector and confined to those who did not participate in literary circles.

It is very important to emphasize the private nature of these relations. The soldiers who write do so in order to give an account of their trajectories to someone, but they do not aspire in any way to have their narrations published. In fact, their autobiographies were not published until this century and then more as documents of historical rather than literary interest. We must therefore exclude any reciprocal influence between their writings. Their formal debts, given the limited nature of the soldiers' education, must be sought primarily in the models accessible to their profession. The accounts of their services, regularly written to request all sorts of gains, while normally drawn up in the third person, must have been a powerful point of reference for the chronological organization of their texts. The sacrament of confession, an oral account of one's deeds (or misdeeds), in the first person, could have shaped the writings' organization, especially in cases such as Pasamonte's. Lastly, Cervantes points out the relationship between the autobiography of certain social groups and the picaresque, and although the soldiers' familiarity with this type of fiction cannot be documented with any degree of certainty, the milieu or many of the situations they present are obviously quite similar. This seems due more to common social grounds and to the self-referential format than to real literary influences.

In the soldiers' autobiographies it is evident that the author-narrator's position is inferior to that of his implied reader's who appears to be invested with authority or power, and before whom one's own actions should be justified. Perhaps there is a certain hope that the narrative will entertain such a reader. Cervantes himself, who aspires to a much wider audience, addresses a public that will judge his work. In general, the situation of an autobiographical writer is always that of someone whose story must be adjusted for the purpose of being well received. An attitude of total independence on the narrator's part does not yet exist.

From the previously mentioned characteristics, that is, an initial subordinate position to a limited public/receiver, one can derive the fact that the autobiography gives itself over to practical objectives, at least for this social group. These individuals do not take on the task—not always an easy one for them—of writing their stories out of a sense of pleasure in leaving a memoir for their families, who in many instances did not even exist, much less out of a sense of aesthetic purpose. They write because, from this communicative effort, they hope for a practical gain, be it an economic benefit, the attainment of social advancement or self-justification. From their point of view, their lives have been useful ones, they have done something valuable and for this reason they should be heard and compensated. Even Cervantes, when he speaks of himself in the *Journey to Parnassus*, assumes this position. It is symptomatic that only individuals of lower military rank write their life-stories; they were subject to more economic misfortune than those of the higher ranks.

It must also be noted that the written version of their stories comes about after previous rehearsals in an oral format. All of them record having told their stories to others in order to move, entertain or incline their public to offer some aid, in situations vaguely similar to those of the false captives in Cervantes's *Persiles*. In the case of the three soldiers observed above, this oral trait is transmitted in different degrees to their prose style.

All these factors come together in such a way that the focus of these narrations' content is mostly events of external activities at the expense of declaration of inner processes for whose exposition the period's lexicon is very limited. In the case of these occasional writers, it is evident that their readers should know what they have accomplished in order to duly appreciate their contributions when the time comes to reward them. It is also imperative that the events narrated be intrinsically interesting, at least from the authors' point of view, because they must maintain the addressee's attention and make possible the practical results they propose to achieve with their narrative efforts. These soldiers have seen the world, their adventures have been many, and the content of their stories have an interest of which they are well aware. The affirmation or definition of the "I" is only conceived through action and not by means of self reflection. Besides, the world of that period values this position; it is a moment in which the great conquests in the New World and the military campaigns in the Old still act on the national consciousness, even if success or victory is not always attained. We are still within the sphere of soldiers and pirates, of the height of theatrical gesture in life and the theater of action in the stage. What is important for the laity of the Golden Age is activity, not theory. Except in the case of religious reflection, to speak of one's own inner world would have been considered almost lewd, and certainly impertinent.

This does not mean that self-consciousness or perception of one's inner evolution is absent, but rather that the manifestation is not carried out by means of explicit verbalization of the sort one expects after Rousseau. The means of expressing the sphere of self vary with each individual: Contreras does it by means of the subjects he deals with and his dialogues, Pasamonte in the revelation of the formulas for prayer, and Castro makes use of a different stylistic level according to the sort of facts he needs to present. Self reflection is hidden behind narrative structures because language itself at this time does not offer a precise lexicon for presenting conditions of mind. In general, the soldiers who write during the Golden Age manifest pride in themselves and who they are or have become through the mere fact of writing their life stories.

The above mentioned characteristics could be extended to include the *Life* of Diego García de Paredes, or Diego Suárez Montañes. In that of Diego Duque de Estrada one notes the incidence of clearly novelesque episodes in addition to a greater literary consciousness.[14] But all are the attempts by which a genre still in its formative stages searches out its own rules of expression.

NOTES

[1] Georg Misch, *Geschichte der Autobiographie*, 4 vols. (Bern: A.Francke, 1950). Georges Gusdorf, *La découverte de soi* (Paris: Presses Universitaires de France, 1948) and also: "Conditions et limites de l'autobiographie," *Formen der Selbstdarstellung, Festgabe für Fritz Neubert* (Berlin: Duncker and Humboldt, 1956) 105-123, translated as "Conditions and Limits of Autobiography," *Autobiography: Essays Theoretical and Critical*, ed. James Olney (Princeton: Princeton Univ. Press, 1980) 28-48. By the same author see also: "De l'autobiographie initiatique à l'autobiographie genre littéraire," *Revue d'histoire littéraire de la France* 75 (1975): 957-994. Philippe Lejeune, *L'autobiographie en France* (Paris: Colin, 1971); Lire Leiris, *Autobiographie et langage* (Paris: Klincksieck, 1975); "Autobiography in the Third Person," *New Literary History* 9 (1977): 27-50; "Le pact autobiographique," *Poétique* 14 (1973): 137-162; "Autobiographie et histoire littéraire," *Revue d'histoire littéraire de la France* 75 (1975): 903-935. The last two articles were included in *Le pact autobiographique*, (Paris: Ed. Seuil, 1975). It would be impossible to mention here all the substantial works concerning autobiography that have appeared in the last decade. A useful bibliography can be found in the Addenda of Jeffrey Mehlman's *A Structural Study of Autobiography: Proust, Leiris, Sartre, Lévi-Strauss* (Ithaca: Cornell Univ. Press, 1974) 170-213.

[2] See in particular his "Le pacte autobiographique (bis)," in *L'Autobiographie en Espagne, Actes du IIe Colloque International de la Baume-lès-Aix*, (Aix-en-Provence: Université de Provence, 1982) 7-26.

[3] In addition to the above mentioned volume, see *L'autobiographie dans le monde hispanique, Actes du Colloque International de la Baume-lès-Aix* (Aix-en-Provence: Université de Provence, 1980). In this volume, the article by Jean Molino "Strategies de l'autobiographie au Siècle d'Or," 115-137 is particularly relevant to our present subject. Considering the amount of available material very little has been written on the Spanish autobiography of the sixteenth and seventeenth centuries since Manuel Serrano y Sanz's introduction to his volume *Autobiografías y Memorias* (Madrid, Nueva Biblioteca de Autores Españoles: Bailly-Ballière, 1905). An important contribution was made by Randolph Pope, *La autobiografía española hasta Torres Villarroel* (Bern-Frankfurt: Lang, 1974).

[4] Lejeune's definition of autobiography is: "A retrospective account in prose that a real person makes of his own existence stressing his individual life and particularly the history of his personality." It has remained invariable since the publication of "Le pact autobiographique."

[5] Originally published in French, Starobinski's "The Style of Autobiography" has been translated into English in the above mentioned volume on *Autobiography*, edited by James Olney.

[6] See Elizabeth W. Bruss, "L'autobiographie considérée comme acte littéraire," *Poétique* 17 (1974).

[7] See my book *Autobiografías del Siglo de Oro* (Madrid: Sociedad General Española de Librería, 1984) where bibliography and more information about these authors can be found.

[8] Pasamonte's *Life* was first published in *Revue Hispanique*, 55 (1922), and reprinted later in *Autobiografías de soldados*, Biblioteca de Autores Españoles, Vol. 90 (Madrid: Atlas, 1956). Pope discusses Pasamonte's autobiography in his above-mentioned book.

[9] Useful information on this subject can be found in *Massive Psychic Trauma*, ed. Henry Krystal (New York: International Univ. Press, 1968).

[10] Even if biased, a good account of the Christian slaves' situation can be found in Fray Diego de Haedo's *Diálogos de la Captividad de Argel* and *Diálogos de los mártires de Argel* included in his *Topografía e Historia General de Argel*, 3 vols. (Madrid: Sociedad de Bibliófilos Españoles, 1927).

[11] Manuel Serrano y Sanz published for the first time Contreras's autobiography in the *Boletín de la Academia de la Historia* 37 (1900). For other editions translations and bibliography see my *Autobiografías de Soldados* 93-94. To the references included there should be added an interesting article by Beverly Jacobs, "Social Provocation and Self-justification in the *Vida* of Captain Alonso de Contreras," *HR* 51 (1983).

[12] Castro's *Life* was first published by Antonio Paz y Meliá with a short preliminary study as: *La vida del soldado español Miguel de Castro* (Barcelona: Biblioteca Hispánica, 1900). Both Paz y Meliá and Alfredo Morel Fatio in "Soldats espagnols du XVIIè siècle" *Bulletin Hispanique* III (1901), refer to the literary limitations of this text. Castro's style has also been very well studied by Pope in his book mentioned above, 201-209.

[13] The following studies deal with Cervantes's autobiographical writings: J.B. Avalle Arce, "La captura (Cervantes y la autobiografía)," *Nuevos deslindes cervantinos* (Barcelona: Ariel, 1975); E. Rivers, "Cervantes' Journey to Parnassus," *MLN* 85 (1970); J. Canavaggio, "Cervantes en primera persona," *JHP* II (1977) and "La dimension autobiographique du *Viaje del Parnaso*," in *L'autobiographie dans le monde hispanique*; F. Márquez Villanueva, *Personajes y temas del Quijote* (Madrid: Taurus, 1975) 92-146; J.J. Allen, "Autobiografía y ficción: el relato del capitán cautivo," *Anales Cervantinos* 15 (1978); M. Gaylord Randel, "Cervantes' portrait of the Artist," *Cervantes* III 2 (1983).

[14] See the important preliminary study by Henry Ettinghausen included in his edition of Diego Duque de Estrada's *Comentarios del desengaño de sí mismo* (Madrid: Castalia, 1982).

CHAPTER 5:
THE PICARESQUE AS AUTOBIOGRAPHY:
STORY AND HISTORY

Edward H. Friedman

Self-revelation of the inner life is perhaps a dirty business. Nevertheless, even in its ugliest forms, we cannot afford altogether to despise anyone who—for whatever reasons—is the humblest and ugliest servant of truth. Human beings are instruments crawling about the surface of the earth, registering their reactions to one another and to things. Some of them are very crude instruments, others exact and sensitive. A human instrument is most exact about objective things when it is most detached from them. The effort to create form and objectivity in literature is detachment: and whoever writes of that which is most close to him—himself—is unlikely to achieve detachment.
—Stephen Spender, "Confessions and Autobiography"

Autobiography is marked by a sense of difference: neither fact nor fiction, objective history nor literary object, it is a hybrid of codes, strategies, and writerly options. Autobiography borrows from narrative, which in turn may recreate its structural source, in the form of an invented life. The reciprocity of the intertext foregrounds the conventions—and counterconventions—of autobiography as device. The Spanish picaresque novel develops, to a degree, from what may be termed an autobiographical impulse, which unites confession (and confessional literature), an acknowledgment of the representative nature of the individual, and the self-consciousness (and self-confidence) of the narrating subject. Be it the explanation of a case, the confession of a repentant sinner, or the experiences of a social climber, the picaresque has as its focal point a "life" recounted in the first person. Not only is the teller in the tale, but he is the tale; the narrative act becomes both form and substance of message production. Revelation lies in the discursive space between event and text, between an amorphous reality and a fixed system of emplotment. The (pseudo)autobiographical trappings of the picaresque illuminate a process of transformation, of temporal and contextual shifts, and an awareness on the part of the authors—real, implied, and fictional—of their audience.

Autobiography, like historiography, is an ordering of events, which Hayden White relates—in *Metahistory* and in essays such as "The Historical Text as Literary Artifact"—to rhetorical or tropological patterns inherent in composition, or to ploys on the part of the writer. The element of truth, which at least nominally separates documental history from fictional narrative, is a more open issue in autobiography, which certainly allows for a subjective vision. In terms of reception, one may expect opinion rather than fact to dominate, meditation rather than exposition for its own sake. Pseudoautobiography—autobiography at play—may flout the motives and the motifs of the authentic form, but the intensification only underscores the rhetorical, personal bent of the narrative. Fictional autobiography is twice or thrice removed from history and from the allegiance to truth which serves as a cornerstone of historiography. Emplotment is the mediating factor in each case, but the writer of fiction enjoys greater creative freedom, less relegation to veracity. Most importantly, perhaps, in fictional autobiography the subject/object dichotomy expands to include the creator of the narrator/protagonist and his (or her) intratextual alter ego,

the "implied author." The implied author (via Wayne
Booth in *The Rhetoric of Fiction* and other narratologists,
among them Seymour Chatman and Susan Sniader
Lanser) is a construct that addresses the author's presence
in the text, as encoder and arbiter of signs, as voice-over
and ironist.

In "The Style of Autobiography," Jean Starobinski
maintains that "autobiography is certainly not a genre
with rigorous rules. It only requires that certain possible
conditions be realized, conditions that are mainly ideological (or cultural): that the personal experience be important, that it offer an opportunity for a sincere relation with
someone else" (288). Starobinski adds that "one would
hardly have sufficient motive to write an autobiography
had not some radical change occurred in his life—conversion, entry into a new life, the operation of Grace" (289).
Autobiography denotes a wish to share experience; every
"I" must have its corresponding "you," every narrator a
narratee. In a paradigm of the genre, the *Confessions* of St.
Augustine, "the author speaks to God but with the intention of edifying his readers. God is the direct addressee of
the discourse; the rest of mankind, on the contrary, is
named in the third person as indirect beneficiary of the ef-
fusion that it has been allowed to witness. Thus the autobiographical discourse takes form by creating, almost simultaneously, two addressees, one summoned directly,
the other assumed obliquely as witness" (288-89). For
Starobinski, the dual audience is not a luxury but a necessity. St. Augustine conveys his gratitude—not information—to an omniscient God, the master of his fate: "By so
openly making God his interlocutor, Augustine commits
himself to absolute veracity: How could he falsify or dis-
simulate anything before One who can see into his in-
nermost marrow?" (289). The secondary addressee, the
human auditor, comes "to legitimize the very
'discursiveness' of the confession. The confession is not
for God, but for the human reader who needs a narrative,
a laying out of the events in their enchained succession....
And thereby are reconciled the edifying motivation and
the transcendent finality of the confession: words addressed to God will convert or comfort other men" (289).

122 EDWARD H. FRIEDMAN

Spiritual autobiography occupies, with idealistic fiction, a prominent position in the picaresque intertext. Picaresque narrative deflates, as it were, the premises and conventions of both models. Following Starobinski's definition, one may point to a modification of the norm, with insignificance substituting for significance and a compromising and decidedly secular situation replacing spiritual pursuits. The primary addressee is no longer God but a gentleman of higher rank than Lázaro who requests an account of what may be—or may have been—a scandal. The secondary addressee in this case is the (implied) reader, recognized, it would seem, for an ability to link linguistic and semantic ironies with social irony. The reader needs to deal with the question of exemplarity (and its underside) and with the text as artistic enterprise, as indicated, somewhat paradoxically, in the prologue. Through recourse to variations of the verb *confesar*, and more abstractly through the form and ideology of his text, the author of the *Lazarillo* acknowledges a debt to St. Augustine. It is, however, Mateo Alemán in *Guzmán de Alfarache* who most closely adheres to the form, if not the spirit—the story, if not the discourse—of confession.

Guzmán's text proposes a setting of repentance and moral instruction for autobiography, yet good spirit is missing from this by-product of a spiritual transformation. Undisguised resentment marks the discourse of Part I. Part II modifies the "intention" to include a self-righteous attitude toward the morality of the first part (Guzmán as a potentially "perfect man") and an attack on the sequel and its author (a reorientation of story and a more bitter discourse). The literary exorcism has ironic consequences: in avenging Sayavedra and Martí, Guzmán and Alemán ignore the effects of the conversion on the wayward protagonist, and they forget that the narrating voice needs to speak for comprehension and forgiveness. Guzmán's "superiority" over Sayavedra lies in roguery and possibly in intellect, but not in morality. Martí and his less than classical tome "survive" in the pages of his enemy and, significantly, redirect the penitential thesis of the narrative.

In his essay on "Confessions and Autobiography," Stephen Spender relates confessional literature to the collectivity of addressees: "All confessions are from subject to object, from the individual to the community or creed. Even the most shamelessly revealed inner life pleads its cause before the moral system of an outer, objective life. One of the things that the most abysmal confessions prove is the incapacity of even the most outcast creature to be alone. Indeed, the essence of the confession is that the one who feels outcast pleads with humanity to relate his isolation to its wholeness. He pleads to be forgiven, condoned, even condemned, so long as he is brought back into the wholeness of people and things" (120). For one who considers himself forsaken by God and his fellow man (as Carroll Johnson contends in "Dios y buenas gentes en *Guzmán de Alfarache*") Guzmán as the archetypal outsider may find release—catharsis, if you will—from the act of writing. The nature of the undertaking gives him a chance to vent his anger, to offer a defense, and to make contact with a reader. He can admit the possibility of winning over his audience and the assurance of interacting with those who remain unpersuaded. As long as there is a book as object and a potential reading public, Guzmán is not alone, just as he is not alone as he objectifies his former self. Guzmán's place in the world is his place in the text. An implied author may undermine his argument—and render it ironic—but cannot eradicate the persona(e) created in the Guzmán's account, a confession in more than one sense.

Because the implied author of the *Buscón* so obviously (em)plots against the narrator/protagonist, the deconstructive process is likewise more evident. Pablos's narration, like his pretensions, seals his fate. Pablos wants to be a nobleman, not to perform noble deeds. He wants to succeed, not to be good. His literary conceits reveal his conceit, and he falls into a deterministic trap set by a hierarchical society and by an implied author working on behalf of the establishment. As an ultimate irony, the implied author, by betraying his presence in the text, demonstrates art imitating life. The illusion of narrative control—of authority—mirrors the lack of control of the marginated person in society. Pablos's genealogy carries more weight than his choices (resignation to subservience or ill-fated rebellion). Within this closed system, delinquency becomes a defense against and an acknowledgment of social determinism. The heavy hand of the implied author converts autobiography and a secular confession into an indictment against upward mobility. The discursive struggle—and its resolution in favor of the authorial figure—establishes a structural parallel between the text and its ideological backdrop. The outsider in society becomes an outsider in the text that bears—but does not necessarily bear out—his imprint.

The "lives" of Lázaro de Tormes, Guzmán de Alfarache, and Pablos [de Segovia] share a point of origin in the spiritual confession, which gives them a formal model to emulate and an ethical course from which to diverge. St. Augustine's *Confessions* seem to be part of *Lazarillo*'s de(con)struction of the idealistic intertext and of humanistic exaltation of the individual. Lázaro hints at confession, while Guzmán strives to re-create the documented history of a conversion. Guzmán forces the addressee to accept his story on faith, when his discursive premises seem made to be broken. His semiotic system emphasizes the problematic space between signifier and signified. Pablos's discourse, on the other hand, and despite its reliance on Baroque excesses, is not particularly ambiguous. It is uniformly ironic, self-parodic, and counterproductive. Wordplay at the same time shields and emits the "truth." Pablos hides his feelings in life and in the text that portrays that life; nonetheless, story and discourse—deciphered—reveal the interior self. The (implied) author protects himself by keeping his distance from—and punishing—Pablos's social radicalism, if not from his wit.

In an attempt to relate the picaresque to principles of autobiography, Jean Starobinski writes: "Traditionally, the picaresque narrative is attributed to a character who has arrived at a certain stage of ease and 'respectability' and who retraces, through an adventurous past, his humble beginnings at the fringes of society. Then he did not know the world, he was a stranger, he got by as best he could, more often for the worse than for the better, encountering on the way all the abuse, all the oppressive power, all the insolence of those above him. For the picaresque narrator, the present is the time of well-merited repose, of seeing oneself finally a winner, of finding a place in the social order. He can laugh at his former self, that obscure and needy wretch who could only respond in hang-dog fashion to the world's vanities. He can speak of the past with irony, condescension, pity, amusement. This narrative tone often requires the imaginary presence of an addressee, a confidante who is made an indulgent and amused accomplice by the playfulness with which the most outrageous behavior is recounted" (292-93). Starobinski makes a brief allusion to *Lazarillo de Tormes* and does not mention other Spanish texts. The above description reflects a rather liberal, and perhaps overly literal, reading of the canon. One would have no choice but to count Lázaro "at the height of all good fortune" and to discount the negative connotations of the "case." The jocular detachment which Starobinski associates with the narrator/protagonist does not take into consideration either the frame of religiosity and repentance that Guzmán would claim as the prime mover of his opus or Pablos's closing statement to the effect that old habits—such as the inclination toward evil—die hard. The assessment presupposes success in the story and in the storytelling, a social and discursive freedom whose absence may be the essence of picaresque narrative.

Is there a text that approaches "pure" autobiography, that secularizes the goals and form of confessional literature, that satisfies ("actualizes") Starobinski's criteria, and that displays the dialectics of time, space, and voice of the picaresque archetypes? I would submit that *Estebanillo González*, an autobiography influenced by picaresque fiction, is perhaps the strongest contender. *Estebanillo González* offers a doubling of the narrator/protagonist through a retrospective vision that recasts history as comedy, as befitting a "present" in which the writer is a buffoon. Both Randolph Pope and Richard Bjornson, in their studies of the work, signal a calculated appeal to a mentor or elevated audience. What poses as the truth may be a version of the truth directed more toward a favorable response than to accuracy. Estebanillo's flouting of the generic rules—tragedy as burlesque, autobiography as entertainment, history as histrionics—calls attention to what is changed as well as to the change itself. The rhetorical flourishes cannot fully conceal the "inner man" or the intertextual ties with confession. The "life" of Estebanillo González may be a synchronic source for investigation of the picaresque as autobiography. It is an idea worth pursuing—appropriately, one might say—at another time and in another place.

WORKS CITED

Arias, Joan. *Guzmán de Alfarache: The Unrepentant Narrator.* London: Tamesis, 1977.

Bjornson, Richard. *The Picaresque Hero in European Fiction.* Madison: Univ. of Wisconsin Press, 1977.

Brancaforte, Benito. *Guzmán de Alfarache: ¿Conversión o proceso?* Madison: Hispanic Seminary of Medieval Studies, 1980.

Chatman, Seymour. *Story and Discourse.* Ithaca and London: Cornell Univ. Press, 1978.

Gusdorf, Georges. "Conditions and Limits of Autobiography." Trans. James Olney. *Autobiography: Essays Theoretical and Critical.* Ed. James Olney. Princeton: Princeton Univ. Press, 1980. 28-48.

Howarth, William L. "Some Principles of Autobiography." *New Literary History* 5 (1974): 363-381.

Johnson, Carroll B. "Dios y buenas gentes en *Guzmán de Alfarache.*" *Romanische Forschungen* 84 (1972): 553-563.

———. *Inside Guzmán de Alfarache.* Berkeley: Univ. of California Press, 1978.

Lanser, Susan Sniader. *The Narrative Act.* Princeton: Princeton Univ. Press, 1981.

Pope, Randolph. D. *La autobiografía española hasta Torres Villarroel.* Frankfurt: Peter Lang, 1974.

Rico, Francisco. *La novela picaresca y el punto de vista.* Barcelona: Seix-Barral, 1970.

Rodríguez Matos, Carlos Antonio. *El narrador pícaro: Guzmán de Alfarache.* Madison: Hispanic Seminary of Medieval Studies, 1985.

Spender, Stephen. "Confessions and Autobiography." *Autobiography: Essays Theoretical and Critical.* Ed. James Olney. Princeton: Princeton Univ. Press, 1980. 115-122.

Starobinski, Jean. "The Style of Autobiography." *Literary Style: A Symposium.* Ed. and trans. Seymour Chatman. York: Oxford Univ. Press, 1971. 285-96.

White, Hayden. "The Historical Text as Literary Artifact." *Tropics of Discourse.* Baltimore and London: Johns Hopkins Univ. Press, 1978. 81-100.

———. *Metahistory.* Baltimore: Johns Hopkins Univ. Press, 1973.

Whitenack, Judith A. *The Impenitent Confession of Guzmán de Alfarache.* Madison: Hispanic Seminary of Medieval Studies, 1985.

Zumthor, Paul. "Autobiography in the Middle Ages?" Trans. Sherry Simon. *Genre* 6 (1973): 29-48.

CHAPTER 6:
THE HISTORICAL FUNCTION OF PICARESQUE
AUTOBIOGRAPHIES: TOWARD A HISTORY
OF SOCIAL OFFENDERS

Anthony N. Zahareas

The fundamental discovery of this essay, which was advanced in a preliminary way years ago (Zahareas, "El género picaresco y las autobiografías de criminales"), is that the structure of traditional and modern picaresque novels resembles closely the narrative structure of modern "case histories" of deviants or criminals. In the past, authors made their fictive anti-heroes, as marginal *pícaros*, tell their own version of their life's history; social offenders explain *presently*, how they broke the law in the *past* and why at a crucial point in their lives they decided to narrate their own delinquent or criminal acts. Today's real social offenders also record their activities and, like the fictional characters of picaresque life-stories (or *vidas*), narrate what, when, and where they broke the law and, given the shift from social offender to writer, discuss how and why they ended up speaking or writing about themselves. In fact, in either traditional picaresque novels or modern criminal case-histories, the narrators are made to marshall the events of their delinquent past in an episodic sequence of cause and effect.

This essay is concerned with four problems within the literary historiography of Spanish Golden Age autobiography as related to historical issues of criminology: first, with a theory of autobiography as narrative structure and, in particular, its applicability to picaresque novels; second, with the degrees to which the contexts of deviance or criminality in picaresque fiction can affect (and even be affected by) the first-person narrative structure in which they are inscribed; third, with the pertinent ways in which the structure of Spanish picaresque narratives are related to modern deviant and criminal (or even "confessional") autobiographies and case-histories; and fourth, with the historiographical dilemmas and interdisciplinary questions which such parallels pose to literary and social historians. The four problems are closely linked; together, they touch upon an immense historiographical problem such as the social history of law-and-disorder, but do so only from the limited angle of "literary" autobiography.

As with most recent comparative and interdisciplinary studies, a historical analysis of picaresque fiction can be subject to sweeping verdicts and confusing interpretations. For this reason I have followed a limited plan of short expositions: a review of the problematic borderlines between fiction and history in autobiographical discourses is followed by the analysis of the structure of traditional picaresque autobiographies; a brief research into modern criminal case-histories is paired with a close comparison of criminal autobiographies and picaresque narratives; and the review of literary analysis of narrative in terms of social history concludes with a reappraisal of the historical function of picaresque autobiographies.

There is a need for a framework that can facilitate a comparative analysis of autobiographical narrative systems; it must be broad enough to encompass not only examples of picaresque, but also variants and other kindred cases. The basic components of the framework must deal with three key historiographical aspects of narrative structures: composition, transmission and reception of all first person narratives—especially those fictive versions that deal with and are recalled by *pícaros*, deviants, sinners, criminals, and all those marginal individuals who are associated with the underworld or lower depths of society. A potpourri of such known works would include two lists: *Lazarillo; The Unfortunate Traveller; Guzmán; Justina; Buscón; Coloquio de los perros; Marcos de Obregón; Estebanillo; Courache; Simplicissimus; Moll Flanders; Periquillo Sarniento; Roderick Random; Gil Blas; Felix Krull; Augie March; The Invisible Man;* maybe even *Pascual Duarte.* The other representative list includes some of the better known first-person lives by historical figures: George Jackson in his "love letters"; the prostitutes taped in interviews with Oscar Lewis; the "happy hooker" about her profession; Caryl Chessman's apologetic remembrances of crime from death row; H. Papillon's proud account of escapes from prison; George Colson's account of having been born again soon after his conviction; E. Bunker's prison experiences in *No Beast so Fierce;* Patricia Hearst's story of abduction and complicity; K. Waldheim's partial recollections of war experiences as German officer; Malcolm X's *Autobiography;* R. Nixon, H. Kissinger, the Berrigans, Caryl Chessman, and R. Baker; and, perhaps, even J. Genet's *Thief's Journal* and the very recent sexual confession of some nuns and that of Jessica Hahn. There are hundreds more and thousands of case histories available in prisons.

I. *Borderlines of History and Fiction in Autobiography*

A generic assumption of all autobiographies is that no one is better qualified to narrate one's full and intimate personal history than the person involved. At the same time, the knowledge, memory, selection and interpretation of past details are historiographically as problematic as any presentation of historical events. The motives alone behind the desire to avow fully before others both the shameful and creditable experiences of one's life are as varied as the results themselves—witness, for instance, the radical parallels and differences between Augustine's and Rousseau's *Confessions*. A preliminary answer to the question "what is autobiography?" involves basic historiographical considerations: the first-person narrative is a continuous process of interaction between the subject as narrator and the narrated events, what historians call the unending confrontation between present and past, between raw personal experiences and their interpretation. The narrative system of autobiography contains within itself, as part of its validating principles, three key relational borderlines: history and its varied modes of narrative presentation; facts and their interpretation; experiences and their transmission.

For example, despite radical differences between one picaresque fiction and another (say, the cases of *Lazarillo* and *Moll Flanders*, *Buscón* and *Augie March*, *Guzmán* and *Gil Blas*, or *Estebanillo* and *Simplicius Simplicissimus*), there are generic resemblances: when one *pícaro* narrates one past and another *pícaro* narrates another, the *structural* pattern is the same, even though its *meaning* may be different. One key presupposition to all picaresque literature is an answer to the implied question of why low-born individuals bother to recount their past life-story which, admittedly, they consider worthless and undesirable; that is, why the contradiction of recalling what is forgettable. The attribution of motives is embodied, directly or indirectly, in the elaborated structure of the first-person narrative. Thus, if there is a set of marks which serve to separate each picaresque novel from all the others (witness the textual analysis of individual works), there is also another set of marks which serve to lump picaresques together as literary autobiographies (witness the generic or comparative studies of the works as a group).

The assumption that very pronounced differences often highlight similarities among autobiographers is to be expected. Nevertheless, the remarkable parallels between traditional picaresque narratives, probably the oldest generic literature about social deviance, and criminal autobiographies or deviant case-histories, perhaps the newest mode of confessional documentary, are striking. If there is any tacit agreement between social historians or criminologists who deal with real cases of deviants and literary critics who analyze fictional versions of *pícaros,* it is on the separateness of historical conditions from fictive situations of deviance. Social and literary historians alike, at least in their practice, seem to have taken for granted the impossibility of encompassing within a single theoretical framework propositions about historical and fictional cases of deviance and crime.

Consider, however, at least as a counter to traditionally rigid views, the two following confessions:

> ...it was repenting after the power of further sinning was taken away. I seemed not to mourn that I had committed such crimes, and for the fact as it was an offence against God and my neighbour, but I mourned that I was to be punished for it.

> ...every story tried to sell off a new piece of me. So I'm dealing with it publicly. Head on. You want to look? I'll show you. Relax, guys, I know what I'm doing.

The first comes toward the end of Defoe's "picaresque" *Moll Flanders,* the other from Jessica Hahn's recent "interview" with *Playboy.* Both confessions are deliberately ambivalent between humility and pride, repentance and defiance. For no matter how inconsistent these two fictive and historical women are, no matter how false, secretive, or disjointed their existence, or how possibly governed by opportunism and double standards, the true reason for their shifts, often from the extreme of crime or sin to remorse and good works, are not arbitrary because they are intimately connected to their narrated acts. The narration in first-person of one's own past misdeeds usually provides, at least implicitly, the very reasons for bothering to write and, supposedly, "to tell it as it is." Thus the one factor that these and other female narrators share is the presentation of a situation in which each narrator, in her own particular way, is extremely conscious. Comparisons are prompted by a general rule of all autobiographical structure whereby the difference between, say, fictive picaresque narrative and historical life-stories is delusory.

Proofs of parallels abound. Consider the case of the radical black activist, Malcolm X, who wrote his *Autobiography* with the help of a man of letters, Alex Haley (published posthumously in 1965). If readers are to capture Malcolm's true identity they must treat each interesting detail of his narrated experience as only one small part of a bigger whole:

> But people are always speculating—why am I as I am? To understand that of any person, his whole life, from birth, must be reviewed. All of our experiences fuse into our personality. Everything that ever happened to us is an ingredient. (150)

Malcolm X started not only with a provisional selection of biographical and historical *facts* but also with a provisional *interpretation* of his entire life in the light of which that selection was made. The narrative play here is to recall his past and, simultaneously, to impose simultaneously on readers his own specified way of reading that past: hence the subtle—and very revealing—shift from the specific "I am" to the general "any person" to the broad, allegorical "our experience" to the somewhat theological "that ever happened to us." The question of which comes first—the facts or their interpretation—is very problematic. In most narrated autobiographies, history and desired meaning are inseparable, necessary and complementary to each to other—even though they may be opposites.

Literary critics can easily recognize Malcolm's interpretive demands as the well-known literary commonplace of the "part and the whole," a ploy which is part and parcel of all medieval confession and fictional picaresque autobiographies. The first fictive *pícaro*, in *The Life of Lazarillo de Tormes* (1554), as if anticipating step by step the historical Malcolm X, had imposed on readers the very same rules for reading his life-story correctly so that they might understand better who he is and what his account is all about:

And since your Excellency has written me for a full
account of this [particular] matter, I thought it best
not to start in the middle, but at the beginning. In this
way the whole story of my life will be revealed...
(xviii)

...Y pues Vuestra Merced escribe se le escriba y relate
el caso muy por extenso, parescióme no tomalle por el
medio, sino del principio, porque se tenga entera
noticia de mi persona...

According to Lazarillo, the detail of his present predicament can be interpreted correctly only if it is read as one
smaller part of a bigger whole. The public scandal surrounding his wife's affair with his employer is a minor
aspect if judged, as it should be according to the narrator,
in terms of the need and struggle to survive which produced it; and the reader needs to be as much aware about
the imposed causes of hypocrisy as is the narrator. To give
an account of his present dishonor without placing it in
context, without revealing the historical factors of hunger
and beatings which have shaped his consensual dishonor
and hypocrisy (factors which only he knows well because
he lived them) is clearly inadequate. Lázaro's *Vida*, like
Malcolm's later *Autobiography*, provides its own codes for
being read or understood and converts these codes into the
structure and meaning of his life-story.

The many differences between the Spanish fictive or-
phan who became a fictive town crier in the sixteenth
century and the American historical black who became a
militant radical are not meant to be dismissed. The parallels are too important for the history of social offenders to
leave unexplained: the past experiences of real autobiographies are often structured and transmitted in the same
way as those fictive life-stories. The structural constant is
historiographical: there is reciprocity, within the first person narrative, of historical events and their recreation,
that is, of verifiable facts and the not-so-easily verifiable
interpretation. Had the fictive Lazarillo not been obliged to
explain his cuckoldry on his own terms, including his
questionable origins, orphanage, cruel apprenticeship,
hunger and basic needs, the morally rigid "Excellency"—

and through him we, the readers—would not have been able to read the complete description, explanation and evaluation of a past life which, according to him, was both shameful and creditable, disastrous and, ironically, triumphant. The same process works in historical accounts too. The factual account of Malcolm X contains an overall view of his true first person which helps him create a far more telling image of himself as a black denizen of white America, and a full time participant in its ritual racism and segregation, than if he had allowed American readers to enjoy and judge the often humorous contents one by one.

Whether by design or not, both fictional and the historical autobiographers become writers who tend to interpret themselves holistically, doing so with various degrees of control, interpretation and, hence, *(un) reliability.* A real autobiography by the black militant Malcolm X, or an anonymous writer's fictive confession of and by the poor *pícaro* Lazarillo, contain, alongside the diverse contents, the summarizing function of them. The rhetorical choice is deliberate and calculating: to limit the scope of the narrative is to choose central topics and narrate several (perhaps exemplary) episodes in light of them. An autobiography assumes, self-consciously, a good deal of compression of historical contents and a deliberate omission of others. Such narrative choices suggest something of the coherence and continuity of any life-story. Malcolm X and Lazarillo are paradigmatic of the fences put up between history and interpretation or fiction in almost all autobiographies.

The issue of recalling one's acts of the past for the sake of the present always involves some kind of interpretation which, acting as a gesture of authorial command, intrudes confidently in the narrative structure, in order to subvert, not the authenticity of historical experiences but the very reliability of authentic data. Both Malcolm X and Lazarillo (as well as, say, the fictive Guzmán, Buscón, Simplicius and Moll Flanders, and the historical Genet, Waldheim, Chessman, Papillon, etc.) suggest in their life-stories that some ways of reading are adequate while others are not; they call on readers for an approach to what they are reading as an arrangement of diverse features which, despite the segmented presentation of the life-story, reveals (consciously or unconsciously) an underlying design of expected response to the whole presentation of the orderly recollection.

Lazarillo and Malcolm are paradigmatic in the ways they structure their dilemma: one must explain apologetically how he came to accept degeneracy and hypocrisy as a way of survival; the other must protest defiantly how he came to accept hate and militancy as social activity. Both dilemmas are structural; they are open to analysis and, within the narrative bounds of autobiography, to common sense. In the narrative itself, either there is or there is not, an accounting of the reasonings for coming to critical decisions. Moreover, the true reasons behind the decisions need not be arbitrary or unconnected to previous acts and decisions. To put it in modern terms: if a subject's radical change of looking at his society is unconvincing, then the long series of episodes would be structurally loose, uncorrelated and (at least according to Lazarillo and Malcolm) surely subject to grave misunderstandings. Accordingly, what autobiographical narrators apparently want of readers is a reaction that clearly reveals the influence of the narrative's strategic terms at which judgments arise.

The rhetorical commonplace of the part and the whole is only one example of internal codes for the reciprocity between a narrator's present and past: Lazarillo and Malcolm portray themselves as part of the present while the facts of their lives belong to their past. The details of the past without a present interpretation are, in an autobiography, meaningless. This is why each autobiography encodes within its narrative structure a central historiographical issue: how have narrators been able to know and select what they have narrated in their life-story. Between authentic and fictionalized history there is the borderline area of autobiography, exposed to influences by both sides. On the one hand, one's own narrated life-story does not exist independently of the narrator; on the other, an unrecorded life-story, historically speaking, is potentially recordable, and thus independent of the narrator's self-portrait. The Grecian Urn, to take a historian's recent example, would exist with or without Keat's poem; likewise, Guzmán de Alfarache's account of social fall and moral recovery, with all its first-person unreliability, would be no less a fact of that fictive thief's biography if the narrative and all other records had not been written down. To update the issue with two diverse but much commented recent cases: Jessica Hahn's real psycho-social trauma of losing her virginity as told to and written by *Playboy*, or Kurt Waldheim's military past in the German army documents and in his own versions—that is, their lived biographies—already have existed and will continue to exist independently of the interpretations of their first-person accounts. The biography of someone may exist without his or her autobiography yet the awareness of the biography is realized through autobiography—herein lies the historical function of autobiographic forms.

II. *The Structure of Picaresque Autobiographies*

The narrative strategy of picaresque *Vidas* was to turn the invented *pícaros* into the first-person narrators of their past social deviance. The perspective employed in picaresque fiction clearly anticipates what modern sociologists such as E. Goffman now call the "presentations of self" to others. The narrative principles are necessarily "performative" or "rhetorical". Picaresque autobiographies embody the ways in which narrators present their past deviant activity to others; the manner in which they guide and control the impression readers form of their narrated deviance; and the kinds of ploys or schemes they may and may not use while sustaining their narrative performance before readers. The designed performance is vital to the transmission of the life-story because an autobiography consists of what is narrated only in terms of what is left out. The narrative versions of one's deviant life presents past events already interpreted by the *pícaro*, literally organized, rehearsed and full of artifice; presumably that narrative stands in some relation to the many events of past life that are real, loose, and not all rehearsed or designed.

Picaresque autobiographies thus place readers between two kinds of reality. One is the historical reality of a *pícaro's* life in which phenomena can supposedly be experientially verifiable. Within that real life is the interpreted version of a packaged life-story narrated by the *pícaro*. To readers, the *pícaro's* narrated version cannot be real in the sense that the life the *pícaro* lived is real. In the narrated life the *pícaro* might suffer the deceptions, indifference, cruelties and miseries of the real life counterpart but, nevertheless, the *Vida* itself differs from the real life in that it is an interpreted or imaginary life, a product of the narrator's recreation. The distinction between these two first-person realities is often deliberately blurred—just as it is in third-person, allegedly "objective", histories.

Now, given its dual form, a picaresque autobiography tends to implicitly validate, in a remarkable series of self-references, its own narrative project of treating the historical facts of one's life in fictional terms. The dual narrative structure of first-person narratives, and the problematic contradiction between one and the other, had of course already surfaced centuries before the appearance of Spanish picaresque fictions in a variety of confessional guises. The Archpriest of Hita had already taken full advantage of the ironic potential of the dual narrative formula in structuring the loose, fragmented episodes of his *Book of True Love;* readers are not allowed to confuse the hero of the bawdy and sinful love experiences with the poet who writes that first-person story at the completion of them. The first-person pattern of narrative had thus a sort of "perpetual present" and kept on serving as a mode for a multitude of varied autobiographical discourses of which two versions are the picaresque novels of Imperial Spain and the deviant autobiographies of modern time.

Picaresque narratives are usually structured as absurd self-portraits of low-born social offenders who mockingly reject as destructive and undesirable everything associated with social deviances such as hustling, lying, thieving and constant mobility. The narrators accept responsibility and blame; they often become aloof by looking upon their previous selves as humorously foolish. The attempt is to purge oneself now of errors committed in the past. By

loading the burden of misjudgment, error and wrongdo-
ing upon himself, the *pícaro*, ironically, turns into his
own scapegoat; he is made to bear all the blame for the
narrator's past vices and social offenses. In this sense, each
picaresque fiction is, as in the *Buscón*, purposefully narrated as a contradiction: Quevedo's *pícaro*, as swindler, is a
clever liar whereas, at the same time, the narrator of social
offenses, is brutally honest; the narrated life-story does not
hide from readers outside the text, what the narrator was
hiding from others inside the text. Hence the necessary yet
subtle difference between the *pícaro* as the social offender
and as the narrator who now recalls his past offenses: picaresque narrators distance themselves from their past deviances in the very act of recalling and narrating them (see
Zahareas "Quevedo's *Buscón*: Structure and Ideology").

A picaresque life-story refers to the first-person narrative of past social offenses and at the same time to the social offenses of that narrative. The readers of Quevedo's
Buscón, for example, must distinguish between the failure
of the swindler to improve his lot in Spanish society and
the success of the narrator to narrate that failure humorously and grotesquely in book form. Now, in terms of historiography, a *pícaro's* past has already passed; the events
that have gone by are, literally, not renewable. It is therefore easy in a picaresque autobiography to confuse a *pícaro's* deviant past with the narrated past communicated
to readers. The attempts at confusion are often deliberate, a
part of a picaresque novel's subtle strategies at narrative
presentation. The story of the past life of Quevedo's
swindler, for example, is not the historical past but rather a
verbal construction by the swindler who is narrating it.
The fictive social offender does in fiction what historians
do in historical narratives. He interprets episodically the
outstanding events of his life by concentrating on the
grotesque aspect of his failures; and by narrating, humorously and burlesquely, various exemplary episodes in the
light of those failures.

A brief paraphrase of some key picaresque *Lives* reveals,
self-referentially, this generic pattern of presenting a re-
membrance of past offenses in the interest of the offender's present. Within the four picaresque representa-

tions that follow, for example, a basic question of all historiography is intricately posed: in what ways can a social offender or *pícaro* reason about his undesirable historical past if he can no longer change it or intervene in its outcomes? After all, a *pícaro* can intervene in his deviant past only as the writer of that past deviance. This is why each Spanish picaresque *life* contains, as an indispensable ingredient of the autobiographical structure, how the narrator became a social offender in the past and why at a crucial turning point of his life he decided to write about these social offenses or deviances.

For example, the poor towncrier of Toledo called Lázaro de Tormes (1554) wrote during the times of Imperial Spain about his terrible experience with poverty, hunger and cruel masters in order to explain why he accepted a situation of moral degeneracy whereby townspeople knew that his wife was cuckolding him with his protector and employer, a powerful archpriest. During 1599-1603, at the height of the Spanish Counter-Reformation, a former thief and now galley slave for life, called Guzmán de Alfarache, recalled his past as if it were an evil life, stressing robberies and frauds in order to explain his change of heart and justify one questionable act: why he had betrayed some fellow prisoners who planned a mutiny and why they deserved to be hanged. Around 1605-1626 a fugitive swindler and fraud known as Pablos the Sharper described his long series of interlinked misfortunes which started with hoaxes and swindling and ended in murder by explaining that he escaped to the New World where not only did he not improve his luck, as he had hoped, but where things turned out even worse than before. One of his aims was to convince readers (in the guise of the commonplace "Señor") that he finally realized that men like him could not improve their lot socially (*medrar* in the acute articulation of Maravall) by hustling and drifting aimlessly from one place to another. In 1646 the court jester of General Piccolomini, Estebanillo González, explains burlesquely how he accepted the debasements that went with clowning because it was the only way of surviving in the midst of war.

The elaboration of the structure of all these picaresque novels is episodic and has its own presentational exigencies. The social offenses of the past are, on the one hand, lumped together as episodes and, while humorous or interesting enough in their place, do wear the miscellaneous look of a past scrap-heap; on the other, there is some kind of underlying unity of the scattered episodes (and often sermons) provided by the narrator who constantly oscillates between past divergence and present coherence. There is a typical textual illustration in the *Buscón*, the picaresque life-story that contains the least number of intrusions in the narrative:

> Yet when misfortunes begin plaguing someone, it seems that they never end, that they are connected as in a chain, link by link.

> Pero, cuando comienzan desgracias en uno, parece que nunca se han de acabar, que andan encadenadas, y unas tras otras. (I, 5)

The narrator now wants to influence readers in the way they ought to read and understand his miserable and undesirable past in its structured totality of connected adversities rather than simply in one entertaining adversity at a time. Readers, however, must confront two structures. One is supposedly historical since it is the life lived out by the swindler, a life full of bad experiences and worse luck; the other is the written discourse of that lived life. Quevedo's fictive *pícaro*, by means of a causal succession of witty, burlesque episodes, is made to narrate his criminal past as if it were a literary discourse—with its rhetoric, strategy, stylistic turns, apostrophes, jokes, euphemisms, images and even ambivalence. The life story of the social offender in the *Buscón*, like most past experiences transmitted in history, is transmitted to readers only as a recreated life.

The structure of Spanish picaresque narratives highlights the well known maxim that beneath disorder lurks order. In the very act of narrating episodically, *pícaros* can predict from the present the chaos of their past lives; in other words, and they could "retrosee" those deviant patterns of behavior which they could not always "foresee" as they were happening in the past. Living a chaotic existence in history corresponds, ironically, to writing about that historical chaos as orderly literature. Being presently aware of one's past unawareness may be the only way for the fictional social offenders of picaresque to give some kind of pattern to the tumult of chaotic happenings. In picaresque autobiographies, "to look back and forth" (a kind of "discursive schizophrenia") is to structure one's past history of loose deviance as an orderly—*structured*—narrative. Necessarily, then, when becoming the narrator of his past life the *pícaro* must explain to the reader why, if his deviant past is, as he claims, not worthy as a way of life, he takes the trouble to portray it for others.

Spanish authors were aware of the paradoxes of such ironic structures. As early as 1605, Cervantes, as part of his parody of literary genres, in *Don Quijote*, in a dazzling display of what is currently called "self-referentiality," dramatizes lucidly the narrative process of turning inward so that a fictional structure, like that of picaresque life-stories, can reflect upon its own constitution. The dangerous criminal, Ginés de Pasamonte, explains without apologies to the inquisitive madman, Don Quijote, that he has already composed his personal history of crime as fiction— as if it were a first-rate picaresque *vida:*

> 'He is speaking the truth,' put in the sergeant. 'He has written his own story, as fine as you please, and left the book behind at the prison...' 'It's so good' replied Gines, 'that *Lazarillo de Tormes* will have to look out, and so will everything in that style that has ever been written or ever will be. One thing I can promise you, is that it is all the truth, and such well-written, entertaining truth that there is no fiction that can compare with it.' (*Don Quijote*, J. M. Cohen translation, Penguin, 176.)

> Dice verdad—dijo el comisario—; que él mesmo ha escrito su historia, que no hay más, y deja empeñado el libro en la carcel... Es tan bueno—respondió Ginés—, que mal año para *Lazarillo de Tormes* y para todos cuantos de aquel género se han escrito o escribieren. Lo que le sé decir a voacé es que trata

verdades, y que son verdades tan lindas y tan dono-
sas, que no pueden haber mentiras que se le igualen.
(Ed. Luis Murillo, Clásicos Castalia, I, 271-272.)

Within the bounds of Cervantes's fiction, a real criminal
becomes an author only in order to narrate the history of
his life of crime—not simply as historical truth, but in imitation of the well known fictive *vida* of the fictive *pícaro*
Lazarillo, that is, history becomes as literature. The deviant facts of his biography are presented as fictions.
Cervantes's parody contains outwardly, as do the picaresque *vidas* inwardly, an awareness of the discursive
system of all criminal confessions or autobiographies.
Whether the reasons are social (like Ginés's wish for his
book to sell better), moral or psychological (the reasons offered by the diverse *pícaros*), the narrative structure of
Spanish picaresque fiction is consciously *pragmatic*. A *pícaro*'s real past is usable or exemplary as present fiction:
"how best to use my past history during my present
quandary and pressure regarding today's decisions" is an
implied question of picaresque narratives. Because history
is treated pragmatically, the crucial events recollected occur twice: the first time as real, the second time as literary,
that is, it puts the past in the service of the present.

It happens that picaresque lives first occur, in history, as
tragic events and next, in literature, as farce and mockery.
This is because the very entertaining laughter of picaresque *vidas* is integral to the first-person structure; it
represents a wicked sense of superiority over the targets of
ridicule. Following the pattern of picaresque narratives,
for example, it is the fictive character Pablos (and *not* the
real author Quevedo) who recalls with grotesque humor
his vain efforts to change identities, to negate his own in-
famous genealogy and become a man of honor. Pablos, the
narrator, laughs at his grotesque failures to change his social status because, implicitly, he is conscious of having
surmounted his silly presumptuousness that has led him
to a doomed search. He can now mock the pretensions of
others as long as his own understanding is finally
"detached," that is, "freed" from foolishness or blindness.
Such detachment might explain why there is no compro-

mising irony in the narrator's humorous yet matter-of-fact depiction of his dealings with himself or others. Pablos's reliance on a harsh, cold humor to narrate his own past has the function of blotting out any sympathy on the part of the stern narrator for this social climber or for similar deceivers.

The implications are very subtle; a *pícaro's* past is denied any reality independent of present needs and wants because, as in many written histories, his life-story is founded on a pragmatic and, hence, "unhistorical" point of view. A telling irony of the pragmatism of autobiographical structures is that the practical narrator does not give up the game of pretense; he gives the lie to his attempts at offering a disengaged account of past events at the very instance when he pretends to be a mocking, distanced reporter. Thus the pragmatic structure of picaresque narratives is both the negation of historical distance and the pretentious claims for it. The contradiction is of significance because it contains historiographical problems which are often not resolved, but which are revealed in the very contradictory structure. The implications are, theoretically and practically, staggering for the ideological studies of almost all history writing: a historian's alleged distance in reconstructing a past may be one of the more subtle attempts to conceal the practical interests of that reconstruction and, at the same time, to transcend the evident contradictions—all in the name of objectivity, unity and coherence.

The undesired social offenses of a *pícaro's biography* become, in his written *autobiography,* the desired presentation of the undesired. Generally, the moment a *pícaro's* deviant life appears in writing as the narrator would want it to appear now, the real author of the novel also shows his hand as far as social deviance is concerned. This double narrative standard of almost all picaresque novels represents the undeclared historical function of picaresque *vidas* as well as the source of an autobiography's ideological potency.

III. *Picaresque Narratives and Modern Autobiographies*

There are four aspects of social offenders that are usually identified within criminology. One is the relations that are being maintained, either factual or imaginary, with the adversary of criminals—the social order and the legal apparatus which work under the ideologies of law and order. The second is the set of relations they cultivate with marginal groups of society: members of strata labelled invariably as lower depths, underclass, social scum, underworld figures, outcasts, outsiders, hustlers, dealers, underdogs, prostitutes, drop-outs, misfits, delinquents and deviants. The third is the relationship with types of social victims that rely on legal protection—those conned, hustled, cheated, roved, terrorized, wounded, violated, killed. The fourth is the existence of another type of victim—the social offenders themselves, that is, the so-called victimization of the victimizer.

One significant feature of modern criminology is how it is constructed to study and deal with the complex problem posed by the individual criminals themselves, particularly if they are insufficiently passive and if they insist on presenting to the society that has condemned them their side of deviance. Social perceptions of crime and punishment, with all of their ideological labels, are nowadays balanced—and at times countered—by a social offender's own *self-concept* of his or her illegalities. Modern social offenders can present their side of deviance; they can explain how and why they have been handicapped or collided with the law and at the same time discourse on offenders through "autobiographies," "letters," "diaries," "memories," "confessions," or "interviews." This is why we know so much about social deviance today; we hear social deviants talking, we are familiar with their ways of thought and their special manner of expression.

However, the further we go back in time the more difficult it is to distinguish the voices of criminal subcultures or the words of social offenders. We do not hear much of outcasts because official and unofficial records of social deviance are rare or unavailable. We can read wills, legal documents, letters, laws, prison lists, court cases, chronicles, etc., which record diverse facts about crime and criminals. These are not, however, personal documents and do not record the individual self-awareness of the condemned, as modern case-histories do. They are *third-party* accounts which reflect the chronicler's own moral positions or dominant ideologies of law and order. Now, in modern times a commonly accepted argument is that a society cannot expect authentic answers to what criminals are doing and why they are doing it unless ways are provided to allow criminals to tell their side of their crime record and, more importantly, to make such personal documents available. Yet there is nowhere available, on the basis of such first-person versions of deviance, a single, global, yet precise and extricable, social history of social offenders.

The biggest surprise, as far a social historiography is concerned, is the lack of viable explanations as to why such a necessary history has not been undertaken. The answer might lie in the available first-person documents that are used to assess concepts of social offenses. In thousands of modern recorded cases social offenders have made themselves the subjects of their own criminal discourse: such case histories offer some kinds of answers as to what social offenses were committed, where and when crimes took place, who was the social offender, why or with what consequences. Historians of law often lack precisely the type of evidence provided by such cases about the real criminals who died long ago, without the chance to explain themselves, so that modern historians can perceive only their collective features; they tend to see them as lawgivers saw them. Past criminals are silent yet their first-person version of crime, if available, would be indispensable for a more comprehensive history of social offenders.

It is here where we might consider the important potential of the historical function of fiction such as picaresque narratives. If real social offenders in the past did not (for they could not) leave behind their life-stories (depriving us of such "historical" documents), the first-person voice of social offenders can be confronted, at least indirectly, in "fiction." From the Middle Ages to our day there have appeared picaresque-type narratives in which deviant and criminal acts were described, explained, and interpreted by the deviants themselves. The third-person accounts about criminal justice, enforcement of laws, and judicial procedures range in information from seating arrangements, to arraignments, to convictions and to methods of torture and execution. These are invaluable documents for understanding past societies but do not yield (as modern case histories) an authentic self-consciousness of the criminals themselves. They usually represent the authorities and are written from the vantage point of law and order. The official language of past legal documents is limited because it often conceals or minimizes the immediate aspects of judgment and moral valuation that are intrinsic to traditional picaresque fiction and modern criminal autobiographies. Thus, for example, the biographies of prisoners in the *Newgate Calendar*, which dates back to the eighteenth century, are an unrivaled source of information about contemporary social offenders and the attitudes of those who represent law and order. These attitudes toward crime, however, are not always pertinent to (and often deliberately exclude) the criminals themselves. Third-person legal documents tend to be absorbed usually by the dominant labels—and ideology—that deviance and crime either do not pay or are sinful; they impose imaginary representations of the special relations between crime and punishment.

Picaresque autobiographies can be many things but, as narrative structures, they always revolve around the life experiences of the "narrator" when he was not a narrator but a wrong-doer or deviant. The formal presentation of these fictive life-stories of social offenders clearly parallels (and perhaps anticipates) that of modern case-histories of deviants. The narrative structure of modern case-histories show that social offenders, in the act of recalling their past offenses, usually divide their own personality and keep fixed two perspectives—that of the deviant's present consciousness and that of memory—and keep outlined the characteristic inward situations of the social offender's present and those of his past. Such a split between the social offender who becomes a writer of his own past misdeeds is the common denominator to most autobiographical story-telling, real or fictional, from the *Confessions* of Augustine to the *songs* of the Archpriest to the *Testament* of François Villon; from the apologetic *letter* of Lazarillo de Tormes to the defiant prison letters of George Jackson; from the *Memoirs* of Moll Flanders to the *Autobiography* of Malcolm X and the *Journal* of Jean Genet.

The narrative structure shared by historical and fictive life stories creates a meaningful and relevant borderline between picaresque narratives and criminal case-histories. The fictive *lives* of Guzmán de Alfarache and Moll Flanders, for example, are presented as "historical" while the real, historical cases of death row Caryl Chessman and the delinquent-turned-radical Malcolm X are often structured like so many "fictions." As for the *journal* of the criminal/writer Jean Genet, it is on all counts and at the same time both history and fiction. Lives can be fashioned into exemplary or entertaining literature; the historical social offender might be as important as the literary version of his offenses. As we saw earlier, Cervantes was alert to the generic potential of picaresque *lives*; the case of the galley slave in 1605 (like that of Genet in these times) clearly anticipates the historical function of literary narratives and the dependence of historical cases on the rhetoric of fiction. Consider only a handful of modern autobiographies in which a contemporary figure reconstructs his or her past experience in order to confess or explain away some kind of criminality, deviance or accusation and suspicion. Puerto Rican prostitutes taped for Oscar Lewis the hardships of hooking as their *lives* (*vidas*); Caryl Chessman wrote a best-seller by relating past viciousness to writing in a death cell; Bobby Baker explains how and why he "wheeled and dealed" in Congress; R. Beck detailed his social experiences as male pimp; Patricia Hearst revealed the inside story of a questionable experience with her radical abductors; H. Papillon bragged of his successful escapes from well-guarded prisons; J. Genet advanced defiantly his perversions during his life as thief and vagrant; J. Blake confessed the vicissitudes of his drug addiction; Malcolm X traced his delinquent past up to his revo-

lutionary consciousness, while before he was killed trying
to escape, George Jackson angrily defended his past violence in and out of prison; and so on with radicals, killers,
terrorists, prostitutes, gang leaders, and counterfeiters,
from the lowest to the highest. Watergate alone led to self-
portrayals most of all the accused and condemned—from
the unrepentant G. Liddy, to born-again Christian George
Colson, to ex-President Nixon himself who, ironically, in
his defiant apology refused the label of criminal on the
grounds that "a president simply could not commit a
crime."

All causes, effects, purposes, motivations and consequences of social deviance are explained, in parallel ways
with picaresque autobiographies, from the *inside out*; that
is, the narrated situation itself (apart from its authenticity
or lack of it) contains explanations for the offender's acts
and changes. For example, there usually is in *the structure
of each narrated* autobiography an accounting *both* of what
happened *and* why there is a need to share that past with
others. In this sense, a social offender's narrative of past
experiences is, historically speaking, the most authentic
available but, given the historical context of presenting
oneself before others, it is also, ironically, *the least reliable*.

Recent cases provide examples for meaningful comparisons. Among recent debated issues are those of so-called
"world criminals" and ecclesiastic "sexual deviance." One
issue being confronted is whether past crimes (usually denied or difficult to prove conclusively) discredit present
accomplishments and contributions. The other issue is exactly the one presented in picaresque narratives: what is it
that the accused themselves have had to say or write about
their past. For example, the recently elected President of
Austria, Kurt Waldheim recalled how he was wounded as
a German soldier on the Russian front, but did *not* include
in his life-story that he later served near Salonica, Greece,
during the World War II Balkan fighting, when thousands
of Greek Jews were deported for extermination and
Yugoslav partisans were executed in retaliation. What is
included in historical records of the time is excluded in the
personal accounts of these experiences. In confessing that
it is impossible to include in one book all details of one's

past life, Waldheim's words imply that, in fiction or history, compression often means conscious omission while coherence indicates planned selectivity. The intricate borderlines between a reliable and unreliable narrator are not only an issue of fiction to be analyzed by literary critics—it is built into the discursive structure of written self-revelations; the case of Waldheim's written and explained lifestory (like that of picaresque and modern autobiographies) betrays more than the writer wishes or suspects. Even if Waldheim "didn't know what was going on," his autobiography is being *amended* to show, unlike the present available versions, that he at least "was there." Whatever he recalls *now* about his *past* will therefore be considered authentic (since he is the only one left alive who really knows what he did); it will be simultaneously unreliable since as President of Austria, he needs to be opportunistic and have a coverup. As in the case of picaresque patterns, the real history of Waldheim, once re-transformed by him into the written life-story, *cannot escape fiction.*

The mutual dependence of two opposites such as authenticity and unreliability will be reflected in the structure of his narrated autobiography; *necessarily*, Waldheim will have to explain why he excluded in the earlier versions of his autobiography what he includes now. The parallels bring us back to the historical function of the picaresque form; the traditional narrated episodes of a deviant's past life (as with the contemporary past of Waldheim which, according to Nuremberg standards, is criminal) are presented to readers, subtly, as the "resolved" or "transcended" cases of contradictory activities. This is why for readers who learn to see what picaresque narrators have learned to hide, Waldheim's autobiography reads like the successful coverup of a noted politician on the make. The other recent example deals with the on-going issue of convent sexuality from the Middle Ages to our day. There are hundreds of third-person documents regarding problems of clerical celibacy (especially in records of Church Councils and Synods) but, except for the purely literary autobiography of the *Book of True Love* (*Libro de buen amor*, c. 1330-1343) by the as yet unidentified Archpriest of Hita, there were (as in the case of social offenses) no first-person accounts of sexual deviance among "avowed" celibates. Now, however, the first-person accounts of "the controversial bestseller" *Lesbian Nuns; Breaking Silence* (Rosemary Curb and Nancy Manahan, eds.) provide immediate documents about hitherto unrecorded attitudes: chaffing under restrictions, hating celibacy, defying edicts yet feeling guilty over incontinent behavior, struggling with conscience but breaking vows of chastity, etc. These personal accounts, unlike the hard rules laid down by the Church, reveal extreme paradox: that chastity need not exclude sexuality.

To reveal what has been hidden is, historically speaking, an already ambivalent situation—especially if judgment of past offenses is wedged between its historical truth and the fictional discourse of that truth. A *pícaro*, for example, may present himself as the earlier dupe of his illusions precisely because, as the narrator of his own shame and guilt, he is no longer the same person and can sarcastically reject his harmful illusions; in a parallel manner, modern criminals tend to be drawn to the ambiguous frontiers between guilt and redemption precisely because, as the composers of their suspect past, they must hide or bypass a reprehensible behavior in view of their more acceptable present success. Denying one's past in the present is, ironically, one way of highlighting, in the very negative representation, all real and potential misrepresentations.

Disengaged accounts of past criminal events are rare: what is usually transmitted to readers is not only a series of authentic events that accurately recollected later but also a series of efforts to cover other authentic events that, ironically, are also accurately ignored. (The ways a recalled criminal past is mediated can be exemplified by innumerable stories written by prison inmates which center on the criminals' personal experiences. They are, of course, structurally—and hence historically—different from the prison accounts of *Newgate* and others we have examined).

It is against this modern background that picaresque novels can be reexamined—both analytically and historically. The following is a fairly representative sample of literary autobiographies (listed chronologically) that, on the one hand, are either picaresque or could be treated as such, and, on the other, contain, with variables, most of the historiographical constants of autobiographies: the dissolute vagabond played by the *Archpoet Golias* (second half of twelfth century); the potentially condemned sinner acted out by Dante in his *Commedia* (1321); the picaresque *Archpriest* and concubinary celibate represented as the poet Juan Ruiz (1330-1343); the imprisoned, blasphemous poet François Villon mockingly composing his *Testament* (1461-62); the cuckolded towncrier, *Lazarillo*, defending his degeneracy and hypocrisy (1554-55); the galley-slave *Guzmán* who justifies, ambiguously, his betrayal of his fellow inmates as mutineers (1599-1603); the female rogue *Justina* played by an alleged prostitute (1605); a scavenging social climber acted out mockingly by a *buscón* or swindler turned murderer (1608-1626); an unstable life as servant of many masters played by an errant dog in Cervantes's *Coloquio*, (1613); a Spanish survivor of the Thirty Years' War played by a court buffoon *Estebanillo* (1646); a German survivor of the same war impersonated by the court jester *Simplicius* (1669); a scavenging *Mother Courage* played by a prostitute (1670); a survivor of brutal political intrigues by the intriguer *Gil Blas* (1715-1742); the notorious *Moll Flanders* condemned to the gallows played by a promiscuous shoplifter (1722); the skillful con man, *Felix Krull*, who turned his social offenses into the aesthetic virtue of deviance (1954); a repentant Republican militiaman about to be executed by the nationalists, played by a backward murderer of his family, *Pascual Duarte* (1941); a southern black underdog who becomes aware that he is an *Invisible Man* to whites (1947); a nice but spineless rogue acted out by the Jewish delinquent, *Augie March* (1949).

Despite radical differences of times, nations, languages and cultures, there is a discursive mode through which authors structured the episodic stories of their *created* social offenders: the version of an offender's fearful quandary *is not reported by a third party*. According to the rules of autobiographical representations (as with most picaresque novels or criminal autobiographies) the social offender himself is the *only one* who, truthfully or falsely, reliably or unreliably, could isolate the devastating experi-

ence of confusion and then dramatize its impact on him—
only after he had time to review the particular decisions or
motives of his deviant past, and only after experience
helped him reflect and think through his problems could
he understand what his search for social improvement
was all about and why it could or could not succeed. It is
consequently the narrator's social being as a social offender
(and what Maravall has called the aspiration of *medro-
medrar*), especially as dramatized in his frank admission
of total confusion, the one factor which at the end usually
determines his consciousness regarding the difference between bad and good decisions or authentic and inauthen-
tic changes.

The archetypal picaresque novel, Mateo Alemán's *Vida
del Pícaro Guzmán de Alfarache* offers a good test case of
the function of autobiographical structure. Moreover, the
unmanageable bulk of the rambling narrative and the
long intrusive sermons have raised questions about the
"outcome" and "point of view." During his earlier years,
Guzmán refined the role of the successful con man; he
mastered the art of begging, lying, stealing, defrauding in-
nocents, procuring—even for his wife. He ended a life in
the galleys from where he wrote his *Life*. Before receiving
a full pardon, this "very famous thief" was a hardened
criminal, flogged almost to death after failing to escape
and, finally, betrayed seven fellow inmates who were
hung as mutineers. Guzmán claims to have repented, but
the criminal's repentance and pardon have two blind
spots in the narrative; he was pardoned; *after* betraying his
inmates and writes his confession *before* the arrival of the
official pardon. Thus, disturbing ambiguities and ironies
surround the *pícaro*'s *life*. Had he acknowledged that the
betrayal was calculated to earn a pardon his repentance
would be a total sham. Guzmán's own disclosures of this
terrible act force readers to confront the ambivalent issue
of whether the criminal's opportunistic treachery discred-
its or at least questions the sincerity of his repentance
dramatized in the sermons of the narrative.

Only Guzmán can explain the sudden, radical change
from criminal to penitent—those are the rules of his author's narrative game. Whether true or false, the galley-

slave's explanation is the dilemma or crisis of the life-story's outcome; the conversion and the crisis that brought it about have determined the structure of all episodes and sermons. It was a personal crisis that he felt head-on when he was, though innocent, brutally flogged. The hardened criminal came to feel not merely the force of cruelty and injustice but also, and above all, the indifference of the other inmates to his suffering; that is, when he needed compassion, he could not count on it:

> And the greatest ... pain I felt in this my misery, was not so much for the pain which I did endure, nor for the false witness that was given against me, as that all of them should have believed that I deserved this punishment and took *no pity on me.*

> Y el mayor dolor que sentí en aquel desastre, no tanto era el dolor que padecía ni ver el falso testimonio que se me levantaba, sino que juzgasen todos que de aquel castigo era merecedor y *no se dolían de mí.* (My italics)

Whether reliable or not, the *pícaro*'s explanation about the terror of his deeply felt alienation is at least "authentic"; because, as the narrator of his past crimes and repentance, the social offender has dramatized retrospectively not only a painful experience but how his retrospective explanation of it can be both "false" and "true," all in the one telling, climactic decision.

Guzmán's *Life* helps identify a key constant in the composition of criminal autobiographies and their transmission to readers. As a vital strategy in representing (for those *outside* the criminal's *vida*) a deviant situation (from the *inside* of the life-story), lies an angle or viewpoint from which the two internal opposites of the life-story—the criminal elements in the first-person structure and their potential ideological referents in the reader—generate and depend on each other. Criminal contents are structured into a first-person narrative only to become, in the dialectical relations between criminal acts and their formal transmission, a mutual dependence of historical criminal contents and a structured presentation.

This structural pattern is repeated, albeit with variables, in almost all the picaresque-type narratives that we have mentioned. In the *Buscón* the deviant past is sarcastically rejected; in *Estebanillo* it is sarcastically accepted; and in *Moll Flanders*, as in *Guzmán*, it is ambiguously indulged. In our times, *Pascual Duarte* dramatizes the sharp change when one thing is renounced and another embraced. We need not limit our comparisons only to fictive picaresque autobiographies. Before *Guzmán*, the Emperor Charles's personal clown, the *converso* Francesillo de Zúñiga, wrote a jest book (*Burlesque Chronicle/Crónica burlesca*), which, structurally, revolves around his court experiences at a time when he was not a chronicler but, for the sake of necessity, an anxious laugh maker: "It is necessary and a reasonable thing for men to seek ways of making a living" (Necesario y cosa razonable es a los hombres buscar maneras de vivir). In our times, the notorious "black prince of letters," Jean Genet (called a "liar, thief, pervert, saint and martyr" by Jean-Paul Sartre) drew on his own criminal experiences for his autobiographical *The Thief's Journal;* he wrote that he was falsely accused of thievery as a boy and was sent to reform school. There (unlike Guzmán the character but, like Guzmán, as the only one who could provide hints) he vowed to reject a society that had wronged him and to become the pervert he was accused of being. The antisocial unrepentance of Genet is as unreliable as the conformity of Francesillo or Guzmán since, ironically, all three benefitted from society according to their autobiographies.

The recent urge to write social history "from below"— from the hitherto excluded view of social offenders or clowns—makes these life stories central to the type of historical interpretations that are dramatically altering the study of both literary and social history. A quick examination of the historical factors which shaped the context not only of past crimes and criminals but also of the fictive autobiographies, might help us trace the progression from an absolute conception of deviance and crime to a more open and relativistic one—the shift, say, from medieval criminals labelled "mad," "sinners," or "heretics" to modern criminals labelled "rebels" or even "heroes" and "saints." The disparity between our present knowledge about criminality and simultaneous ignorance of its historical past is due to the as yet unexplored study of the historical function of picaresque related literary autobiographies--especially since they are often the only personal documents available about social offenders.

Conclusions

The phenomenon of social deviance is one with which everyone has to come to terms in a century which knows more about social offenders than any other in recorded history. By the very nature of their impact on modern society, however, social offenders are not easy to analyze satisfactorily, surrounded as they are by the extremes of "crime and punishment," "reality and labelling," "blame and responsibility" and "individual and society." The real social historiography of deviance, in spite of a remarkable accumulation of data, is only just beginning. Sociological studies of case-histories have not led to either textual analyses or historical studies. Thus it is perhaps not without significance that recent attempts to conduct research of marginals comes not only from historians but also from cultural and literary scholars. The question to be asked about such interdisciplinary attempts is whether they may hold some interest for the specialists and the social historians. Therefore, it might be useful here, as a way of conclusion, to report briefly how I have gone about this interdisciplinary research project and what are the differences between concrete findings and speculation.

1) One starts with standard formalist studies of picaresque autobiographies, treating them as literature and highlighting their structural and stylistic characteristics—above all, the subtle and humorous ways *pícaros*, as narrators, recall, supposedly from a "distance," the social and moral wrongs that they committed; 2) a side effect of textual scrutiny is the emergence of a remarkably diverse lexicon used in the descriptions of social deviance and criminal subculture, that is, there are extra-literary elements on the linguistic level of picaresque texts; 3) assuming that the

past vocabulary about social deviance was in its time contemporary, one can conjecture whether the fictive situations of picaresque narratives might offer potentially a
"visitable" past that could be analyzed both in terms of its
structure and the historical conditions of law and order to
which it refers; 4) upon undertaking a preliminary investigation of social deviance one realizes that almost all social studies, though full of indispensable information,
concentrate on data, theory and almost exclusively on the
modern period; 5) a telling clue to the abundant information in our times is the effective use of first-person
accounts—interviews, confessions, case histories, letters,
etc. 6) one fails to find similar first-person accounts in the
past while, surprisingly, there are no histories written of
past social offenders, that is, we can conjecture that the
lack of deviant life-stories by the social offenders themselves is somehow connected to the lack of histories about
them; 7) while examining modern case-histories one
notices the important and relevant parallels between the
structure of criminal autobiographies and those of
picaresque fictions or medieval confessions; 8) if structural
similarities are indisputable, the historical interpretation
of them, given socio-historical variables, seem highly
problematic; 9) one common denominator of historical
and fictive autobiographical accounts is a telling but
understandable contradiction: social offenders tend to
recall a past they burlesquely consider unworthy or
undesirable and, therefore, they deal with this paradox by
providing explicit or implicit reasons for bothering to
write; 10) what literary scholars analyze as "narrative
distance" turns out to be, coincidentally, a pivotal point of
modern theorists of historiography: deviant *pasts* are
constructed discourses by the social offenders who are *now*
reconstructing them and, therefore, like readers of all
history, must be alert to all (deliberate or unconscious)
confusions between past events and the present transmission of those events; 11) the historical function of the
narrative structure of picaresque autobiographies, no
matter how elusive, becomes evident; and 12) a good part
of the problem lay in modern ahistorical approaches—in

criminology by pragmatic social scientists; and, in the humanities, by textual "literalist."

The problem is that, like any genuine reappraisal of a canonized genre, this project faces a dilemma: how to seek solutions that might lie outside the framework of established standards and practices while struggling within that framework. There is no simple way out of this dilemma for it is built into the situation of Hispanic studies. Yet the self-sealing ways of textual analysis, though invaluable, are by themselves no solution (nor is the reaction of outright rejection of the canon). Investigating the historical function of picaresque autobiographies in a field such as ours just happens to be difficult. Hopefully, however, the friction between two disciplines might be a sign that the problem of social deviance, in history and fiction, can nudge in a meaningful way. Unlikely as it seems (to borrow an optimistic metaphor from scientists), the tiny air currents that a butterfly creates travel across thousands of miles, jostling other breezes as they go eventually changing the weather.

To conclude with the title of the essay, there is a need to stress the difference between the "general" function of forms of literature and the "specific" historical function of picaresque texts. A general function refers conceptually to the "nature" of forms in texts without the need to deal with the specificity of the available modes of writing. The historical function of a particular Spanish picaresque text, on the contrary, must refer concretely, among other things, to dates, age, social context, and modes of production. An opposition is thus created between a text's fictionality and the historical referents of that fictionality. The urgent question, then, is whether it is possible to develop an inclusive analysis of forms that represents a genuine synthesis of "historical" and "formalist" perspectives. An attempt at such a synthesis must confront serious theoretical and empirical issues but it should no longer be bypassed by labelling it a pseudo-problem.

WORKS CITED

Alemán, Mateo. *Guzmán de Alfarache.* 2 vols. Ed. B. Brancaforte. Madrid: Cátedra, 1979.

———. *The Rogue (or the Life of Guzmán de Alfarache).* Trans. James Mabbe. London: 1924.

Alighieri, Dante. *Inferno (The Divine Comedy).* Trans. J.D. Sinclair. New York: Oxford Univ. Press, 1961.

Anonymous. *The Life of Lazarillo de Tormes. His Fortunes and Adversities.* Trans. Harriet de Onís. New York: Barron, 1959.

———. *La vida de Lazarillo de Tormes y de sus fortunas y adversidades.* Ed. A. Blecua Madrid: Castalia, 1974.

Bellow, Saul. *The Adventures of Augie March.* New York: Viking Press, 1960.

Cela, Camilo José. *La Familia de Pascual Duarte.* Barcelona: Destino, 1955. English title: *The Family of Pacual Duarte.* Trans. A Kerrigan. New York: Bald/Avon,1964.

Cervantes, Miguel de. *Don Quijote de la Mancha.* Ed. Luis Murillo. Madrid: Castalia, 1978. English title: *Don Quixote.* Trans. J.M. Cohen. London: Penguin, 1976.

———. *The Dog's Colloquy* in *Exemplary Novels.* Trans. W. Starkie. New York: Signet Classics, 1963.

———. *Novelas Ejemplares (El Coloquio de los Perros).* Ed. J. Bautista Avalle-Arce. Madrid: Castalia, 1982.

Charrière, Henri. *Papillon.* Trans. J.P. Wilson and W.B. Michaels. New York: Pocket Books, 1971.

"The Confession of Golias", in *The Goliard Poets.* Trans. G.F. Whicher. Cambridge, Mass., 1949.

The Confessions of St. Augustine. Trans. Rex Warner. Ontario: Mentor Books, 1963.

Defoe, Daniel. *The Fortunes and Misfortunes of Moll Flanders.* New York: Modern Library, 1950.

Ellison, Ralph. *The Invisible Man.* New York: Vintage Books, 1947.

Espinel, Vicente. *Vida del escudero Marcos de Obregón*. Ed. Mª Soledad Carrasco Urgoiti. Madrid: Clásicos Castalia, 1972.

Fernández de Lizardi, J.J. *El Periquillo Sarniento*. Mexico: Ed. Porrúa, 1969.

Genet, Jean. *The Thief's Journal*. Trans. B. Frechtman. New York: Grove Press, 1964.

Goffman, Erving. *The Presentation of Self In Everyday Life*. New York: Doubleday, 1959.

Grimmelshausen, H.J. Chr. Von. *Simplicius Simplicissimus*. Trans. G. Schulz-Behrend. New York: Bobbs-Merrill, 1965.

———. *The Runagate Courage*. Trans. R.L. Hiller and J.C. Osborne. Lincoln: Univ. of Nebraska Press, 1965.

Hahn, Jessica. "The Confessions of Jessica Hahn to Playboy." *Playboy* (October 1987).

Jackson, George. *Soledad Brother: The Prison Letters*. New York: Bantam Books, 1970.

Le Sage, Alain René. *Histoire de Gil Blas de Santillane*. Ed. M. Bordon. Paris, 1955.

Lesbian Nuns: Breaking Silence. Eds. Rosemary Curb and Nancy Manahan. New York: Warner Books, 1985.

Lewis, Oscar. *La Vida*. New York: Random House, 1967.

López de Ubeda, Francisco. *La pícara Justina*. In *La novela picaresca española*. Ed. A. Valbuena Pratt. Madrid: Aguilar, 1962.

Malcolm X. *The Autobiography of Malcolm X*. New York: Grove Press, 1966.

Mann, Thomas. *Confessions of Felix Krull, Confidence Man*. Trans. D. Lindley. New York: Signet Classics, 1963.

Maravall, José Antonio. *La literatura picaresca desde la historia social*. Madrid: Taurus, 1986.

———. "Relaciones de dependencia e integración social: criados, graciosos, y pícaros," *Ideologies & Literature*, Vol. I, No. 4 (Sept.-Oct. 1977) 3-32.

Nashe, Thomas. *The Unfortunate Traveller or The Life of Jack Wilton.* New York: Everyman's Library, 1966.

The Newgate Calendar (or Male-Factors Bloody Register). New York: Capricorn Books, 1962.

Quevedo, Francisco de. *La Vida del Buscón llamado dos Pablos.* Ed. D. Ynduráin. Cátedra. 1980. English title: *The Scavenger.* Trans. H. Harter. New York: Las Américas, 1962.

Ruiz, Juan. *The Book of True Love.* Bilingual Ed., Daly/Zahareas. University Park: Penn State Univ. Press, 1977.

Sartre, Jean-Paul. *Saint Genet.* Trans. B. Frechtman. New York: Mentor Books, 1963.

Smollet, Tobias. *Roderick Random.* New York: Signet, 1964.

Spadaccini, Nicholas and Anthony N. Zahareas, Eds. *La vida y hechos de Estebanillo González, hombre de buen humor. Compuesto por él mesmo.* 2 vols. Madrid: Castalia, 1978.

Teresa of Avila, Saint. *The Life Of Saint Teresa.* Trans. J.M. Cohen. London: Penguin, 1957.

Theoretical Perspectives on Deviance. Ed. by R.A. Scott and J.D. Douglas. New York, 1972.

Villon, François. *Complete Works.* Trans. Anthony Bonner. New York: Bantam Books, 1960.

Waldheim, Kurt. *In the Eye of the Storm.* New York, 1985.

Zahareas, Anthony N. "El género picaresca y las autobiografías de criminales," *La Picaresca: Origenes, Texto y Estructuras.* Madrid: Actas I., 1979. pp. 631-663.

―――. "Quevedo's Buscón: Structure and Ideology," *Homenaje a Julio Caro Baroja.* Madrid, 1970. 1055-1089.

Zúñiga, Francesillo de. *Crónica burlesca del Emperador Carlos V.* Ed. D. Pamp de Avalle-Arce. Barcelona: Grijalbo, 1981.

Helen H. Reed

Antonio Pérez published all of his *Historical Accounts
(Relaciones)* from exile, although they were partially written before he left Spain, in response to political events
there and in defense of himself. Subsequently, the adversity of exile provided further impetus for his writing, and
he achieved much of his literary renown abroad. His elo-
quence evolved according to its use, from the early diplomatic correspondence to highly rhetoricized, apologetic
forms of discourse. Pérez had been the intimate political
advisor and finally Secretary of State to Philip II, as had his
father, Gonzalo Pérez, before him. In 1579, Philip surrepti-
tiously removed Antonio Pérez from office and replaced
him with a rival. Pérez had orchestrated the assassination
of a political undesirable, Juan de Escobedo, for reasons
that may never be entirely clear, but probably with the
king's tacit approval (Marañón, *Antonio Pérez* 274-326).

Thirteen years later, after a protracted legal and psychological battle with the king and in danger of his life, Pérez finally fled Spain. In exile, from 1591 until his death in 1611,
he lived hectically, moving from one foreign court to another. He vacillated between France and England, instigat-
ing political intrigues supported by an elaborate correspondence. A consummate letter writer, as were his humanist friends, such as Francis Bacon and the Earl of Essex,
Pérez became one of the most exquisite practitioners of the
art. He was also one of the most prolific.[1]

Pérez was a brilliant rhetorician. He had been educated
in the humanistic tradition, hence, in part, his predilection for letter writing, an art cultivated to sustain friend-
ships among the humanists, especially by those separated
geographically. As Pérez himself states in the following
aphorisms, "The Breath of Life: letters from distant
friends" ("Respiración de Ausentes: las cartas de los amigos") or "The pen: a sixth sense for those absent in place of
the five they can't use" ("La pluma: sexto sentido para los
ausentes por no poder usar de los cinco").[2] Gracián describes Pérez admiringly in his *Wit and the Art of
Ingenuity (Agudeza y arte de ingenio)* as "the prime example of serious, epigrammatic and natural style" ("el
primer ejemplo del estilo grave, conceptuoso, y natural")
and cites a letter from the *Historical Accounts (Relaciones)*
by way of example (qtd. in Ungerer, *A Spaniard* II, 325-
327).[3] Pérez wrote facilely in several languages besides
Spanish—Italian, Latin, French, and English—and may
best be described both ideologically and stylistically as a
mannerist, particularly in the disillusioned later years of
his exile (Ungerer, *A Spaniard* II, 324-362). His literary production is chiefly autobiographical and concentrated in the
appropriate genres, commonplace during the sixteenth
century, the memoir, historical account *(relación)*, narrative letter *(carta de relación)*, and epistle. His private
correspondence was later published in collections, sometimes as "personal letters" *(epístolas familiares)*, letter-es-
says that portrayed in many ways their writers' characters,
thoughts, and feelings: at first self-revelations for private
circulation, they increasingly became contrived self-
glorifications for public consumption. Pérez also exercised

some influence as a political thinker.[4] His political ideas were expressed intermittently in his autobiographical accounts in the form of mini-treatises or aphorisms relating to the narrative material. The aphorisms, some of which were political maxims, often appear as marginalia to the narrations and were later gathered into separate collections and published, as were the letters.

In regard to the *Historical Accounts (Relaciones)*, an abbreviated Spanish version of the three related, but diverse, narrations was first printed in 1591 in Pau, the city to which Pérez fled after leaving Spain. In 1594, while Pérez lived in England under the tutelage of the Earl of Essex, he published a longer Spanish version, presumably directed to readers in Aragón and the Netherlands. This essay will concentrate on the expanded version of the *Relaciones* published in Paris in 1598, the year that Philip II died. Some new material has been added in the form of documents, notes, and more direct accusations of the king's dubious role in events.[5] The narrations are preceded by several introductory dedications and followed by a detailed index. Additionally, some letters to the powerful individuals to whom Antonio Pérez sent his "little book" *(librillo)*, the third of the narratives, are included. Finally, a collection of aphorisms culled from the *Relaciones* and letters have been added to the same bound volume. These aphorisms were published together in 1616 in Paris, but circulated in various separate collections both in England and France from 1598.[6] Some of them provide a key to the design of the *Relaciones*. Eloquently phrased traditional *topoi*, political maxims, or truisms, they state Pérez's underlying assumptions and interpretive conclusions in regard to his unfortunate experience. The indices and glosses added to the margins similarly demonstrate the effort to coherently organize or orientate historical data. Moreover, each aphorism in the final anthology is followed by a page number locating the illustrative material from Pérez's life. This is a didactic autobiography written to exemplify or discover some general truths, replete with an elaborate system of cross references.

In the present essay, I will undertake to describe what some consider essential to autobiographical discourse, the design elicited from (or imposed on) the narrative material, its "figuration" or way of ordering the facts (Pascal and Fleishman). To interpret his life, Pérez recurs to certain conventional paradigms prevalent in Renaissance thought, but further relates these patterns and events to the exploration of some pressing political issues. He not only demonstrates an effort to structure his life's story, but also to define a past self and reassemble a present one from the vestiges of the past (Beaujour and Olney). This attempt at self-portraiture is somewhat incomplete and disjointed. The imagery utilized, which appears inspired both in past persecution and present exile, is striking both in itself and in its resemblance to that of other Baroque or mannerist writers describing characters in similar predicaments. Another salient feature of the text is Pérez's skillful incorporation of epistles into his narrative, even taking into consideration a literary horizon of expectation conspicuously dominated by that form of discourse. The vast majority of Golden Age autobiographies, whether fictional or historical, are couched in terms of a letter written to someone, and often the person addressed *(destinatario)* wields power over the writer.[7] Pérez addresses his accounts to various audiences and influential people, but also includes within the narrative judiciously selected letters from himself and other renowned individuals. By this means, he imparts information, authenticates his account, and diffuses the narrative perspective. All the *Relaciones* are apologies written to justify past actions, stave off future disaster, or persuade people to pursue a course of action that will benefit the author. However, as mentioned, Pérez also adapts a highly interpretive stance in regard to his experience, drawing political and philosophical conclusions from the narrative content. Like other contemporary works, such as *Guzmán de Alfarache,* the story is heavily laced with doxy and serves an exemplary purpose. Ironically, in the process of this theoretical effort, what appears designed as an apology or self-defense also becomes an attack on the system and, therefore, in some ways, negates its original motivation. In regard to the author's political and economic advantage, it may have even become self-defeating.

The *Relaciones* were all ostensibly written by Antonio Pérez to win political support and later patronage, most specifically to exonerate his role in the murder of Juan de Escobedo or to protest the injustice of his persecution by the king. His defense rests on the claim that he acted as executioner rather than assassin, a vassal obeying the command of his sovereign, Philip II. According to Pérez, in 1578 Philip II deemed it necessary to the state's interests to eliminate Escobedo, the Secretary of Don Juan of Austria, without due process of law. Pérez expresses the view that Philip was alarmed by Escobedo's active fostering of Don Juan's ambition to become King of England by marrying Queen Elizabeth. Following the crime, rumors immediately began to circulate that linked Pérez and his probable accomplice and paramour, Ana de Mendoza, the Princess of Eboli, as together responsible. More than a year later, in response to the complaints of Escobedo's family and machinations of political enemies, Antonio Pérez was apprehended. He was for years merely confined to his home, left free to associate with whom he pleased, but harassed by secret investigations and attempts to confiscate his personal papers. The prolonged conflict between Pérez and the king may be explained by Philip's wish to divert public attention from his own part in Escobedo's assassination. He seems to have feared that Antonio Pérez would reveal damning documents about his role in the affair, as well as other state secrets. Pérez apparently hoped to obtain royal pardon and some return to favor. He resisted disclosing the contents of his papers, but also relinquishing them to the king and leaving Spain. In June of 1585, at the highly irregular, secret "Trial of Investigation" ("Proceso de la Visita"), he was officially condemned for the first time and was thereafter treated with increasing severity, alternating with brief periods of leniency. He was several times incarcerated, tortured, and subjected to lengthy and complex legal proceedings. Houdini-like, he twice escaped from prison, the first time in 1590 to flee to Aragón, under whose autonomous legal system he was removed from the strict jurisdiction of Philip II. His second escape was to abandon Zaragoza, having taken advantage of the confusion caused by a popular uprising in support of his cause.

Pérez crossed the border to France in November, 1591, because the king had sent an army to quell the rebellion and to return Pérez to the Inquisitorial Courts of Castilla to fulfill his death sentence. In order to survive, no other recourse remained save self-imposed exile (Marañón, *Antonio Pérez* 274-618).

All the *Relaciones* are recounted by a first person narrator about a third person character, "Antonio Pérez," though the narrator often designates himself, or signs the various manuscripts and letters as, "Rafael the Wanderer" (Rafael Peregrino). This consistent differentiation between Antonio Pérez past actor and present writer seems in part designed to make the historical account appear more objective. It distinguishes the historical events from their emotionalized interpretation, and distances the narrator from his other (former) self. Although the notion of third person autobiography appears paradoxical, as Philippe Lejeune points out, the subject in the process of self-writing inevitably divides, both a narrating and a narrated self. In third person autobiographies this duality is especially emphasized or boldly proclaimed *(Je est un Autre)*. Here, it seems to me, the separation enables Pérez to enjoy the best of two worlds, to illuminate his conniving past from his present state of moral indignation. He can appear to be dispassionate on one level, while on another unleashing his rhetorical skills to persistently play on the readers' sympathy. The inclusion of numerous letters from famous and politically eminent individuals, to which Pérez had been privy as Secretary, further verifies events and supports his case. Thus, Pérez makes use of a shifting perspective and varies epistolary, autobiographical, and historical narrative structures. The highly rhetorical commentary seems intended to amuse the reading public and demonstrate the author's virtuosity, as well as win sympathy for his cause.

The use of third person for an autobiography is a narrative technique also employed in some classical chronicles, notably Caesar's *De Gallo Bellico*, as well as some modern autobiographies, such as the *The Memoirs of Richard Nixon* and *Roland Barthes sur Roland Barthes*. Here the continual mention of Pérez's proper name appears imita-

tive of the chronicle tradition and designed to dignify him
as a public figure of historical importance. In fact, the third
person subject pronoun is never used when referring to
him. By this means and others, the text is colored by
Pérez's sense of himself as a tragic historical personage, a
once mighty statesman now unjustly persecuted by his
sovereign and brought low by contrary fortune. With one
of his typically pictorial images, for example, he refers to
himself as "a persecuted man that carries with him wherever he goes, the wrath and rage of his Sovereign attached
to his shadow" ("un perseguido que lleva adondequiera
que va, atada a la sombra la ira y enojo de su Príncipe"
[Pérez, *Relaciones*, p. a]). Yet, at the same time, one senses
a self-deprecatory or ironic note in some of the rather contrived metaphors and historical reminiscences. When describing his flight to France, for example, he writes: "he
crossed the Rubicon, I mean to say, the Pyrenees" ("pasó el
Rubicón, digo, los Pirineos" [Pérez, *Relaciones* 107]), as if to
mock his own propensity for classical references and
abrupt shifts in voice. More importantly, the distancing of
himself from himself in the light of other features of the
text may connote a self-disgust or horror, a desire to mask
or maintain a separation from some of the more loath-
some aspects of his person. Such an interpretation, I
would suggest, is also substantiated by the mannerist imagery and fragmented structure of the text.

The earlier two memoirs, and the last in order in the
text here studied, are the most pragmatic. The third account included in the *Relaciones*, the so-called "little
book" *(librillo)*, was written in a desperate attempt to miti-
gate the dangerous circumstances in which he found himself. It was circulated only after repeated requests for
clemency and includes many of those letters to the king
and others together with their replies. Pérez had recently
escaped to Aragón to avoid probable execution. Upon arrival, his worst suspicions were confirmed, for he learned
that he had been tried *in absentia* by the Inquisitorial
Court on trumped up charges of heresy and witchcraft. He
was sentenced to be drawn, hanged, and quartered, and his
estate was to be sequestered. He attempted to publish the
librillo in Zaragoza and, failing that, had thirty copies re-

produced from prison and distributed to the judges and other powerful persons. The manuscript was finally printed in Pau after his escape and widely circulated throughout Europe (Marañón, *Antonio Pérez* 505-24). In it, Pérez accuses the king as author of the death of Escobedo and presents abundant documentary proof. Even so, he proceeds with tact and caution, casting the blame on the king's advisors and dwelling on his father's and his own loyal service as former Secretaries. He still maintains that he is as faithful and obedient to the Royal Will "as clay in the hand of its Potter" ("como el barro en la mano de su Hollero" [Pérez, *Relaciones* 167]), to my mind a strangely submissive image given his present state of rebellion. His defense rests on stating the reasons for Escobedo's removal, chiefly his politicking to further Don Juan of Austria's ambitions, and in presenting supporting evidence in the form of correspondence between all the principals involved, including Philip II. As always, he invites the reader's compassion. For example, in an elaborate series of metaphors he compares himself to a ship that has sailed through fair and foul winds of fortune. In the following passage, he describes the calm before the storm:

> ...in the middle of that sea, so tranquil with the soft breezes of favor and tokens of love never before granted to a person of his sort (as the same documents will show), he wanted to withdraw and secure his poor boat and family in any hideaway, fearing the storm of Envy and recognizing the terrible winds and whirlwinds of persecutions that were coming over him.

> ...en medio de aquella mar tan sosegada de gracia jamás vista en persona de su suerte con el más fresco aire de favor y prendas (como los mismos papeles constarán) que deseó apartarse y meter en cualquier rincón su pobre barca y familia, temiendo la tormenta de la Invidia y conociendo los terribles vientos y torbellinos de persecuciones que sobre él venían.
> (*Relaciones* 215)

This vision of himself as a victim is typical, both in its emblematic dramatization of his plight and recourse to the *topos* of fortune's vicissitudes.

The distribution of the *librillo,* together with several anti-Inquisitorial lampoons,[8] Pérez's pathetic physical appearance after torture by the Inquisition, and his oratorical gifts won him short-lived popular support in Zaragoza. A mob rose in rebellion as Pérez was transferred from the Charter Prison to the Prison of the Inquisition, lynching the King's viceroy, the Marquess of Almenara, and setting Pérez free. The history of these events is recorded in the second *Relación, Concerning What Happened in Zaragoza, Aragón, on September 24, 1591, in behalf of the Liberty of Antonio Pérez; and Concerning its Laws and Justice (Relación de lo sucedido en Zaragoza de Aragón 24 de septiembre del año de 1591 por la libertad de Antonio Pérez y de sus Fueros y Justicia).* This brief piece was first published anonymously in Pau in 1591 as part of Pérez's propagandistic effort to foment a revolution in Aragón and Catalonia from exile, an absurd enterprise that ended in failure. It is a vivid account centered on an issue and related event, with theorizing kept to a minimum. It jubilantly describes the popular uprising in Zaragoza in hopes of its being imitated on a wider scale. Both the history of the laws *(fueros)* of Aragón, Philip's violation of Aragón's regional autonomy, and the illegalities of Pérez having been handed over to the Inquisitorial Court to be tried are briefly discussed. Pérez offers many convincing descriptive details and anecdotes that demonstrate popular enthusiasm for his cause: for example, the story of the fruit vendor that gave him not only fruit but ten coins *(reales),* the attempt by the armed populace *(pueblo)* to carry him off on their shoulders, and the clamorous shouting of the people in defense of his liberty. He cites a biblical parallel in which God responded to the cries of the people of Israel by descending from Heaven and implies divine intervention will be God's likely response to the present circumstances:

> ...from now on I think it also ought to be said that the voice of the People is the voice of God; because from where the People finish their complaints and crying out to God as a last resort, he begins with his marvels and magnificence.

...que de aquí pienso que se debió también de decir voz
de Pueblo, voz de Dios; porque de donde el Pueblo
acaba, que son sus quejas y voces a Dios como último
remedio, comienza él con sus maravillas y grandezas
(*Relaciones* 153).

Thus, the expressed will of the people is equated to divine approval for Pérez's cause. However, the populace of Aragón did not actually favor the legal autonomy provided by the regional laws and resulting feudal privileges accorded to the nobility. It is just that Pérez, through skillful use of propaganda and sheer demagoguery, had manipulated the mob and temporarily exploited the issues to his advantage (Ungerer, *A Spaniard* I, 204-205; Marañón, *Antonio Pérez* 525-618).

The longest and to my mind the most interesting of the *Relaciones*, the memoir that most approaches in scope an autobiography, is the first. This summary account of the whole matter is stylistically and ideologically adumbrated by the shorter histories. It differs in treating matters from a more theoretical, critical, and bolder perspective, not surprisingly, since it was written from the relative safety of exile. A narrative performance in response to public curiosity, it is mainly directed to a foreign audience and particularly to several politically powerful individuals such as Henry IV King of France and the Pope, though Pérez still hoped to gain support in Spain. Here Pérez obviously attempts to give a cohesive shape to the history of his life, but does not entirely succeed. He expresses regret at not incorporating all the material from other *relaciones*, which the reader must consult to fully grasp the situation, yet does not wish to repeat himself. Thus, this version is an incomplete or truncated autobiography, that he perhaps hoped to supplement. Moreover, transitions are abrupt, and the arrangement of autobiographical elements is sometimes clumsy. This fragmentariness, I would suggest, indicates Pérez's reluctance or inability to fully portray himself or complete a definitive version of his life. He appears to have regarded himself with both narcissistic fascination and fear. There were also practical reasons for not confronting his reflection too truthfully. He not only depended on the clemency of foreign princes for political asylum, but also may have considered the welfare of his wife and children who remained imprisoned in Spain. The Princess of Eboli was also imprisoned, but died in 1592, soon after Antonio Pérez escaped to France.

The *Summary Account (Relación Sumaria)* is prefaced by letters to Henry IV of France, under whose protection he then resided, to the Pope, to Everyman, and to the Curious. As he sought favor in foreign courts, Pérez's letters, always eloquent and diplomatic, became increasingly obsequious, unctuous, and mannerist in their bizarre and sensuous imagery. The prefaces here are not as precious or perverse as Pérez's private correspondence with Francis Bacon and others, for example, but they are more self-consciously rhetorical than the earlier writings. With stylistic devices reminiscent of Mateo Alemán, he attempts to persuade the reader of the truth of his history, not only through argumentation but also through affecting his sensibilities. In both the prefaces and the text that follows, he utilizes some of the same rhetorical techniques to play on the readers' emotions that Cros summarized under the rubrics of *amplificatio* and "actualization" on analyzing *Guzmán* (Cros 247-72; Ungerer, *A Spaniard* 324-62). These include use of definitions, enumeration, illustrative anecdotes, dramatic oppositions, as well as elaborate pictorial similes and even allegories. Through these means Pérez attempts to establish a powerful image of himself as unjustly persecuted martyr.

No reader of Michel Beaujour's recent book on autobiography as autoportrait could fail to note Pérez's inclination to portray himself visually with words and even to accompany his text with illustrations that represent him and his plight symbolically. The 1594 edition of the *Relaciones* is subtitled "living portrait of Fortune's natural man" ("retrato al vivo del natural de la Fortuna"). An art collector, Pérez especially admired Titian, whom he had met in Italy, as did Philip II. He owned ninety-six superb and valuable paintings, a large number of them Mannerist in style (Ungerer, *La Defensa* 70-72). He seems to have regarded writing as another representational art, even one superior to painting, and to have considered personal letters *(cartas familiares)* to be verbal portraits or mirrors of their authors, as testified by the following aphorisms:

> Letters declare more about a person's nature than a face reveals to a physiognomer.
> Another man called letters the portrait of the soul.
> As the brush portrays bodies, the pen paints alive the virtues of souls.
> The brush: a dead pen; the pen: a brush alive with the virtues of immortal souls.
> There's no brush that paints as well as the pen.

> Las cartas familiares declaran más el natural de una persona que el rostro a un fisiógnomo. (*O.C.* 740)
> Retrato del ánimo llamó otro a las cartas familiares. (*O.C.* 742)
> Como el pincel retrata los cuerpos, la pluma pinta al vivo las virtudes de los ánimos. (*O.C.* 1018)
> El pincel: pluma muerta; la pluma: pincel vivo de virtudes de ánimos immortales.(*O.C.* 1018)
> No hay pincel que pinte tan bien como la pluma. (*O.C.* 742)[9]

The preface dedicated to Henry IV makes use of both painterly and nautical imagery. Pérez stresses his sincerity, claiming that although men paint themselves with the most favorable colors possible before kings, he will confess intimately as though before God "his imperfections and human passions, I mean those of ignorance, grief, anguish, and miserable, misguided, and even dangerous grievances" ("las imperfecciones y afectos naturales, digo de ignorancia, de dolor, de desconsuelo, de quejas miserables, perdidas y aun peligrosas"). The king has ordered him to relate the "sources" *(manantiales)* of his persecutions. Thus, he enumerates his sufferings somewhat chaotically and finally presents a hyperbolic, summarial image of them. He states that bad fortune sometimes leads to unexpected good and cites the example of leaving a sinking ship (tactfully implying his pleasure in arriving at the "port" of France). A dichotomy is established between bad Philip II and good Henry IV. Accordingly, he suggests allegorically the exemplarity of his account as a mirror for princes: great seamen learn best from the errors of their peers that no rock is more dangerous to great ships than passion, particularly those sailing under full sail of absolute power. The name of Henry IV will become the Hieroglyph of Piety and Justice (it is implied, because of his anticipated kindness to Antonio Pérez).

The text's didactic purpose is restated and amplified in the letter to "Everyman" *(Todos)*. It is now also specifically designated an "anatomy for the education of princes' favorites" ("anatomía para enseñamiento de privados de príncipes"). Pérez begins by discussing two devices that represent graphically the evolution of his relationship with Philip II and his motivations for change. Both devices picture a minotaur in the center of a labyrinth, the first with his finger held to his lips and the words "IN SPE" written above. In the second, the labyrinth is broken, and the minotaur's finger is pointing toward heaven with the adage "VSQUE AD HOC" inscribed above. Long imprisoned in his labyrinth of silence and hope, Antonio Pérez finally spoke, breaking free at the point he became disillusioned *(desengañado)*. In effect, the contrasting states of bondage and freedom from bondage indicate the future action of the *Relación* and orient the reader to the shape of the narrative. The emblem of the minotaur also appeared as a seal on Pérez's letters and many of his belongings—books, writing desk, bed-curtains, jewels and so on. In fact, the first half of the emblem had also been used by his father.

The symbol of the minotaur—half bull/half man trapped in a labyrinth—is followed by other images of monstrosity to describe himself, the most frequent of which is that of a "monster of fortune" ("monstruo de la fortuna"). This expressive and complex metaphor is the crux of a network of related ideas. It immediately calls to mind the analogous epithet of Lope de Vega, "monster of nature" ("monstruo de la naturaleza"), and the less frequent "monster of wit" ("monstruo del ingenio"), sometimes applied to Calderón (Ungerer, *A Spaniard* II, 330-336). In any case, one meaning is surely that of an extreme, unbelievable, and bizarre example of something - in this case misfortune. Linked with Pérez's frequent mention of himself as a "wanderer" *(peregrino)* speaking in barbarous

or Babylonian languages, the implication is that the depri-
vation of his political power and role as Secretary of State
made him a monster, a barbarian outside civilized society.
Similar metaphors of the self may be found in *Life is a
Dream (La Vida es Sueño)*, where Segismundo, denied his
birthright as heir to his father's throne, i.e., his political as
well as his familial rights, is reduced to a state of bestiality.
He is violent and angry, clad in animal skins, and lives in
dark, labyrinthine mountains. Similarly, Rosaura, a social
outcast for having been seduced and abandoned, arrives in
the same labyrinthine mountains astride the back of a
mythical monster or hypogryph. Unmarried and deprived
of her honor, she is dressed as a man. These aberrations of
nature have been prevented from fulfilling their expected
social role and perceive of themselves as animalistic, un-
civilized, or abnormal.

Another aspect of his monstrosity that Pérez plays upon
is that he is interesting as a rarity on display—a monster to
excite the curiosity of spectator, to produce wonder. That is
the gist of his argument on hoping to be given asylum in
the court of Catherine of Navarre, the sister of the French
king Henry IV.

> ...and just as Nature's strange animals and monsters
> are presented to Princes and received with courtesy
> and curiosity, there will present himself before Your
> Highness a Monster of Fortune; they have always
> been admired more than the others, for showing the
> effects of more violent causes.

> ...y como a los Príncipes se les presentan y admiten
> con gracia y curiosidad los animales raros y mon-
> struos de la Naturaleza, a Vuestra Alteza se le pre-
> sentará un Monstruo de la Fortuna: que siempre fueron
> de mayor admiración que los otros, como efectos de
> causas más violentas.

In the late Renaissance, such bizarre beasts as elephants,
tigers, and rhinoceri were sometimes displayed in court, as
Pérez mentions in a letter to the Earl of Essex (qtd. in
Ungerer, *A Spaniard* I, 333), again suggesting that he, as a
monster of fortune, would be at home in the midst of

these monsters of nature. During the same era, c. 1550-1650, the *kunst* or *wunderkammer* flourished, museums or, literally, "wonder cabinets", housing collections of bizarre and amazing objects with the sole purpose of causing wonder (Mullaney 40-67).[10]

Likewise, Antonio Pérez presents himself as reified, a spectacle of strangeness. He not only displays his own monstrosity, but in a letter christens his mistress, the Princess of Eboli, a "Cyclops" (Ungerer, *A Spaniard* I, 457), the origin of the horror figure in the myth of Polyphemus and Galatea and the subject of Góngora's poem. In other passages of the *Relaciones*, Pérez refers to himself as a little ant, albeit a prodigious one, expressing surprise that "such a little ant has embarrassed such a great king for such a long time" ("tan pequeña hormiga se ha embarazado tanto tiempo a un rey tan grande" [*Relaciones* 123]). In letters, he quite frequently recurs to the obsequious image of himself as a dog, usually at the feet of the noble and powerful (Ungerer, *A Spaniard* II, 197-202; Marañón, *Antonio Pérez* 345 ff.), calling to mind the composition of numerous Renaissance portraits. In one passage of the *Relación Sumaria*, he combines his monster of fortune image with the idea of a bull-fight, referring to his court battle as the "festival of fortune's monster" ("fiesta del monstruo de la fortuna" [p. 73]). In the final pages of the *Relaciones*, Pérez returns to the bull motif with an elaborate metaphor that describes his emotional state and reasons for deciding to flee:

> ...when Antonio Pérez saw the naked horns of the bull (as they say) about to reach him and a violent end so imminent, both men decided that he should jump, get behind the safety barrier, and not be foolhardy any longer.

> ...viendo ya Antonio Pérez al descubierto los cuernos del toro (como dicen) en su último alcance y llegarle tan cerca la violencia, se resolvieron los dos en que diese el último salto y que se metiese en barrera, y que no fuese más tiempo más temerario. (107).

This time, rather, the bull represents his pursuers. In most cases, these images of animality and, sometimes, violence describe him in relation to an other, usually someone of power and authority before whom he exhibits himself ostentatiously as diminished, dehumanized, or monstrous.[11]

After the introductory letters, the body of the text commences with a statement of purpose and definition, i.e., that it will summarize the imprisonment and persecutions of Antonio Pérez, who was Secretary of State to the Catholic Monarch Philip II. Pérez asserts that the account contains details and copies of papers not published before, but worthy of the public's notice. Fundamental to the narration is the notion of a privileged statesman falling from favor due to the envy of rivals and persecution by his sovereign. He refrains from describing his previous state of grace since it is common knowledge, a static given in the design of a narrative almost entirely devoted to life after the fall. This long process of further decline is, however, both eventful and dramatic. His childhood, youth, and the part of adult life when he was in power are excluded. Only his genealogy, falsified by what it omits in order to establish his family's prominence, and his vertiginous downfall are recounted. This is a world inhabited by persecutors and victims. Pérez mentions in passing the Princess of Eboli and her years of misery and enumerates in greater detail his own sufferings (deaths, misery, imprisonment, etc.). Suddenly, he introduces the theme of his family history. He presents a succinct genealogy of his paternal ancestry, a preamble to establish his identity. He begins by describing his great-grandparents and clarifying some mistaken impressions about their birthplace. He emphasizes his family's, and especially his father's, contributions to political life and his link to the family tradition. No mention is made of his mother, maternal relations, illegitimacy or descendance from a family of Jewish converts (conversos).[12] Immediately afterward, he abruptly jumps forward to the death of Escobedo, stating unequivocally that the king had resolved that he should die without the customary court procedures. The precipitating factor in the tragedy's unraveling is the murder of Escobedo, and Pérez relates the events that follow with care. He includes letters from his political enemies, particularly Mateo Vázquez, his replacement as Philip's Secretary, to further illustrate the destructive qualities of Envy and Passion in the powerful. He also includes what he introduces as an eloquent (more accurately, indiscreet, angry, and impertinent) letter from the Princess of Eboli, undeservedly persecuted like himself, the contributions of her husband Ruy Gómez, former Secretary, now unappreciated. Her story, like his own, exemplifies the commonplace of a fall from grace precipitated by the ingratitude of the powerful. Her emotional accusations impart pertinent information and discredit his enemies without compromising his own position. Pérez also dwells on the hardships his wife suffered—a miscarriage in the eighth month of pregnancy, imprisonment with a bevy of small children, and interrogation by the Inquisition. (Both women fared badly, for they were incarcerated without trial for the rest of their lives.) Pérez emphasizes his own physical sufferings and hardships, as in this passage describing his flight through the Pyrenees:

> He walked with such difficulty for being a delicate man; his tribulations had made his bones grow thin, and both his inner and outer person were so exhausted that it was necessary to carry him through many icy mountain passes and in others throw capes down over the frozen patches where he might step.

> Caminaba con tanto trabajo por ser hombre delicado, y tenerle los trabajos muy adelgazados los huesos, y muy fatigada la persona exterior y interior, que era menester pasarle en brazos muchos pasos de los helados, y en otros echar las capas sobre los hielos por donde pisase. (108)

This harmoniously cadenced verbal picture of his infirmities and consequent actions is well designed to evoke the reader's pity.

Pérez is masterful in teasing the public's curiosity without revealing what might be detrimental to his cause. He capitalizes on his notoriety and tantalizes interest through the inclusion of new documents, such as letters from other famous persons, or refusing to divulge something he assumes readers are eager to know, such as the details of his escapes from prison. He sometimes corrects false impressions and at others confirms hearsay. It is really through this dialogical relationship with his audience that he fashions a self contrived to counteract adverse public opinion. It is for the most part a defensive and somewhat vain portrait, since he virtually never berates himself or admits to any fault. On the contrary, he appears to delight in enhancing remarkable or admirable aspects of his reputation, exhibiting his astrological knowledge, artistry at prison escapes, and persuasiveness as orator. He also plays on the public's curiosity in regard to the Princess of Eboli, implying that she scorned the king as a suitor and that Philip, jealously and mistakenly, imagined that Antonio Pérez enjoyed her favors. An engraving of Ticius, for example, was included with the 1598 edition and also functioned as a seal for some of Pérez's letters. Ticius attempted to seduce Latona, the mother of Apollo and Diana, who together killed him after being ordered to do so by Jupiter, their father and Latona's lover. His body was eternally exposed to the ravages of birds of prey. At the foot of the engraving is a Latin verse, comparing Pérez's lot with Ticius, but declaring his innocence. He, guiltless, has suffered for merely arousing the suspicions of Jupiter. By this means and others, Pérez kept the legend of the love triangle alive and reiterated in a new way the theme of his persecution.[13]

The *Relación Sumaria* reflects a conscious effort to present a coherent life's history, but really only examines in detail the years of Pérez's political discontent. It is intended as a mirror for princes with Philip providing a negative illustration, as well as a mirror for secretaries of state. Pérez stresses his own exemplary service and loyal obedience to his Sovereign's wishes, in contrast to Philip's sorry behavior. He recommends reliance on good ministers and advisors, "that serve as the eyes and minds of their kings" ("que sirven a los reyes como de ojos y entendimientos" [113]) in governing the state. Pérez's mistreatment also became the perspective from which to examine certain political issues theoretically. In his zealous effort to eliminate Pérez without implicating himself, Philip badly abused the legal system. Pérez does not discuss in any detail a sovereign's right to implement political murders, that is, to summarily execute individuals thought to be inimical to the state's interests. He merely reports that justification for Philip's decision. He does express outrage against the illegalities and arbitrary procedures of his own treatment in court: for example, secret proceedings, torture, corrupt judges, false testimony, false charges, and abuse of the legal autonomy of Aragón. Some of his aphorisms lodge specific complaints against the abuse of power or suggest its natural limitations, such as the following:

> A judge that has in his mind's eye the Will of his Prince for the picture he must paint may judge badly.
> Power can give possession, but not the right to it.
> A Prince's persecution of a vassal, lack of authority for the Prince, authority for the vassal.
> Temporal power is a great burden for those that carry it too far.
>
> Mal puede juzgar un juez que tiene a vista del juicio la Voluntad de su Príncipe, como idea de lo que ha de pintar.
> El poder puede dar posesión, no derecho.
> La persecución de un Príncipe contra un vasallo, desautoridad del Príncipe, autoridad del vasallo. (118)
> Gran cargo de los que alargan más de lo justo el Poder Temporal. (122)

His criticisms also sometimes take the form of brief political treatises that constitute digressions from the narrative, and afterwards, Pérez remarks more than once that he will return to his "Relación". He apologizes for the length of his Relaciones, perhaps indicating his belief that he is modifying the conventions of his chosen genre by including his political ideas.

Pérez also relates the events of his life to analogous occurrences from history. The classical historian most often cited by Pérez is Tacitus,[14] who in his Annals and Histories of Imperial Rome maintained a consistently anti-imperialistic stance. Pérez concurs with Tacitus's idea of the educational value of history and also with his political views and is influenced to cast his history in the same mold. "What would Cornelius Tacitus have done had he chanced upon Antonio Pérez's papers?" ("¿Qué hiciera Cornelio Tácito si topara con los papeles de Antonio Pérez?"), he slyly queries, adding that Tacitus's intent was to write about the nature of princes and their passions *(afectos)* and inclinations so that no one might mistake them for anything else but men (35). The susceptibility of the powerful to human failings—especially passion—is a leitmotiv of Pérez's account, and many of his wittiest aphorisms are devoted to the subject. He asserts that the purpose of writing history is didactic—to teach the human species how to improve. Reminiscent of one of Mateo Alemán's justifications for *Guzmán's* exemplarity is his explanation of how the ancient historians extracted from the "poison" of historical events an antidote to human misfortune, which consists in their telling its tale:

> ...from various contrary poisons reduced by distilla-
> tion they extracted the fifth essence and antidote to
> human failure, which is to tell about it; the main
> purpose of history is to serve as a warning for men's
> edification.

> ...como de venenos varios y contrarios reducidos a
> destilación, sacaron la quinta esencia y el antídoto
> contra los caios humanos, que es la noticia dellos
> para el enseñamiento y escarmiento de los hombres, y
> el fin principal de las Historias. (34)

In other passages, he stresses analogies between incidents from his own experience and from the histories of Tacitus. Frequently, his selections treat statesmen or ministers in disfavor, for example, Pison, who was executed for the poisoning of Germanicus, having failed to disclose to the Senate that he had been acting under orders from the Emperor. Antonio Pérez, then, reveals Philip II's role in the murder of Escobedo,

> in order not to find himself in Pison's predicament,
> similar to Antonio Pérez's, about whom Cornelius
> Tacitus tells in the Life of Tyberius; for his refusal to

> divulge his written orders from his monarch and trust
> in the various promises of Sejanus...cost him his life.

> por no verse en lo que se vio Pison, ejemplo como el de
> Antonio Pérez, de quien dice Cornelio Tácito en la
> vida de Tyberio que por no descargase con los billetes
> y mandatos que tenía de su Príncipe y por confiarse en
> las varias promesas de Sejano...le costó la vida. (71)

Other parallels are drawn from the Bible—such as David, "God's great favorite" ("privado grande de Dios"), whose kingdom suffered the miseries of hunger (138). Saul's clemency in pardoning his daughter Micon is cited in contrast to Philip's cruel treatment of Doña Juana, Pérez's faithful wife. Both women helped their husbands to escape the wrath of their monarchs. Pérez also mentions that both the Law of Fernán González and Civil, Common, and Canonical Law absolve a wife for acts committed in defense of her husband (56, 57). Suffice these examples to demonstrate that Pérez frequently contextualizes and highlights his story with historical comparisons in some way favorable to his argument. He thereby indirectly, as well as explicitly, criticizes the royal abuse of power.

Thus, the narration is consciously, but imperfectly, shaped to illustrate general truths, some of them political in nature and others philosophical. These generalizations, in turn, illuminate the events to the author's purpose. Oppositions are established between virtue and vice, the unjustly persecuted and the tyrant, the loyal vassal and the ungrateful sovereign. Equally dramatic are the contrasts caused by fortune's vicissitudes or the differences between the just, pious princes, such as those whose favor Antonio Pérez was presently seeking, and those motivated by Envy and Passion, whose favor he had forfeited. Pérez churlishly dwells on the all too human weaknesses of the latter, particularly in his aphorisms, as the following examples demonstrate:

> Kings have passions like anyone else; but they
> repress them in public, because the people's adora-
> tion depends on holding them in esteem.

A fool he who plans to possess his Prince through confiding secrets in him.
Princes elevate more men for their ambition than for their merits.
There's no Prince alive that doesn't enjoy gossip.

Los reyes tienen sus afectos como cada cual: pero reprímenlos en lo público por la adoración de las gentes, que depende de la estimación. (24)
Necio el que piensa poseer a su Príncipe por secretos y confianzas. (17)
Los Príncipes levantan más hombres por apetito, que por méritos. (17)
No hay Príncipe que no guste de chismes. (25)

One understands that these pithy, barbed adages are inspired by the behavior of one particular prince, but it is also implied that none of these faulty individuals should rule by divine right and without limitations set by law. Pérez, capriciously, sometimes claims the favor of Divine Providence and the will of the people in support of his own cause. Providence even occasionally intervenes in his behalf. For example, Pérez gleefully reports that a judge in his trial (*visitador*) who viewed him unfavorably died of a sudden apoplexy without confession before stating his decision.

Like other Renaissance "self-fashioners" (Greenblatt 9-26), Pérez defined himself in relation to authority. Given the loss of his status, role, and milieu, he evolved into a Satanic figure intent on undermining the sovereign that had unjustly treated him as scapegoat. Displaced from center stage, he shrilly voiced his discontent as if from the wings, creating an elusive, histrionic self-image through the power of language and use of emblems and metaphors visually conceived. His narrative also reflects a sense of self-diminution that expresses itself in increasing hypochondria and servility. His obsessive recounting of physical suffering is complemented by abject images of his insignificance. For example, in relation to royalty, he describes himself as an ant, dog, or clay in the hand of the royal potter, albeit perhaps facetiously. Bulls, monsters of fortune, and minotaurs are other animal symbols of his entrapment and persecution. This metaphoric dehuman-

ization and self-cancellation is offset by repeated mention
of his signature, i.e., proper name, and suffering body, as if
to reaffirm his very existence. Equally persistent is his ab-
sorption with a courtly context, his narrative self-fashioning always an attempt to define himself in the service of
royal authority and even in close proximity to the king's
person, for example, as "clay in the hand of his Potter"
("barro en la mano de su Hollero"), "eyes and mind of the
King" ("ojos y entendimiento del Rey"), or "a persecuted
man that carries attached to his shadow the rage and wrath
of his Prince" ("un perseguido que lleva...atada a la sombra
la ira y enojo de su Príncipe"). Although theoretically he
deprecates absolute monarchy, he remains in thrall to it, a
fawning caricature of his former eminence. In the process
of the narration, he portrays his state of loss and also his
other, his Sovereign, whose favor he once enjoyed but
now lacks and who plays the role of persecutor to his victim. They are posited as two terms of an opposition. In
fact, Pérez proposes in one passage of the *Relación
Sumaria* to write a biography of the king. Such a
manuscript has never been published to my knowledge;
however, a manuscript entitled *In Praise of the Life and
Death of Philip II by his Secretary Antonio Pérez (Elogio a
la vida y muerte del Rey D. Phelipe 2 por el Secretario
Antonio Pérez)* has recently been discovered in the
municipal archives of Ubeda (Valladares Reguero 98).

Frequent editions of the *Relaciones* were printed during
the seventeenth century and probably interested readers in
much the same way as modern autobiographies of notorious murderers or prominent political figures. Pérez's autobiography also shares the high degree of intentionality of
other Renaissance historical accounts and letters
(relaciones y memoriales) usually written to solicit some
favor from the powerful. Antonio Pérez first wrote of his
life (in his *Memorial)* to save his life and then wrote his
life to save his reputation and secure patronage. Literature,
and especially life-writing, became his best means of
livelihood, as well as a symbolic attempt at self-restoration
and gesture of revenge. As Pérez points out: "The pen is
more cutting than the sword." ("Las espadas cortan menos
que las plumas" [qtd. in Marañón, *Antonio Pérez* 734]).

Fortunately, the text is salvaged from its somewhat re-
dundant design by the occasional ironic detachment and
rich pictorial imagination of the author, who recreates
himself best through emblematic metaphors, verbal images with enormous visual impact.

For reasons I've tried to suggest, the *Relaciones* didn't
fare as well as they might have, nor quite as intended, either as a literary or a propagandistic text. The moralizing
digressions, lack of organic unity, and status as non-fiction
prevent them from forming part of the modern literary
canon. As (putatively) self-serving memoirs, they portrayed the author too fully and presented too strong a case
against absolutism to advance his fortunes. Though kings
might delight in Pérez's wit and welcome his criticism of
Philip II, they could hardly have sanctioned his attack on
the institution of kingship nor appreciated his cynical, and
even venomous, remarks on the nature of kings. Pérez's
anti-imperialistic convictions undermined the system
from which he hoped for protection and prevented him
from recovering any vestige of his former eminence during his lifetime. Nonetheless, Pérez's letters, aphorisms,
and *Relaciones* seem to have exercised some influence
among political thinkers and contributed to the contemporary debate on limited monarchy. His rhetorical skills
and wit may have found better expression in the *bon mot*
and the brief *tour de force* than in the sustained effort of
his longer narratives. Yet, the dramatis personae of his
somewhat mendacious autobiographical histories have
lived on in the popular imagination for literally centuries
and frequently in accordance with Pérez's portrayal of
them. The so-called Black Legend of the evils of Philip II
and the love story of Antonio Pérez and the Princess of
Eboli have continued to attract interest and inspire diverse
fictional and historical interpretations. For example, two
centuries after the writing of the *Relaciones*, Philip II and
the Princess of Eboli were elaborately fictionalized in the
tragedy by Schiller, *Don Carlos*, and, following that, in
Verdi's opera of the same name. And Pérez, in the process
of his self-defense and theoretical articulation, i.e., in the
fictionalization of his own life's history, became a writer
and increasingly regarded himself as such. In the early

days of his exile, he already refers to letter writing as "mea occupatio et recreatio animi" (qtd. in Ungerer, *A Spaniard* I, 299). Toward the end of his life, ill, living in a small house in Paris, and denied the company of courtiers and kings, writing seems to have been his only solace. As he was fond of saying,

> I have no other friend save this pen. Look, sir, at what this century's friends are worth: when a pen (How little it weighs!) is worth more than a friend.

> No tengo otro amigo que esta pluma. Mire vuestra merced cuánto valen los amigos de este siglo: pues una pluma, ¡cuán poco pesa! vale más que un amigo. (qtd. in Marañón, *Antonio Pérez* 735)

NOTES

[1] Gustav Ungerer describes Pérez as an "epistolomaniac" and mentions that he claimed to have written 850 letters in Latin alone between July, 1595, and January, 1597 (Ungerer, *A Spaniard* I, 298-302; II, 362-363). Pérez was also a glib conversationalist and persuasive orator. In exile, he led the busy and precarious life of a foreign courtier currying favor. At court, he was championed for his wit and considerable charm, but suspected for his nationality, religion, and affectations. A Renaissance dandy, he dressed ostentatiously, reeked of perfume, and fancified his speech with elaborate conceits. His luxurious tastes, probable bisexuality, and devious politicking caused comment and consternation at home and abroad. He was often pursued by spies and surrounded by body guards, who sometimes served as double agents. (See Ungerer, *A Spaniard* I, 189-203; Marañón, *Antonio Pérez* 76-79; 304-313; 340-360; Muró, 60-68.)

[2] Pérez, *Las Obras* 42 and 740. When quoting Pérez, I have modernized the spelling. All translations from this text and others are my own.

[3] Gracián, *O. C.* (1944) 282-83.

[4] See Marañón, *Antonio Pérez*, 732-741; Ungerer, *A Spaniard* I, 203-215. Pérez's *Relaciones* and especially his account of the revolt of Aragón may have influenced some British pamphleteers and political theorists, such as Francis Bacon, Henry Wotton, and Christopher Goodman. Two separate political treatises, *El Norte de Príncipes* and *El Conocimiento de las Naciones*, sometimes attributed to Pérez, were

probably written by Alamos de Barrientos (Marañón, "El Conocimiento" 317-347). Pérez's aphorisms best represent his political philosophy and have not been much studied, according to Ungerer (*A Spaniard* II, 346-361). They influenced Gracián, Quevedo, and French political thinkers. *Las Migajas* have been falsely attributed to Quevedo and are for the most part a literal transcription of Pérez's aphorisms, with a few extracts from Virgilio Malvezzi (Ungerer, *La Defensa* 10).

[5] This edition was reprinted quite frequently in more or less the same form during the seventeenth century and thereafter much less often. It is interesting to note that an English translation by Arthur Atey and a candid review by Henry Wotten, which Pérez and Essex had sponsored in 1593 hoping to appeal to an English speaking readership, were never published. The Tudors censored historiography, and Queen Elizabeth could not have tolerated Pérez's seditious ideas. (See Ungerer, *A Spaniard* II, 208-18, 247-253; and Pérez, *Un pedazo de Historia*, prologue by Antonio Pérez Gómez).

[6] Pérez's first attempts at writing aphorisms appear in the text and marginalia of the enlarged editions of the *Relaciones* of 1593 and 1594. The first set to be published was appended to the octavo (not the cuarto) of the Paris editions of 1598. About 1601 there were two different Paris editions of the aphorisms taken from Spanish and Latin letters and published together with them. In 1602 Pérez sponsored a French translation entitled (with characteristic lack of modesty) *Aphorisms ou Sentences d'Orées*. In 1603 aphorisms from the letters and relaciones were first published together. (See Ungerer, *A Spaniard* II, 346 ff.)

[7] On the importance of the epistolary tradition in Renaissance Spain, see García de la Concha, *Nueva Lectura* 47-70. Of course, letters were the only means of communication between those separated by distance, hence both their practical importance and profound effect on literary discourse. Picaresque narratives, *relaciones*, and autobiographies often adopted an epistolary structure and were written as replies to a request by an interlocutor, for example, Sor Juana Inés de la Cruz's *Respuesta a Sor Filotea* and Santa Teresa's *Libro de su Vida*.

[8] See Pérez, *Un Pedazo de Historia*, "Apéndice Primero. Composiciones satíricas publicadas durante los disturbios de Zaragoza."

[9] Qtd. in Ungerer, *A Spaniard* II, 363. The idea of the *carta familiar* as self-revelatory or representative of a man's measure is also suggested by the following quotation from Antonio de Guevara's *Cartas Familiares*, 123: "The madman or the wise man is recognized in three ways: to wit, in how he controls his temper, governs his household, and writes a letter; for these things are so difficult to achieve that they can neither be bought with wealth nor even loaned for the sake of friendship." ("En tres cosas se conoce el hombre loco o el hombre cuerdo; es a saber, en re-

frenar la ira, en gobernar su casa y en escribir una carta, porque estas cosas son tan difíciles de alcanzar, que ni se pueden con hacienda comprar, ni aun por amistad emprestar.")

[10] Mullaney notes that Francis Bacon, a friend of Pérez's, refers to the *wunderkammer* in his essay, *The Advancement of Learning*, as a "substantial and severe collection of Heteroclites or Irregularities of Nature" (40).

[11] Both "monstruo" and "mostrar" are derived from the Latin verb "monere", to warn or advise.

[12] Antonio Pérez's birth is shrouded in mystery. Gonzalo Pérez had become a priest by the time he was born and sent the baby to be brought up in the country. A document exists in which Charles V declared him legitimate in 1542. His physical resemblance to Ruy Gómez, his mentor and close friend, as well as the husband of the Princess of Eboli and Philip's Secretary of State until 1573, was so noticeable that Ruy Gómez was rumored to be his true father. (See Marañón, *Antonio Pérez* 18-62; Ungerer, *La Defensa* 10 ff.; and Muró, 62-64.)

[13] Ungerer, *A Spaniard* I, 197; Ungerer, *La Defensa* 11, 77-80; and Marañón, *Antonio Pérez* 222-47.

[14] Pérez, like his mentor the Belgian humanist Lipsius, was a Tacitean scholar and owes to him many of his stylistic proclivities, including his love for adages and marginalia. (See Ungerer, *A Spaniard* II, 337 ff.)

WORKS CITED

Beaujour, Michel. *Miroirs de l'Encre. Rhétorique de l'auto-portrait.* Paris: Seuil, 1980.

Cros, Edmond. *Protée et le Gueux.* Paris: Didier, 1967.

Fleishman, Avrom. *Figures of Autobiography: the Language of Self-Writing in Victorian and Modern England.* Berkeley: Univ. of California Press, 1983.

García de la Concha, Víctor. *Nueva Lectura de Lazarillo de Tormes.* Madrid: Castalia, 1983.

Greenblatt, Stephen. *Renaissance Self-Fashioning. From More to Shakespeare.* Chicago and London: Univ. of Chicago Press, 1980.

Guevara, Antonio de. *Cartas Familiares*, 2nd ed. Buenos Aires: Espasa-Calpe, 1946.

Lejeune, Philippe. *Je est un Autre: l'autobiographie de la littérature aux medias*. Paris: Seuil, 1980.

Marañón, Gregorio. *Antonio Pérez. El hombre, el drama, la época*. 9th ed. Madrid: Espasa-Calpe, 1969.

——. "El Conocimiento de las Naciones y El Norte de Príncipes ¿Son obras de Antonio Pérez o de Alamos de Barrientos?" *Estudios Dedicados a Menéndez Pidal*. Tomo I. Madrid: C.S.I.C, 1950.

Mullaney, Stephen. "Strange Things, Gross Terms, Curious Customs: The Rehearsal of Cultures in the Late Renaissance." *Representations* 3 (1983): 40-67.

Muró, Don Gaspar. *Vida de la Princesa de Eboli*. Madrid: Imprenta de Aribau, 1877.

Olney, James. *Metaphors of the Self. The Meaning of Autobiography*. Princeton: Princeton Univ. Press, 1972.

Pascal, Roy. *Design and Truth in Autobiography*. Cambridge: Harvard Univ. Press, 1960.

Pérez, Antonio. *Las Obras y Relaciones*. Ginebra: Samuel Chonet, 1654.

——. *Relaciones de Antonio Pérez, Secretario de Estado, que fue, del Rey de España Don Phelippe deste nombre*. Paris: 1598.

——. *Un pedazo de Historia. De lo sucedido en Zaragoza de Aragón a 24 de septiembre del año de 1591*. Prologue by Antonio Pérez Gómez. Opúsculos Literarios Rarísimos. Valencia: Duque y Marqués, 1941.

Ungerer, Gustav. *A Spaniard in Elizabethan England. The Correspondence of Antonio Pérez's Exile*. 2 vols. London: Tamesis Books, 1974-76.

——. *La Defensa de Antonio Pérez contra los cargos que se le imputaron en el proceso de la Visita, 1984*. Zaragoza: Institución "Fernando el Católico", 1980.

Valladares Reguero, Aurelio. "Tres Obras de Quevedo y dos atribuidas a Antonio Pérez en un manuscrito del Archivo Municipal de Ubeda." *RLit* XLVIII, 95 (1986): 95-99.

CHAPTER 8:
THE WOMAN AT THE BORDER:
SOME THOUGHTS ON CERVANTES AND
AUTOBIOGRAPHY

Ruth El Saffar

> Portraits of myself are very rare.
> I have never been too concerned with my own face.
> —Picasso

Autobiography introduces to the issues of writing and
identity some limit conditions that make it a form especially valuable to consider when assessing a writer's view
of his craft. What most stands out in Cervantes's work is
his resistance to the first-person narrative structure that
attracted so many of the writers of his age, particularly in
the form of the picaresque novel. In Cervantes's version of
the rogue narrative, as, for example, in *Rinconete y
Cortadillo* or *El coloquio de los perros*, he refuses for his
character-narrators the place of the isolated narrating "I,"
insisting either on the placement of that "I" within the
context of a listening other, or directing the attention of
the first-person narrator away from himself toward the
lives of others.

The narrative structure of *Don Quijote* itself could well be analyzed as a commentary on autobiography, since the isolated country gentleman turned knight of La Mancha in effect took up arms in order to have his life story written, in order to generate a scribe who would take upon himself the task of converting his deeds into written text. To become the subject of narrative, however, as Cervantes apparently understands it, one must first of all adopt a persona distinct from one's given identity, and one must entrust the narrative that will follow to an Other who turns out to be not only enemy, but who literally writes in an alien tongue. The process of being transported out of the flesh and into a written text, in other words, is one that involves in Cervantes both a severing from communal life and submission to an inevitable and ongoing act of betrayal.

In the deflected autobiography that Don Quijote creates with the help of his fictional scribe Cide Hamete, Cervantes shows not only the necessary self-splitting that is required to transform an ordinary being into a subject of narrative, but the correlative loss to that split-off self of autonomy and self-definition. To choose the place of the hero, as Don Quijote has done, is paradoxically to submit to the laws of community which degrade that which is lofty and make common currency of that which is unique. The pair Don Quijote/Cide Hamete functions as commentary on the nature of all writing, as it highlights the process of deflation that takes place when a repeatable series of linguistic signs becomes the vehicle through which that which is non-repeatable and convention-escaping can be brought to consciousness. As the author makes clear through his multiplication of narrators, translators and scribes, something invariably gets lost in the translation.

Cervantes's resistance to writing out of the self about the self extends past the borders of his fiction into the arena from which authors normally address the reader as an audience absent from the scene of writing. In his prologue to *Don Quijote* Part I he very quickly introduces into his studio the voice of a friend who relieves him of the nearly overwhelming burden of writing to an unknown destinary. The Prologue to the *Persiles* also becomes the transcription of a living discourse between Cervantes and another, in this case a student, whom he meets on the way to Madrid. Even in the Prologue to *Don Quijote* Part II, where Cervantes's "I" is caught raging against the absent but terribly present Avellaneda, his narrative instincts quickly take over, transforming that so uncomfortable open statement of the isolated self in pain into the more familiar discourse of the storyteller.

It looks very much as if, for Cervantes, the self-reflexivity basic to autobiography is regularly skirted or subverted in his works. Either the narrator of his life story is given an interlocutor, so that the tale is *spoken* not written, or the isolated writer is given a subject separate from himself on which to elaborate. Cervantes's "I," in other words, is a *speaking* subject. As writers his narrators function as reporters, as historians, as transmitters of the lives and deeds of others, but never as the creators of their own personae.

The *Casamiento engañoso-Coloquio de los perros* provides a good example of how Cervantes eludes in his work the picaresque confluence of writer and fabricator of self. The double *novela* is made up of a series of self-narratives, each told to an interlocutor, and each embedded within the narrative of the one preceding it, working in from the story the Ensign Campuzano tells his friend Peralta to the story the dog Berganza tells his canine companion Cipión, to the one the witch Cañizares tells Berganza. The series of stories of the self is so constructed that each is contained within the one that precedes it: Berganza's story belongs within Campuzano's narrative, and Cañizares's, in Berganza's.

Complicating the structure of the *Casamiento-Coloquio* is the fact that each container is also contained within the tale it holds. The story the witch tells not only refracts Berganza's back to him, but tells the story he could never know, the story of his pre-history and of his birth. So also does Campuzano hear himself named in the colloquy he transcribes, and finds in Berganza's failed aspirations a mirror of his own life. Instead of Chinese boxes, the structure of the *Casamiento-Coloquio* resembles more closely the conundrum of the Moebius strip, or the Klein bottle. The case of the *Casamiento-Coloquio* suggests that for

Cervantes the story of the self may only be found in the story of the Other, or, more radically, that the truth about the self can best be told by that which the self rejects or refuses about itself.

Of course Cide Hamete—however envious and perfidious he may seem to a great partisan of Don Quijote like the Second Author (or even like Unamuno, who, in *Our Lord Don Quijote* echoes the Second Author's adulation of the hero)—gives us a fuller picture of his tormented, demented character than the shadowless one Don Quijote would have him write. In the first-person inset tales in Part I of *Don Quijote* we see further examples of the self's capacity for self-deception, and clear signs of the ways that Cervantes elides in his works the notions of isolation, literacy, self-reflexivity, madness and death. Cervantes populates his works of the middle period, in fact, with a whole host of Alonso Quijanos, Tomás Rodajas, Grisóstomos and Cardenios whose repressions of the instincts and of the feminine encloses them within a world of fantasy and solitude.

The case of Cardenio is instructive because it shows how Cervantes works with respect to autobiography. Cardenio's story of himself—that he is victim of Fernando's higher social claims on his beloved Luscinda, and, as a corollary, that she has been unfaithful, effectively seals him off from life itself. Telling his version of himself, however erroneous, as Don Quijote invites him to in Chapter 24, has the result of bringing him to the place where he can finally hear himself in the story of another, in the story of the debased and yet somehow redemptive woman his own story cannot name. By listening to Dorotea, Cardenio begins, as did Campuzano in the *Casamiento-Coloquio,* the process of recovery from insanity and near-death.

If Cervantes refuses the position of autobiographer, if he insists on framing each narrating "I" within a larger narrative context, and if he allows self-stories to be *told* and not written, it is surely because the entire fabric of his opus is spun out of the voice of the Other. Cervantes's great genius consists not only in questioning the Name of the Father but,[1] but in opening his narrative again and again to the voice of the outcast and the repressed. In this context the distressed damsel that Don Quijote is so desperate to rescue throughout Part I can well be understood as his own corporeal self in mourning.[2]

Freud, in his commentary on the famous Irma dream founders at the point where the mystery of the confabulation escapes the integrative powers of the interpreter, the point where the three women, persistently cast as "recalcitrant" in his dream, might conceivably yield to the one who would "open her mouth" (*The Interpretation of Dreams*, 111). At just the point in his commentary where this figure appears Freud interrupts his interpretive construct, footnoting:

> I had a feeling that the interpretation of this part of the dream was not carried far enough to make it possible to follow the whole of its concealed meaning.... There is at least one spot in every dream in which it is unplumable—a navel, as it were, that is its point of contact with the unknown. (*Interpretation,* 111, note 1).

In the *Coloquio* Cervantes confronts his philosopher dogs with a place where the efforts of reason also fail. At the structural center of Berganza's tale, a place that functions as a vortex, it is the witch who opens her mouth. In her discourse she undoes Berganza's life story, bringing him with her words over the threshold of rationality and of consciousness, back into the pre-conscious, pre-verbal world ruled over by the conjurings of witches and centered around the issues of transition, and of identity. At the end of her discourse the dogs are left only with riddles: Are they dogs? Are they men? Can witches so control the mysteries of life that the men could be transformed into dogs? Are Berganza and Cipión in fact siblings? Do they have a common origin that both have forgotten? The questions, which threaten to collapse the reasonable construct Berganza and Cipión have built out of their words, have only to be escaped, as Freud escaped them, by pulling back from the abyss, and settling instead for an agreement which, if unsatisfactory, at least makes going on possible.

Cipión, who has heard the witch name him as Berganza's twin, takes the tack of total denial. Referring to the three witches who threaten to undo his patronymic as philosopher (Scipio) he says:

> Camacha was a false sorceress, and Cañizares a liar, and Montiela foolish, lying, and wicked—excusing the expression, just in case she is the mother of the two of us, or yours, for I don't want her for a mother. (48)

> la Camacha fue burladora falsa, y la Cañizares, embustera, y la Montiela, tonta, maliciosa y bellaca, con perdón sea dicho, si acaso es nuestra madre, de entrambos o tuya, que yo no la quiero tener por madre. (490)

Berganza, in his reply, is quick to follow suit:

> From what you have said I conclude and believe that everything that has happened to us so far, and what is happening now, is a dream, and that we are dogs. But not on that account are we going to deprive ourselves of the pleasure of this gift of speech which we possess.... (48)

> de lo que has dicho vengo a pensar y creer que todo lo que hasta aquí hemos pasado y lo que estamos pasando es sueño, y que somos perros; pero no por esto dejemos de gozar de este bien de la habla que tenemos. (490)

Each denial is tainted with doubt, however. The mystery is never really effaced. The dogs, having listened to the witch/whore/mother, have only to wonder as their talk continues toward dawn. Perhaps the mystery not only of their degradation but also of their redemption hides in the unsavory story of dogs who might, were the powerful brought down and the lowly raised up, as Cañizares prognosticates in her riddle, be restored to their true promise as men.

The dogs' glimpse of the vortex threatens not only their concept of themselves but the structure of their narrative, as three times Berganza is tempted to tell out of order the story of the witch Cañizares, to tumble down his narrative slope into the beckoning and terrifying center where her questions dwell unanswered. However undermining to self-concept and narrative order, the witch nonetheless also energizes self and structure, forcing against her lure the effort of consciousness to create a ground on which to stand, and offering, against the rationalizations and deferrals the dogs construct, the hope that her story contains the key to their transformation. And thus not only do Cipión and Berganza agree to lay uncertainty aside to get on with the pleasures of telling and listening, as do Peralta and Campuzano in the frame narrative, but they also carry into their ensuing dialogue the mysterious sense that they may be more than they are.

The witch's tale has another effect also. The series of masters Berganza encounters before he meets Cañizares reflected the official fathers of his early formation: the butcher, the shepherd, the merchant, the constable, the soldier. After his night journey with the witch, Berganza's masters are other. They represent the heterodox, darker fact of Spanish society: the Morisco, the poet, the playwright, the madman, the saint. It is out of these figures that the mother's son, that Berganza has willy-nilly become, will forge his new identity, just as Campuzano, in the frame story, will move from the soldier and lady chaser of his earlier days to writer after his night in the Hospital of the Resurrection.

The witch at the center of the *Coloquio* represents its crux, its crossroads. A figure of mystery and fear, the witch, Hekate, has long been associated with the place between places, the dangerous place of decision where the conflicting vectors of consciousness meet. It was at such a crossroads that Oedipus killed Laios, "where the roads from Delphi [home of the oracle, of the unconscious, of the "navel of the world"] and Daulia meet" (*Oedipus the King*, 56, 959). Just there Oedipus, like the rationalist Cipión, solved the riddle of the Sphinx, leading him later to boast, against Tiresias's warnings, "I silenced her, I destroyed her, I used my wits, not omens, to sift the meaning of her song" (41, 538-9). And again like the dogs, Oedipus peers into the vortex of his own identity at the center of a text that teases at the borders of origin, a text that questions certainty, and that mocks the one who presumes to know his own identity.

The kingdom established on such assumptions, like the one Cervantes depicts his hero inhabiting in Part I of *Don Quijote*, purchases order at the price of fertility. The cultural crisis for which Oedipus carries the blame at the beginning of *Oedipus the King* has perhaps more to do with the ruler who pretends to have destroyed the Sphinx than with patricide and incest. Like the penitents at the end of *Don Quijote* who carry the Virgin in mourning in their processions against draught, the people of Thebes complain that "nothing grows, wheat, fruit, nothing grows bigger than a seed. Our women bear dead things" (24, 37-39). *Don Quijote* Part I, like Sophocles's drama, portrays the frailty of those certainties of self forged out of the letter, imposed by a decree of intellect.

Under the sway of the preconceived text—the letter forged of intellect at the place of crossroads where mystery in fact dwells—the isolated hero is both most vulnerable and most likely, like Oedipus, to cry "I know who I am" (I, 5). In *Don Quijote* it is the hero without an interlocutor, the hero alone who dares to assert identity. Yet, as Chapters 5 and 25 show, that "I" who says he knows is a fragmented "I", scanning helplessly the pages that flap in his head: "I am Valdovinos," "I am the captive Abencerraje," "I am the twelve peers of France," "I am Orlando," "I am Amadís." Underground, meanwhile, in the forbidden places where the sham of code and structure are made known, the man who really knows, the protean figure who interrupts the seeming certainties of social structuring, can only say with the Don Juan, the trickster of Seville, "I am a man without a name."

The *Casamiento-Coloquio* gives out the secret of the unnamable self through the mother/witch/sphinx who presides over its center and disturbs every pretense to certainty that the talking dogs had managed to muster. Thinking precisely of the disorienting nature of woman in the self's quest for identity, Claude Levesque can be heard asking Derrida in a symposium on autobiography:

> If, on the one hand, man's substantial, effective life is
> in the State, in science but also in war and in work—
> that is, grappling with the vast external world—
> and, on the other, if woman, with her irony, her
> veils, and her lies, is allied with the singularity of
> the unconscious, then can one say that autobiogra-
> phy—if it would see itself through to the end—can be
> produced only as the autobiography of the woman, in
> both senses of that genetive? In autobiography, only
> femininity would lend itself to understanding; only
> femininity would lead one to hear and understand the
> singular secret that constitutes it. Only a feminine
> writing can (even as it cannot) tell its story as the un-
> relenting quest of that terrible thing which opens
> language to its own beyond. (*The Ear of the Other*,
> 76).

The Campuzano who narrates his story, which is the
story of a life caught in the mystery of bewitchment and
transformation, writes and tells across a borderland. He
writes the colloquy he overhears from the bed of the hospital to which syphilis, following his dalliance with a
prostitute, had consigned him. He tells of his fall into lust
and deception from the other side, having left the Hospital
of the Resurrection and entered the gate of the city. If
Campuzano's story, told inside the city walls, narrates a
fall from grace, Berganza's, told outside, in the hospital at
night, recounts a rise from degradation to saintliness. The
trajectories of the lives of man and dog crisscross and in-
tersect as do the moments they trace as they trek in and out
of walled cities, in and out of law, in and out of the structures and hierarchies of consciousness.

Cervantes, writer of the in-between *par excellence*,[3]
questions autobiography as he questions the autonomy of
the self, the absolutisms of language[4] and the univocity of
cultural codings.[5] His insistence that the life be told, not
written, transforms the notion of "I" from a fixed entity
outside of time to one being woven from moment to
moment, made of the matter spun out between con-
sciousnesses, between selves who speak. Certainly, as
Carlos Blanco Aguinaga pointed out long ago, Cervantes
writes his rogues against the would-be transcendent consciousness of Mateo Alemán's fictional autobiography.

Critical commentary has by now caught up with the sham of Guzmán's conversation,[6] the point of cross-over that places the rogue on the other side of desire, from which fixed standpoint he can define as past all that which as thief and vagabond he was.

Cervantes is clearly skeptical of such transitions, aware of their alliance with death. In his only overt presentation of autobiography's impossibility, he has his master rogue, Ginés de Pasamonte, tell Don Quijote that the picaresque novel he writes in jail can have no end since he won't be around to narrate his own death.[7] Ginés's vitality and his creativity depend on his persistence as rogue, on his ongoing attention to the vicissitudes of life, and, finally, on keeping his work continually in progress.[8] Without a standpoint outside himself from which to write, the hero of his own life is cut off from precisely that which would give it shape and definition: the access to the boundary land where transitions take place. What the hero cannot see, while writing, is "the terrible thing that opens language to is own beyond"—Hekate at the crossroads.

The autobiographer against whom Cervantes writes, the hero as convert, Guzmán de Alfarache, seeks escape from time, from the recognition, offered by Georges Gusdorf, that "any autobiography is a moment in the life it recounts" (43). Lawrence Sterne, whose fictional autobiography *Tristam Shandy* offers an extended meditation on the narrative impossibilities of the effort of the self to tell itself, has his narrator observe:

> I am this month one whole year older than I was this time twelve-month; and having got...almost into the middle of my fourth volume—and no farther than to my first day's life—'tis demonstration that I have three hundred and sixty-four days more life to write just now, than when I first started out; so that instead of advancing, as a common writer, in my work...I am thrown so many volumes back. The more I write, the more I shall have to write. Write as I will, and rush as I may into the middle of things...I shall never overtake myself.

Fully conscious of his place at the crossroads, the obsessive-compulsive Tristam depicts himself seeking to embrace in writing the ever-receding point which would mark the beginning of his being while keeping track of that point at the other end of the temporal spectrum toward which he is being borne whether he likes it or not. His place, "writing in the in-between," is not only at an undefined spot on a trajectory that leads from birth to death, however. It is also a place between defining his life and being defined, between the purposive act of writing, and the revelation, through it, of the utterly contingent, irrational basis on which that life was established. Tristam Shandy's probing of beginnings, like Ginés's commentary on endings, marks the autobiographer as caught in a web of contingencies and inconsequentialities without definitory power, lacking all authority.

What gives structure, that is, what determines the beginnings and endings that give narrative shape, is the Other. The case is made at a simple level in the *Casamiento-Coloquio*, where Peralta serves as both receptacle and check on Campuzano's potential for excess, just as Cipión corrects, limits, and contains the flow of Berganza's story. The Other, however, is no safer an entity, ultimately, for established authority and truth than is the self. The Other offers a container for the self's story, but, in all the cases Cervantes presents, that container also seeks containment, also exists under the sign of incompletion and provisionality.

Cipión and Berganza's conversation is enacted not only between them but beyond them. It is recounted in another frame and in another medium as it passes from the consciousness of the two dogs to that of the two friends. And yet the authority that figures outside the frame might confer on those within it continues to elude. The questions, which are ultimately the witch's questions, remain: has all this really happened, or does it happen only in the imagination? In the last analysis we escape the delusions of Cañizares in exactly the way she does, simply by dropping our efforts to distinguish dream from truth, fiction from reality, by letting it all go, as Peralta does at the end of the reading of the *Coloquio* when he says, "Señor alférez, no volvamos más a esa disputa. Yo alcanzo el artificio del *Coloquio* y la invención, y basta. Vámonos al Espolón a recrear los ojos del cuerpo, pues ya he recreado los del entendimiento." (502)

The writer's task, in Cervantes, looks more and more like one that would render authority marginal, that is, that would invert, using Derrida's terms, the "law of the rational community" which "always represses femininity" (Glas). Autobiography, if such is the case, would be the most threatening of all narrative forms, for it would either force the unflinching author to reveal the secrets of the self's transgressive nature that society is least able to acknowledge (à la Rousseau), or it would push a more conniving and manipulative narrator into bald-faced lies or bad faith, (à la Lazarillo, or the Buscón) in order to satisfy his need to be incorporated into the social order. In either case, whether the narrator verges toward the repressed or the conventional, toward the mother or the father in consciousness, it is still out of ego, out of the "I" that he writes.

In what remains here I would like to press a little further the question of margins, and the feminine which finds its home there: to search in the folds of Don Quijote Part I at the juncture where narrators and characters can be found traversing borders for signs of the feminine that Cervantes appears to have sought somehow to refract in his works against the social and linguistic norms designed to repress her.

Like the Campuzano who finds himself spoken in the story of the dogs, the figures to whom the authorship of Don Quijote I is consigned always manage somehow to catch a glimpse of themselves across the barriers that would seem to separate them from their characters. No speaker or writer in Cervantes's work, in other words, succeeds in escaping being named by that which he names. "Cervantes" turns out to be a friend of the Curate (I, 6). His tracings are left in La Galatea, found among Don Quijote's books in Chapter 6, and in the trunkful of stories in manuscript from which the characters read "El curioso impertinente" in Chapters 33-36. Off to the side, easily missed among the gallery of figures that fill up the place of the in-between in Cervantes's novel, a writer called Cervantes, and a rebellious captive called Saavedra (I, 40) challenge the author's pretense to authority, his writerly pose of dominion.

The problem Cervantes presents again and again in his text is the same one that Paul Eakin addresses in his discussion of Paul de Man on autobiography:

> The referential basis of autobiography is...inherently unstable, an illusion produced by the rhetorical structure of language. Both critics...and autobiographers...try in vain to "escape" the constraints of language; their 'reinscription' within the textual system is necessary and inevitable. (186)

The question is not only "who is writing whom?," but "what writes?" When, as was pointed out at the beginning of this paper, Cervantes has his Christian knight written by a Moorish scribe, he is highlighting the alien quality of all transcriptions of life into text, and also the ultimate incapacity of the would-be heroic subject to govern the medium through which he is represented.

In Chapter 16 the carter (*arriero*) who joins with Don Quijote in creating such havoc over the body and image of the prostitute Maritornes pulls the fictitious author Cide Hamete into the world he has been authorized to reproduce. Suddenly the narrator is not our Moorish historian, but an unnamed other (the translator?), who tells us that Cide Hamete made particular mention of the carter because he knew him well and was even known to be a relation of his.

The point at which the crossings over become most vertiginous, however, is at that delicate intersection between the original Parts I and II of the 1605 *Don Quijote* when all might well have been lost, when the life of both Don Quijote and *Don Quijote* appear to be in doubt. The episode is worth probing in some detail, since it reopens, at yet another level, the question of boundaries that is at the heart of the problem of representation, and the problem of self, which, taken together, are the issues autobiography brings before us.

The Second Author has crossed over already, or to use Lewis Carroll's image, stepped through the looking glass. Up until Chapter 8 he had been a reader, according to his own account. Like the Cervantes who is both writer and soldier, or the Cide Hamete who is both historian and carter's cousin, the Second Author moves into a field that is at once within the text we are reading and outside it. In that borderline between the end of Chapter 8 and the middle of Chapter 9, the Second Author opens out a fold of text that reveals a world familiar to Cervantes's contemporaries—the marketplace in Toledo. Somewhere, out in the peripheries of the present drama, Don Quijote and a Basque gentleman face one another with swords raised. Have we stepped out of the "fictional" picture and into the "real" world of the frame, where readers and authors live and breathe? Or, have frame and picture been transposed, so that reader and author are now the subjects of a story Don Quijote and the Basque gentlemen watch from beyond in fascination? Or, finally, could it be that the boundaries that mark picture and frame are illusory, that, like the weavers and the woven in Velázquez's "Las hilanderas", process and product are both painted onto the same canvas? However the transition is understood, we have crossed, between Chapters 8 and 9, which also marks the borders between the original Parts I and II, a magical and indefinable space that renders everything on the other side apparently quite different.

In Chapter 9 the once anonymous reader of Part I emerges in the first person to narrate a struggle for the recovery of the text that bears, on closer examination, intriguing resemblance to the story that now frames it, the suspended tale of Don Quijote's battle with the Basque gentleman. In Chapter 9's "real world" of seventeenth-century Toledo where the Second Author finds Cide Hamete's Arabic manuscript, and the Morisco hired to translate it, we discover that, like the royal highway along which Don Quijote and Sancho ride in search of adventure, deviants from the ideal are everywhere. If Don Quijote, in search of damsels and knights finds instead prostitutes and pig gelders, so the Second Author, searching for an Arabic-speaking translator in the heart of the "Imperial City", finds Jews and Moriscos in abundance: "anduve mirando si parecía por allí algún morisco aljamiado que los leyese, y no fue muy dificultoso hallar intérprete semejante, pues aunque le buscara de otra mejor y más antigua lengua, le hallara" (I, 9).

Neither the royal highway along which Don Quijote and Sancho travel nor the imperial city to which the Second Author has been drawn belongs to the images that would define them. Monarchical Spain, in Cervantes's rendering of it, is the home of marginals. It is a place not of stasis, but of movement, commerce, exchange, transit and translation among people going to and coming from elsewhere.

As if further to underscore the center's marginality, the borders in which the heart of the issue hides, Cervantes has it that the first thing the Morisco translator reads from the newly recovered Arabic manuscript is not something from Cide Hamete's own text, but the marginal notes of another reader. And what that reader has inscribed at the edges of this marginalized text are words that once again efface the comfortable distance that script normally imposes between reader and character at the same time that they deflate the pristine object of Don Quijote's desire. The extraneous notes read: "esta Dulcinea del Toboso, tantas veces en esta historia referida, dicen que tuvo mejor mano para salar puercos que otra mujer de toda la Mancha" (I, 9).

While the Second Author maneuvers to free this Arabic text both from its destiny as pulp and from its imprisonment in the linguistic universe of the Other, out in the center-turned-margin where Don Quijote's battle with the Basque gentleman hangs suspended, a similar rescue operation is being enacted. The lady Don Quijote has decided needs rescuing is a Basque woman crossing the heart of Spain en route to Seville where her husband is preparing to embark for America. Like the Second Author, Don Quijote faces two enemies as he struggles to save the woman who for him is a princess being carried off against her will: the Benedictine friars, who, like the paper seller in Toledo, have in fact little to do with the matter, and the Basque gentleman, who, like Cide Hamete, has actually been entrusted with the task of carrying the lady across the heartland of Spain unscathed.

Who, then, is this transiting figure whom Don Quijote in the frame of Chapter 8 and the Second Author of

Chapter 9 have determined to rescue? Both heroes manage to chase off the false captors, but neither can free the endangered subject from its more intimate guardian. The Basque woman will eventually ride off again with her Basque escort, and the Second Author will have to content himself with hearing the story of Don Quijote through the filter of an Arab historian and a Morisco translator.

Could this lady, and this text as lady, this pristine yet adulterated figure embody the conflict at the center of writing, at the center of the text? In more than one place Cervantes has expressed his sense of poetry as the highest and most vulnerable of literary creations, and has imaged that literary figure as a tender maiden (in *Don Quijote* II, 16, and in *La Gitanilla*). Don Quijote says of this figure: "pero esta tal doncella no quiere ser manoseada, ni traida por las calles, ni publicada por las esquinas de las plazas ni por los rincones de los palacios...No ha de ser vendible en ninguna manera" (II, 16). Cervantes's own placement of his text in the marketplace suggests the betrayal to which his work has been subjected: the impossibility for him of translating into words the tender feelings of that so-distressed damsel.[9]

Beneath that sense of his own betrayal of the tender damsel lurks the sense of her as betrayer. It is expressed, for example in the Second Author's reference to the damsel who would go to her grave "tan entera como la madre que la había parido", and in the unlikely decorum of the married Basque woman traveling without her husband to Seville. It is expressed in the constant pairing, throughout *Don Quijote* and the *Novelas ejemplares*, of virgins and non-virgins, of idealized figures of the pastoral, like Marcela, with the prostitutes found in the inns—the Maritornes, the Tolosas, the Molineras. And, most tellingly, it is expressed in the figure of Dulcinea herself, the first one to be named in the recovered manuscript, a Dulcinea who, far from enshrining the perfection Don Quijote would find in her, seems instead to be best at salting pigs.

In his *Contributions to the Psychology of Love*, Freud connects the boy's sense of betrayal on learning of his parent's engagement in sexual activities to the tendency

among men to split the original beloved mother figure
into a still-idealized and untouchable image on the one
hand and a degraded female through whom his desires
can be expressed on the other:

> We can now understand the motives behind the boy's
> phantasies mentioned in the first of these
> "Contributions", which degrade the mother to the
> level of a prostitute. They are efforts to bridge the
> gulf between the two currents in love, at any rate in
> phantasy, by debasing the mother to acquire her as
> an object of sensuality. ("Universal Tendency," 183)

In a related article Freud further notes:

> Where they love they do not desire and where they
> desire they cannot love. They seek objects which they
> do not need to love, in order to keep their sensuality
> away from the objects they love" ("A Special Type,"
> 183).

It is precisely on the basis of Freud's analysis of the
Oedipal drama that Doug Carey and Phil Williams, in
their excellent study of confessional narrative, relate the
text to the image of the mother, and further, to the mother
as prostitute, to, in short, the witch, to Cañizares:

> The text itself is the cultural artifact *par excellence*,
> multi-determined by the paternal interdict to forsake
> the mother and choose another "body" to explore.
> The book as a concrete embodiment of language, while
> traditionally spoken of as the "child" of the author,
> is perhaps more suggestively seen as that which
> stands in place of the mother. In this view of the text
> as a kind of maternal prostitute, the book substitutes
> for the lost maternal object. (43)

And so it turns out that the Basque woman, like the text
in the marketplace, is a figure in transit. The fantasy of pu-
rity projected on her by Don Quijote and his ideal reader
the Second Author suggests that she is in need of rescue.
In her sullied form she is marketable merchandise. Where
is the center and where is the frame? Where is the woman
who is at once a tender maiden and a physical object up for

sale? The further we reach into this central and yet constantly deferred problem, the less we find resolution.

When Don Quijote, at the borders of his own self-construction, brings into being out of the chaos of Alonso Quijano the discrete and definable entity he named Don Quijote, he began with his armor. Only after selecting and naming his horse does he declare his own name, and only after that does he invent Dulcinea. Is she ancillary or central to his project? The narrative voice is of little help, asking us to image the knight's lady at both extremities: "a knight errant without a lady was [like] a tree without leaves or fruit, and a body without a soul" (I, 1) ("el caballero andante sin amores era árbol sin hojas y sin fruto, y cuerpo sin alma"). The analogies suggest that the lady is both center (alma) and periphery (hojas). Don Quijote's belated invention of his lady further brings into question her importance. Regarding her, he asks himself only:

> Would it not be well to have someone to whom I could send him as a present, so that he could enter and kneel down before my sweet lady and say in tones of humble submission: "lady, I am the giant Caraculiambro... etc.?" (I, 1)

> No será bien tener a quien enviarle presentado, y que entre y se hinque de rodillas ante mi dulce señora, y diga con voz humilde y rendida: Yo, señora, soy el gigante Caraculiambro...etc.?

What *Don Quijote* puts into questions, as the above reflections are designed to suggest, is the place of the center, and, correspondingly, the place of the margin. In Foucault's meditation on Velázquez's "Las meninas" he imagines a void between the work of art and its subject which frees representation from that toward which it points, returning it back on itself as pure form.[10] In my reading of the figures who author *Don Quijote*, I find a different problematic being offered. Instead of subject-void-object, a distribution that locks "art" and "reality" into chambers mutually remote, I see in the work of Cervantes a tendency to populate precisely at the no-man's land where those borders touch, to populate, in other words, the void itself, to be in the place of the void, which is the place between places.

What further reflection on the "void" reveals, however, is that, far from being a place of absence, it is the place of fecundity, that unnamed and unnamable center turned periphery from which life issues, the limit place beyond which consciousness cannot go. In Freud's dream of Irma the void where language and interpretation stop is contained in the body and voice of the woman. In Cervantes's dogs' colloquy it is the place of the witch. Lacan describes/elides the void with the female genitals, as does, pictorially, Picasso, whose last paintings are filled with the image of the female body, or, more accurately, with the image of the artist's effort to capture in painting that body's mystery of generativity. The face that contemplates not that beyond, which the female body as mother/whore evokes, but the image of itself, however, shows a different figure. One of Picasso's last paintings, a full-face self-portrait, shows the artist now as facing himself in his own death, his own horror.

As Derrida has pointed out, the Name of the Father is death:

> The mother is living on, and this living on is the name of the mother. This survival is my life whose shores she overflows. And my father's name, in other words, my patronym? That is the name of my death, of my dead life. (16)

He also notes:

> She [the mother] gives rise to all the figures by losing herself in the background of a scene like an anonymous persona. Everything comes back to her, beginning with life; everything addresses and destines itself to her. She survives on the condition of remaining at bottom. (38)

To become the object of one's own contemplation is to transform oneself into that which can be contained within the symbolic, that is, within the system that wins unification at the cost of the mother, and of the Other. The Cervantes, the Picasso, the Velázquez who catch them-

selves in that Other's gaze, who give the center to the desired and desiring body of the woman, or of the child, ally
themselves paradoxically, not with that symbolic order but
with the process by which the real is constantly being
transformed into the symbolic. Stationed between the two
realms, between the world of the mother and the world of
the father, between the referent and code, these artists of
the in-between offer, in the figures at the margins, the
possibility of redemption at the center.

Nothing could be more telling of Cervantes's sense of
the vitality of marginality—the vitality captured in the
androgynous tricksters Chirinos and Chanfallas in "El
retablo de las maravillas" and in the figure of the master
actor Pedro de Urdemalas—than in own final writing of
himself. In the Prologue to the *Persiles* Cervantes narrates
his encounter with an enthusiastic student as the two
journey toward Madrid. In that narrative "Cervantes" pre-
dicts his death against the student's more hopeful dietary
suggestions for remedy, and, after offering heartfelt good-
byes to friends and to life, that same part that emerged
through the voice of the student persists in asserting itself.
The last words Cervantes wrote go to his benefactor, to
whom he promises more, and yet more.

This Cervantes, this voice of ongoing creativity and
generativity, that insists after all predictions of death, is the
Cervantes who sought his self's story always in the story of
the Other, who found himself best being named in those
whom he named, who allied himself with the artist, the
actor, the trickster. From such a position the self is always
in question, as is the language in which it is represented.
The sense that, beneath the surface of text and self lurks
the Sphinx, the witch, the Other, takes the breath from autobiographer, and reduces to vanities his efforts to tell
himself.

NOTES

[1] The phrase "nom du pere" made famous by Lacan, puns "nom" and "no," homophonous in French. The Word of the figure of authority, which is the word of the unified self, is "no": no to mother, no to the vulnerable, no to the heteronymous, the extraneous, the contingent aspects of the self. It is worth noting, in this context, that Cervantes chose his mother's name. For a full discussion of the significance of Cervantes's *matronymic*, see Louis Combet. For more on Lacan's Name of the Father, see Ellie Ragland-Sullivan.

[2] The notion of mourning and its association both with the celibate woman and with infertility is captured in the final scene of *Don Quixote* Part I, where Don Quixote attacks penitents carrying a statue of the virgin in mourning, demanding of them her release. In "Unspeakable Thoughts" I discuss this scene. For more on Don Quixote and his relation to the body, see Efron.

[3] The reference to the "in-between" comes from the subtitle to Diana Wilson's excellent study of the *Persiles*, a subtitle that comes in its turn from the writings of Helen Cixous as she envisions a writing that would not seal off self from other. See her "The Laugh of Medusa."

[4] For an excellent study on language in Cervantes, see Spitzer's by now classic essay on perspectivism in the *Quixote*.

[5] For a study of Cervantes's minoritarian status in seventeenth-century Spain, see Carlos Otero's prologue to his translation of Chomsky.

[6] See, for example, studies by Carroll Johnson, Joan Arias, and Benito Brancaforte which challenge the long-held assumption that Guzmán's was in fact a tale of spiritual conversion.

[7] When Don Quixote asks Ginés if his *Vida de Ginés de Pasamonte* is finished yet, Ginés replies: "¿Cómo puede estar acabado, si aún no está acabada mi vida? Lo que está escrito es desde mi nacimiento hasta el punto que esta última vez me han echado en galeras." (I, 22)

[8] Cervantes's identity with that early rogue figure is made clear in what are probably his own very last words, written as he dedicated his posthumous *Persiles* to the Count of Lemos. After having said that he has received extreme unction, and imaged his death coming shortly, he ends the dedication saying: "Todavía me quedan en el alma ciertas reliquias y asomos de las *Semanas del jardín* y del *famoso Bernardo*. Si a dicha, por buena ventura mía, que ya no sería ventura, sino milagro, me diese el Cielo vida, las verá, y con ellas fin de *La Galatea*, de quien se

está aficionando vuesa excelencia; y con estas obras, continuando mi deseo, guarde Dios a vuesa excelencia como puede." Echoing in the background we hear Ginés's question magically, wistfully, reversed. It is no longer, "How can my work be finished if my life isn't?," but "How can my life be finished if my work isn't?"

9 John Weigler has nicely studied the place of Cervantes's view of poetry as that view is transplanted into the world of *Don Quixote* Part I, and most particularly as he makes his text apparently marketable in Chapter 9. Mary Gaylord Randel has shown, in her study of poetry in *La Galatea*, how Cervantes makes impossible the task of the poet who dreams of recovering true feeling in any text, poetry as well as prose.

10 See Foucault, *The Order of Things*.

WORKS CITED

Arias, Joan. *Guzmán de Alfarache: The Unrepentant Narrator*. London: Tamesis, 1977.

Blanco Aguinaga, Carlos. "Cervantes y la picaresca. Notas sobre dos tipos de realismo." *Nueva Revista de Filología Hispánica* 11 (1957): 313-42.

Brancaforte, Benito. *Guzmán de Alfarache: ¿Conversión o proceso de degradación?* Madison, Wisconsin: Hispanic Seminary of Medieval Studies, 1986.

Carey, Douglas, and Phillip Williams. *Hierologies of the Eccentric: The Limit Texts of Spanish Confession in the Lazarillo de Tormes and San Manuel Bueno, Mártir*. Unpublished manuscript.

Cixous, Helene. "The Laugh of Medusa." *New French Feminisms: An Anthology*. Ed. Elaine Marks and Isabelle de Courtiron. Amherst: Univ. of Massachusetts Press, 1980.

Cervantes Saavedra, Miguel de. *The Adventures of Don Quijote*. Trans. J.M. Cohen. New York: Penguin Books, 1980.

———. "The Dialogue of the Dogs." *Six Exemplary Novels*. Trans. Harriet De Onís. Woodbury, New York: Barron's Educational Series, 1961. 1-61.

Combet, Louis. *Cervantes ou les incertitudes du désire.* Lyons: Presses Universitaires de Lyons, 1980.

Derrida, Jacques. *The Ear of the Other: Otobiography, Transference, Translation.* Ed. Christie V. McDonald. Trans. by Peggy Kamuf. New York: Schocken Books, 1985.

———. *Glas.* Paris: Galilee, 1974.

Eakin, Paul J. *Fictions in Autobiography. Studies in the Art of Self-Invention.* Princeton: Princeton Univ. Press, 1985.

Efron, Arthur. *Don Quixote and the Dulcineated World.* Austin: Univ. of Texas Press, 1971.

El Saffar, Ruth. "Unspeakable Thoughts: Some Words on Parody in *Don Quixote.*" Unpublished manuscript.

Freud, Sigmund. *The Interpretation of Dreams.* Trans. and ed. James Strachey. New York: Basic Books, 1955.

———. "On the Universal Tendency to Debasement in the Sphere of Love." *Contributions to the Psychology of Love.*

Gusdorf, Georges. "Conditions and Limits of Autobiography." *Autobiography: Essays Theoretical and Critical.* Ed. and Trans. James Olney. Princeton: Princeton Univ. Press, 1980. 28-48.

Johnson, Carroll. *Madness and Lust in "Don Quixote".* Berkeley: Univ. of California Press, 1985.

Otero, Carlos. "Introducción a Chomsky." *Aspectos de la teoría de la sintaxis.* Trans. Carlos Otero. Madrid: Aguilar, 1970. xxv-xxviii.

Ragland-Sullivan, Ellie. *Jacques Lacan and the Philosophy of Psychoanalysis.* London: Croom Helm, 1986.

Randel, Mary Gaylord. "The Language of Limits and the Limits of Language: The Crisis of Poetry in *La Galatea.*" *Modern Language Notes* 97 (1982): 254-71.

Sophocles. *Oedipus the King.* Trans. Stephen King and Diskin Clay. New York: Oxford Univ. Press, 1978.

Spitzer, Leo. "Perspectivism in the Don Quixote." *Linguistics and Literary History: Essays in Stylistics.* New York: Russell and Russell, 1962.

Sterne, Lawrence. *The Life and Opinions of Tristam Shandy, Gentleman.* New York: Boni and Liveright, 1925.

Unamuno, Miguel de. *Vida de Don Quijote y Sancho.* 3rd ed. Madrid: Espasa-Calpe, 1938.

Weiger, John. *The Substance of Cervantes.* Cambridge: Cambridge Univ. Press, 1985.

Wilson, Diana. "Cervantes's Labors of Persiles: 'Working (in) the In-Between'." *Literary Theory/Renaissance Texts.* Ed. Patricia Parker and David Quint. Baltimore and London: Johns Hopkins Univ. Press, 1985.

CHAPTER 9:
POETRY AS AUTOBIOGRAPHY:
THEORY AND POETIC PRACTICE
IN CERVANTES

Jenaro Talens

*(translated by Gwen Barnes
and Steven Suppan)*

In his autobiography, the chief exponent of the *nouveau
roman* made a surprising and, apparently, provocative
declaration: "I have never spoken of anything but myself."
(Robbe-Grillet, 1984). The sentence points to a fundamental problem which has traversed contemporary theoretical
discussions, namely, who speaks in a text, what a text
speaks of, and from where it speaks. On the one hand, we
know that the limits of our language are the limits of our
world, that is, that we can *think* our relation with the real
only in terms of discourse. On the other hand, when one
speaks, it is impossible to not say "I." How, then, does one
resolve what, in these terms, appears to be such an irreducible contradiction? How do we claim objectivity when
we know that it is not possible to transcend our bodies, to
feel with a skin which is not our own; to look with eyes
that, for a moment, forget the untransferable place which

our own history makes them occupy? How, on the contrary, does one narrate his or her own life with words which exist precisely because they cannot belong to anyone. As Lautréamont wrote, "these eyes are not yours. From where have you taken them?" In one form or another, this vicious circle frames and traverses most contemporary writing. Its problematic, however, is not unique to this writing and, in large part, it has guided the historical development of literature.

A paradigmatic case may be the discourse of lyric poetry in which the frequent use of the first person does not always necessarily imply the presence of an "I" that speaks of itself. Yet, the frequent absence of anecdotal-argumentative support leaves bare procedures of composition and structure and allows one to analyze the traces which are no less real for being invisible. A life is drawn not only from what one tells of it, but also from what is silenced. A gesture, the choice of a certain perspective for approaching some matter, the predilection for an adjective, all tell more than a thousand anecdotes. In this sense Cervantes's poetic work can be seen as paradigmatic, despite the fact that it has not enjoyed much critical acclaim in literary history.

The work of Miguel de Cervantes is composed of three parts which are well defined in their limits as well as in their function. He is not only the peerless prose writer and creator of a genre in its modern sense, but also the author who, together with Shakespeare, has managed to produce an entire literary continent. Secondly, he is a playwright who breaks his own paths, distinct from those of Lope de Vega. Finally, he is the poet who perseveres in a task which brings him nothing more than sorrows and none of the praise commensurate with his estimation of its worth. And if critics have been occupied with his novel, and have paid attention, though perhaps not enough, to his theatrical work, his poetry has not enjoyed the same fortune. The attitude towards this portion of Cervantes's work is particularly unjust, above all if, as I will attempt to demonstrate, we can see in it not only its substantive value as poetry (with respect to its original conception of poetic work), but also a small-scale model of his entire literary world. The constancy with which Cervantes applies himself to the unpleasant task of *writing verses* throughout his life would not otherwise have very much justification.

Cervantes begins his poetic adventures in 1569, at the age of twenty-three. The four compositions included by his teacher, Juan López de Hoyos, in his *History and True Tale of the Sickness, Happy Death and Magnificent Funeral Rites of the Most Serene Queen of Spain, Our Lady, Doña Isabel de Valois*,[1] are, indeed, the oldest of his works to have come down to us. In them, there are, as in all beginners, the marks of the teaching of his elders. At the same time, when read from the perspective of his later works, one observes what will become his fundamental tendency: the adoption of the *cancionero* lyric and the Italian model, a double tradition in which he inserts himself and manages to transform. This function of playful craftsmanship—which will make of him later one of the great and original innovators—is what catches one's attention in his poetic work from the very beginning. Such work may be understood as a method on the one hand, and as *salvation of man by beauty* on the other. Both aspects are joined from the beginning, if we consider the simple comparison of texts that are so far apart in time as the "Elegy" of 1569 and that which Dorotea and Clara hear sung at the beginning of *Don Quijote* (I, 43):

> He who always enjoys tranquillity in his state of being
> and whose effect leads him to hope
> and of what he wants, nothing is changed:
> It is said that one may have
> little confidence in he
> who enjoys and sees with
> limpid eyes good fortune.
> ("Elegy," v. 133-138)

> Sluggards do not deserve
> The glory of triumphs or of victory;
> Good luck will never serve
> Those who resist not fortune manfully,
> But fall weakly to ground,
> And in soft sloth their senses all confound.
> ("Don Luis's Song" 388)[2]

Nearly half a century of Cervantes's poetic activity compels us to pay more attention to this work. That activity responds to a vocation that was stated in the prologue to *The Galatea*: "by which I can prove the inclination towards poetry which I have always had" ("para lo cual puedo alegar de mi parte la inclinación que a la poesía siempre he tenido"), repeated only two years before his death in the fourth song of the *Journey to Parnassus* (*Viaje del Parnaso*):

> Since my tender years I have loved the sweet art
> of agreeable poetry and in it
> I will always try to please you.[3]

Ricardo Rojas takes this vocation for granted as does Gerardo Diego who likewise states that "without the divine calling no poet is legitimate.... Miguel who was born a poet, died a confessed poet" ("sin la divina vocación no hay poeta legítimo.... Miguel que nació poeta, poeta confesado murió"). The tendency of his critics to confuse poetry and verse and not to take into account the same presuppositions with which Cervantes confronted his work as a poet, have led even modern editors such as Vicente Gaos to say that Cervantes "was not a born poet."

Cervantes had a high esteem for poetry, an esteem almost like that of a religion, as Schevill and Bonilla note in their 1922 edition, but his relation with poetry turns out to be somewhat ambivalent. He never published a book of poetry. These facts, however, should lead us to reformulate the matter of his poetry in other terms, without judging the results of Cervantes's poetry from presuppositions other than those that he himself established. Perhaps we could break a long critical tradition, initiated in Cervantes's own time, that undervalues his poetic production.

The passages that follow cannot be taken literally, especially in an author who uses irony and *double entendre* constantly in his work. First there is the shopworn citation of the third tercet of *Journey*:

> I have always striven and was vigilant
> to appear that I have the poet's wit
> that heaven didn't want to give me.[4]

There is also the sentence uttered by the Licenciado Vidriera: "I haven't been so foolish as to begin to be a bad poet, nor so fortunate as to have deserved to be a good one" ("No he sido tan necio que diese en poeta malo, ni tan venturoso que haya merecido serlo bueno"). Finally, there are the allusions to poetry scattered throughout his works. Witness, for instance this one from *Don Quijote* (I, 6): "That Cervantes has been a great friend of mine for many years and I know that he is more versed in misfortunes than in verse" (62) ("Muchos años ha que es grande amigo mío ese Cervantes, y sé que es más versado en desdichas que en versos"). Yet, there are also many other quotations that are not so often glossed which would lead us to different conclusions. I cite three fragments from *Journey to Parnassus*:

> Pass on, inventor rare, further advance
> With thy subtle design, and aid supply
> To Delian Apollo, of vast weight—
> Or ere the vulgar squadron comes to call
> E'en more than twenty thousand seven months old
> Poets, whom so to be are much in doubt.
> (Ch. I, v. 223-228)

> Mercy on us! What poetasters rise.
> (Ch. II, v. 396)

> He said, Shall it be possible that in Spain
> There be nine bards with laureated crowns?
> (Ch. VIII, vs. 97-98)[5]

One cannot take Cervantes's ironic statements seriously as did Valbuena Prat (1943), Schevill and Bonilla (1922) or even Alborg (1966), who speak of "painful confession," "bitter realization," etc. Rather, it is necessary to underline, as did Blecua, their humorous and sly character.

For Cervantes, poetry was grounded in the cult of beauty so that a poem could not lower itself to be a commercial object directed towards a pleasure-seeking public. In *Don Quijote* (II, 16) he states that poetry should be kept out of reach of "the ignorant vulgar, who are incapable of recognizing or appreciating her treasures" (569). For this very reason, he considers himself a poet by avocation (*afición*) rather than by vocation (*oficio*). He states as much in *The Gypsy Girl (La Gitanilla)* and in *Don Quijote* (II, 18). The distinction between avocation and vocation has supported those critics who have interpreted Cervantes's attitude towards poetry as being contrary to the normal work of the artist; as being a mere pastime. There is little substance to this view, however, for while Cervantes does not want to lower art to the daily vulgarity of a remunerable job, he does not stop considering poetry as constant and tiring work. This exclusive attitude already is manifest in the fourth book of *La Galatea*:

> ...despite the low esteem in which [poets] are held by princes and common people alike, they communicate with their intellects their lofty and strange concept, without daring to make them known to the world, and in my opinion, Heaven should order the world in this fashion, because neither the world nor our maligned century deserves to enjoy such tasty repasts for the soul.[6]

A detailed analysis of Cervantes's poetry shows, as much from the point of view of his theoretical statements as from that of his concrete practice, that if we seek to discover his work, it requires us to speak of its articulation based on two presuppositions: consciousness and a search for balance. From the latter will come the elements of Cervantes's poetic scaffolding: 1) the objectification of lyric sentiment and 2) the existence of shrewd talents that guide the compositional work. The preceptive zeal is evident throughout his extensive poetic career, but Cervantes possesses a poetics without a code, a theory rather than a normative program. His is a poetics which defends the principle of invention, provided that it does not carry with it the corruption of art in order to submit itself to the dictates of the public, and provided that it does not violate the laws of reason. His rules of composition are flexible, variable and never rigid. Thus, they are less evident than are those of his contemporaries. His theory allows for the modification of what is established by the norms of verse, provided that such modification is submitted to a harmonic scheme fashioned by an intellect controlled by rea-

son and in an analogical relation with the natural processes of the universe. His theory of poetic expression concerns more a meta-aesthetic system of ideas than a treatise
on poetic art. He can make a mockery of the rules, given
their particular character, in contrast to the scope of the
universals in which the poem operates and shows itself,
and can laugh at sterile erudition because of its apoetical
nature (*apoeticidad*). His rules of composition are, as a
consequence, a habit of thought more than norms and orders. His critical scruples as well as his distrust of academic
literary judgments derive from that habit. There is nothing but irony and humorous sarcasm behind the "Privileges, Decrees and Regulations that Apollo Sends to Spanish Poets" in the Appendix to the *Journey to Parnassus*
(Privilegios, ordenanzas, y advertencias que Apolo envía a
los poetas españoles):

> The first essential is that poets be as well known
> for the slovenliness of their persons as for the fame of
> their verses.
> Also, should any poet say he is poor, that he in-
> stantly be credited on his word, without any other
> oath or verification whatsoever.
> It is required that every poet be of a mild and be-
> coming mental habit, and that one should not look at
> stitches, albeit they appear in his stocking.
> Ditto, should any poet touch at the house of a
> friend or acquaintance, and should stay there for ma-
> terial sustenance, that although he swear that he
> has eaten, let it not be believed, save that he be
> made to eat by force, which in that case will be no
> great thing.
> Ditto, that the poorest bard in the world, though
> neither Adams nor Methusalems, may say that he is
> in love, though he be not so, and should give as the
> name of his lady, now styled Amaryllis, now
> Anarda, now Cloris, Phillis, or Filida, or Juana
> Tellez, or any other name at will, all may be done
> without asking reasons why.
> [...]
> Again, notify that he be not held for a thief who
> would appropriate others' verses, and pass them off
> for his own, whether in conception or in part, in
> which case he is as much a thief as Cacus.[7]

Likewise we can say that humor and sarcasm are hidden behind the serious thoughts of the sick poet in *The Dialogue of the Dogs* (*El coloquio de los perros*) when he complains of the failure of his work even while he takes great care to respect "what Horace orders in his *Poetics*" ("lo que Horacio manda en su *Poética*"). If Cervantes's poetics is a habit of thought, his theory is a method of resolving specific artistic problems at a level that is superior to that of codified precepts. In this sense Cervantes associates poetry with life, which he likewise does not subject to precepts. Indeed, his artistic formula is applicable as much to the composition of a poem as to vital processes in general. That principle even appears to rule the world of military affairs, as he states in some verses in the first act of *The Siege of Numancia* (*El cerco de Numancia*) in Scipio's speech:

> If an army, however small,
> is subjected to military order,
> you will see that it shines like the bright sun
> and achieves the victories it desires;
> but if the army conducts itself with indolence,
> although the world sees itself condensed in it,
> in a moment it will be routed
> by a more forthright hand and stronger heart.[8]

In his study *Cervantes's Theory of the Novel*, E. C. Riley noted that the origin of Cervantes's idea on the function of imaginative literature was one of "instructing while pleasing" (*instruir deleitando*). Cervantes reconciled this classical concept of the artistic with the antinomy inherent in the accomodation of neo-Platonic aesthetic ideas with a plan of life ruled by reason. León Hebreo, whom Cervantes had read and assimilated, according to Américo Castro and Francisco López-Estrada, had established a way of articulating this antinomic relation in his *Dialogues of Love* (*Diálogos de amor*). In the *Dialogues* Filon describes the method to grant to him, a bit paradoxically, first a poetic fiction, a Cabalistic meaning and, later, a pedagogical function. This is, in principle, something apparently contradictory but Hebreo saves the antinomy by assigning both elements to differentiated powers:

1) Hermetic, intellectual knowledge is grasped by "creative faculties suitable for divine and intellectual matters and a mind which preserves and does not corrupt the true sciences of those matters."

2) The matter of beneficial instruction (*provecho*) is assigned to three kinds of minds: a) "the less intelligent can only take from poetry the story with the ornament and melody of verse," b) "the more intelligent can digest the moral sense, in addition to the story," c) "the most intelligent can digest, in addition to the story and the moral sense, the allegorical repast, not only of natural philosophy, but of astrology and theology as well."[9]

Cervantes's position does not differ much from that of León Hebreo. He reserves the knowledge of universals to a select few and assigns the "instruction while pleasing" to those not apt for the highest knowledge. In prose, this double purpose of serving everyone can be realized, even if not everyone benefits in the same fashion by what is offered to them. In poetry, however, this realization is not possible because of its very high position in the scale of the harmonic. Poetry aspires to produce pleasure and a supreme good and, therefore, its use is forbidden to the "ignorant vulgar, who are incapable of recognizing or knowing her treasures" ("ignorante vulgo, incapaz de conocer y estimar los tesoros que en ella encierra") as he affirms in Don Quijote's speech (I, 16).

For Cervantes, the fundamental objective of the poem is enjoyment in the contemplation of beauty. The poem's beneficial effect consists of enriching itself with the truth of this graciously received gift. That thought is similar to what is expressed in the treatises on Christian piety in the sixteenth century. One thinks, for example, of Fray Diego de Estella, who writes in his *Most Devout Meditations on the Love of God (Meditaciones devotísimas del amor de Dios* [1576]): "He who says that he loves You and keeps the Ten Commandments of Your law only or chiefly because You give glory to him, should consider himself abandoned by that glory" ("El que dice que te ama y guarda los diez mandamientos de tu ley solamente o más principalmente porque le des la gloria, téngase por despedido della"). This thought coincides with that of Don Quijote when he speaks of his consecration to his lady Dulcinea (I, 31). There he speaks, in neo-Platonic fashion, of the transfer of concepts of universal courage from the sacred to the profane and vice versa.

According to these ideas, prose, as well as poetry, occasion responses in accord with a reader's specific sensibility. But the poem, in contrast to prose, also has the function of producing what is impossible for prose, namely, mental and spiritual therapy by means of the cessation of emotive processes. This kind of therapy is possible only for those who know how to interpret poetry. This pseudo-mystical position, of Plotinian derivation, is also characteristic of León Hebreo. From this perspective, we can understand the definition of poetry which Cervantes gives in *Don Quijote II*, insisting that it is "made of an alchemy of such virtue that he who knows how to treat her will receive in turn the purest gold of priceless worth" ("es hecha de una alquimia de tal virtud, que quien la sabe tratar la volverá en oro purísimo de inestable [sic] precio"). In Cervantes this vision of poetry as an exclusive artistic labor is joined by the consciousness of having both the creative genius and technical competence necessary to convert this mental schema into verbal discourse. At the same time, he knows that not all of his poetic peers possess this virtue.

In effect, in the length and breadth of his poetic production, Cervantes shows himself to have mastered a fairly ample formal and metrical repertory, including troubadouresque, Italianized and popular styles. Moreover, even his own variations within the fixed schemas are intricately woven and superimposed without ever privileging any of these modes of composition. A simple examination of his work shows not only technical and strophic variety, but also the balanced perfection with which it is employed. Examples of this perfection include his sonnets; the *silvas* which appear with the same ease and fluency in *Nine Petrarchan Songs (Nueve canciones petrarquistas)*— fashioned from the news of the defeat of the Invincible Armada in 1588; the poem "To the Ecstasies of Our Blessed Mother Theresa of Jesus" ("A los éxtasis de Nuestra Beata

Madre Teresa de Jesús") of 1615; and the ballads or *romances* which, together with those of Lope de Vega and Luis de Góngora, must have influenced the formation of the *Romancero Nuevo*.[10] If his *romances* were considered well made by his peers, the same can be said of his *zéjeles*, and *villancicos*.[11] In short, Cervantes's formal range encompasses virtually all known varieties of verses and strophes used in his time.

The lack of esteem for one meter compared to another does not imply an eclecticism or indecision, but rather the clear conscience of an instrument for putting into practice what really matters: form, understood as composition, as configuration of all the elements integrated in the superior unity called a poem. Already in *La Galatea* this particular approach to the matter of meter appears, generically speaking, as a form in which the poetic material is embodied, the material which, in the last instance, determines the form and grants value to it. A clear example of this approach is to be found in the eclogue of the third book of *La Galatea*, when Orsenio reiterates in two successive instances the same theme with different versification.

> The fruit that was sown
> by my constant work,
> has arrived in a sweet season,
> the fruit that with happy destination
> was delivered in my power.
> And hardly did I succeed in arriving
> at such incomparable ends,
> when I came to know
> the occasion of such pleasure
> to be of sorrow for me.
> (v. 473-482)

> To my sight was shown
> an opulent lair full of a thousand riches;
> I triumphed in its conquest,
> and when I was more serene,
> vile fate showed itself to me
> transformed into black darkness.
> (v. 557-563)[12]

Likewise, this approach to meter can be seen when two octaves of the same eclogue, in the words of Crisio (v. 223-

238) appear reformulated as a sonnet, in the words of Cardenio in the first act of *La Entretenida*:

> My slim and weak hope flies
> on feeble wings and although the flight
> rises to the zenith of the beautiful heaven,
> never will it attain the point to which it aspires.
> I come to be the dead ringer
> for that youth who left Crete's soil
> and, rivalling his father's zeal,
> propelled himself into the heavens.
>
> Melted by the amorous fire,
> my audacious thoughts will fall
> in the turbulent and cold sea of fear;
> but the violent courses
> forewarned by time and death,
> will not carry my name
> into oblivion.[13]

Meter and the combination of meters lose their determinate value so that the strength of the poem resides in the structural-compositional form and in the internal order of distribution of the poetic material. In this way the craftsman-like artifice of the poet-writer is fundamental. And what counts for Cervantes, at the end of the process of writing, is fulfilling the lyric intention and the conceptual and technical harmony of the parts.

In the same way, the function of the acoustic in the poem is a problem of structure, so that its meter and prosody cannot be judged by the metric and prosodic norms of the Castilian poem, but from Cervantes's particular use of both in his form of conceiving the poem. The greatest attack on Cervantes's poetry has taken place nearly always in the territory of prosody. Yet, it is something that few critics have tried to explain.[14]

In prosodic terms, Cervantes's verse lacks acoustic value in itself. Its value is relative to the structure and function of the poem. The relation is not established between the voice and the phonic group, but between the architectonically elaborated thought and the phonic group which is rhythmically disposed and is subordinated to the harmony of the concepts. This Cervantine characteristic comes from the enormous importance conceded to the voice that sings and is not limited to speaking the verse. Indeed, the phonological schemas of song do not correspond to those of spoken language. We cannot, of course, determine from a written text what its musical cadence would be, but in view of Cervantes's constant preoccupation with the form of rhythmically linking strophes, we could envisage the possibility that it would be (structurally speaking) repetitive and balanced.

Only in this fashion can one comprehend that a poem that fails prosodically to our ears may be considered pleasant and sweet within the work. The melody would lend the necessary acoustic harmony, so that it would correspond to the structural harmony. However, since neither all poems included in texts written in prose, nor are the individual poems sung, it would be worth exploring what happens in these cases. It is worth remembering that in the years in which Cervantes initiates his poetic career, the matter of prosody was not part of metric theory. Herrera, in his *Annotations* to Garcilaso, complained of the strictures of rhyme in 1580: "As those who write in this genre of poetry know, this difficulty of rhymes, which disturbs many beautiful bits of wisdom; they cannot be recounted with so much ease and clarity."[15] In that same year, Miguel Sánchez de Luna in his *The Poetic Art in Castilian Romance Poetry (El arte poética en romance castellano)* confronts the problem of the measured verse that sounds worse than unmeasured verse and he gives it a practical solution:

> The poet should guide himself by sound more than by any other path; and for this purpose some composers usually sing what they are composing.... It is necessary that each composition have its melody. When I was studying, my teacher read Virgil to me by chanting, because in that way, he said, one felt better the smoothness of the verse. He said that Virgil sung them also as he was composing them.[16]

Cervantes, who was very much a poet of the sixteenth century, would probably have used a melody to look for the fluency and smoothness of his verse. Cervantes's preoccupation with music has already been pointed out by Miguel Querol and by Adolfo Salazar, so that it is not too daring to think that the melody, in its specific concept of poetic composition, could make smooth and faint what to our ears seems harsh today. This manner of focusing on the problem had ceased to be the dominant one in the Baroque period.[17]

Despite what has been said above, the use of a musical leitmotif to overcome the formal pitfalls of prosody is not an excuse for the deficient acoustic qualities that many of Cervantes's poems may have. But that use explains how someone with so much facility for discovering the errors of others could compose verses which seem imperfect to us. Perhaps, in the long run, Cervantes himself might have come to think that, within these particular rules of composition without a code, the superficial, mechanical and acoustic structure was something secondary to the global structure of the poem which was, in the last instance, the fundamental consideration.

Cervantes structures his poetry with the precision of a painter, but the important thing for him is not the painterliness of verbal clusters, as Jorge Guillén perceptively noted with respect to Góngora, nor the melody of sounds that thereafter become inlaid in words, as Valle-Inclán said of Valéry's "The Marine Graveyard" ("Le cimetière marin"). Rather, he is interested in the conceptual scaffolding that sustains the verbal clusters. And if the painterly aspect does not appear at times in a specific text, it is because he has decided truly to lay bare that structure, or scaffolding. Therefore, his procedures are of a global nature and attend to the ordering, cohesion and intensification of the signified. This means that figures and tropes are nearly always secondary; they are resources of a cellular function and are accessories to procedures of greater significance: correlation and reiteration, verbal play, the secularization of sacred themes, and the reformulation of the themes and fragments of others, as well as his own. These procedures allow him to say to the Cervantes of the fourth chapter of *Journey to Parnassus* that he has always seen his poetry "dressed in spring colors" ("vestida de color de primavera").

Cervantes's organizing model for his verse was, as stated earlier, a concept of harmony analogous to that of the natural processes of the universe. More specifically, we can allude now to the human body. Already in *La Galatea* he signals his concept of the rhythm of the art of poetry, the relation between the parts of the poem and between the poem and each part (that which some avante-garde theorists refer to as the great discovery of Baudelaire and that, in fact, dates back to Cervantes). He says that the natural correspondence of this relation is the human body:

> But just as physical beauty is thus divided into two parts, living and dead bodies, likewise can there be love of physical beauty that may be good. One part of physical beauty shows itself in the living bodies of males and of females, and this consists in that all the parts of the body are good in themselves and that together they all make a perfect whole and form a body proportioned in members and smoothness of colors. The non-living beauty of the physical part consists of pictures, statues, buildings, a kind of beauty which can be loved without the love with which one loves being vilified.[18]

It is a concept of the rhythm of beauty that Cervantes will not only apply to his verse production, but to his own novels as well. In *Don Quijote* (I, 47) he critiques the romances of chivalry in large part for lacking proportions:

> And even though the principal aim of such books is to delight, I do not know how they can succeed, seeing the monstrous absurdities they are filled with. For the delight that the mind conceives must arise from the beauty and harmony it sees, or contemplates, in things presented to it by the eyes or the imagination; and nothing ugly or ill proportioned can cause us any pleasure. What beauty can there be, or what harmony between the parts and the whole, or between the whole and the parts, in a book or story in which a sixteen-year-old lad deals a giant as tall as a steeple one blow with his sword and cuts him in two as if he were made of marzipan? And when they want to describe a battle, first they tell us that there are a million men fighting on the enemy's side. But if the hero of the book is against them, inevitably,

whether we like it or not, we have to believe that
such and such a knight gained the victory by the
valour of his strong arm alone. Then what are we to
say of the ease with which a hereditary Queen or
Empress throws herself into the arms of an unknown
and wandering knight?[19]

For this formal scheme to be a poem, it needs to be in-
carnated in a word that represents it. Poetic representation
is, for Cervantes, a matter of configuration that subordi-
nates meter and prosody to a structural balance (or to an
imbalance motivated by an ironic or burlesque function
that demands it) and the active disposition that demands
it. Poetic representation orders and distributes elements at
the same time that it binds them, with procedures more
discursive than imaginative, in the poetic totality. The
rhythm of beauty will be the lexicalized construction that
enables the embodiment of what was only embryonic
thought.

An emblem of the image that is offered to us by rhythm
and representation is given by the "most beautiful damsel"
of the poet-page in *The Gypsy Girl*; by the nymph, "the
universal lady" of *Journey to Parnassus*; and by the tender
damsel of the second volume of *Don Quijote*. Rhythm
produces unity and representation produces clarity, while
rhythm and representation combined produce harmony or
consonance, the three characteristics of universal beauty,
according to Thomas Aquinas (*Ad pulchritudinem tria re-
quiruntur integritas, consonantia, claritas*). These three elements, in turn, motivate the image of a beautiful world
condensed in the poem, in the same way that the beauty of
the universe condenses it in the physical beauty of man. In
the last instance, it is clear that Cervantes is looking for a
beauty beyond the reach of man, because although the
poem searches for perfection, it cannot be in itself perfect,
as he already said in the fourth book of *La Galatea*: "the
beauty of which I speak cannot be enjoyed perfectly and
entirely...because it isn't in man's capacity to enjoy perfectly something that is beyond him and is not all his" ("la
belleza de quien hablo no se puede gozar perfecta y entera-
mente... porque no está en mano del hombre gozar

cumplidamente cosa que está fuera dél y no sea toda suya").

What the poem may contain is an approximation of the beauty thought by the poet. And it is that mental design that validates the invention and what justifies, in the interior of Cervantes's work, the valorization of the force of writing, of showing it as such a force in the same poem. When Vicente Gaos defines Cervantes as an uncomfortable poet because he transmits to the reader the sensation of the painful effort that the writer appears to have experienced in shaping his verses, he points to another element of Cervantes's originality. It is not a question, as Francisco Ynduráin said of *Novels to Marcia Leonarda,* to make the work for the public eye, without artifice or *trompe d'oeil,* but to imply to the reader that he suffers.

The essence of this mental design would be the configuration structured in the thought of an image or a concept. It can be the mental design of a face, such as the one that Andrés requests of the poet-page in *The Gypsy Girl:*

> Look, Clemente, the star-studded veil
> with which this cold night
> competes with the day
> of beautiful lights adorning the sky;
> and in this resemblance to the day,
> if your divine wit perceives so much,
> you'll perceive that countenance
> where the utmost beauty is present.
> (v. 108)[20]

Perhaps that is why Karl Selig considers *The Gypsy Girl* to be Cervantes's macro-metaphor for poetry.

Despite everything thast has been said, it is indisputable that many of Cervantes's poems can be characterized as "bad." The problem of bad poems underscores the importance of Cervantes's adventure. The higher one aims, the greater the error if the target is missed. The emphasis on the mental plane is transformed sometimes into a wall against which the verbal achievement explodes. While the verses of Garcilaso, Herrera, Lope or Góngora leave a mark on the eyes and ears, Cervantes seeks to impress our intellective capacity without entering through the senses. More than an error, this is a trademark. There exists in Cervantes a certain mistrust of sensible perception that shows itself with clarity in the *reductio ad absurdam* of the value assigned to the senses in Don Quijote's tale of what he has seen in Montesinos Cave (II, 23):

> I opened and rubbed my eyes, and saw that I was not asleep but really awake. For all that, I felt my head and my bosom to make certain whether it was my very self who was there, or some empty and counterfeit phantom; but touch, feeling and the coherent argument I held with myself assured me that I was there then just as I am here now.[21]

An example of the intellective, non-sensorial mechanism of his conception of structure as formal manifestation are in the following verses of the first book of *La Galatea*: "a thousand incomparable, indescribable charms/ have made me fog to the amorous wind" ("mil gracias que no tienen par ni cuento/niebla me han hecho al amoroso viento"). These verses, which undoubtably have a high affective level, perform their function within their context (the nine octaves of dialogue between Elicio and Erastro as a counterpoint to the verses that close the previous octave: "and other things I saw blinding me/have made me fuel for the invisible fire" ("y otras cosas que vi quedando ciego/yesca me han hecho al invisible fuego"). The syntactical and compositional parallelism (each verse is at the end of the preceding octave) puts two worlds into contact: that of the poetic shepherd, Elicio, who refers to "fuel," "invisible," and "fire" and that of the historical shepherd, Erastro, who refers to "fog," "amorous" and "wind." The worlds are related, harmonizing the universal (poetic) and the particular (historical) to sing to the woman they both love. It is not the isolated verses that count, but the verbal artifice of counterpoint that permits the figure portioned from the whole.

In addition to Cervantes's refusal to commercialize his poetry, this notion of poetry in the totality of the works, rather than in the singular works, is a possible answer as to why he did not publish an independent book of poetry, except for the *Journey to Parnassus*. His entire body of poetic work is a kind of frame where he integrates his proposal as a poet. Thus, the intercalated poems are not really isolated "exceptions," but are part of the fabric of the prose in his narrative and of the verse necessary to the dramatic plan of his theater. If we extract the poems from his novels and plays, we decontextualize them and, as a result, they lose most of their meaning. In this manner, the poems integrated in *La Galatea* are not simple excurses in the traditional fashion, but a form of inscribing his critique of the pastoral genre.

Operating in Cervantes's work is what Emilio Orozco has defined as Baroque integration, in contrast to the merely accumulative character of Mannerism. "The Song of Crisóstomo," for example, in *Don Quijote* (I, 14) (where Garcilaso's *Third Eclogue* is cited: "Let them leave with the suffering soul outside" ("salgan con la doliente ánima fuera"), explains a suicide, whereas the narrative text in which it is inserted only speaks of the death of love. Even in single poems, his tendency to integrate genres is evident.

There is a truly paradigmatic example of this integration in the sonnet "To the Funeral Casket of Phillip II" ("Al túmulo de Felipe II"). That boasting which at the end of the poem visualizes what seems to be the neutral voice of the lyric poet, making of him a soldier and holding him responsible for as much as he says, has a great deal of theatricality. On the other hand, he does not seem to have much interest in conserving individual poems as discrete entities. Some of his compositions would end up being integrated, with few variants, in his works, whether narrative or theatrical. Such is the case of the "Letter to Mateo Vázquez" ("Epístola a Mateo Vázquez") that coincides, with slight changes, with Saavedra's speech in the first act of *Los tratos de Argel*, or some of the verses of Elicio's song in book II, of *La Galatea* which is reproduced in the same play:

> Elicio:
> It is so easy for my faint fortune
> to see bitter death
> joined with sweet life
> and see grief dwell where joy resides.

> Between opposites I see
> hope wane, and not desire. (v. 43-48)

> Saavedra:
> In the fast track
> I see the hurried hours of fleeting time
> conspire against me with heaven,
> with hope left behind, not desire.[22]

Finally, before speaking of *Journey to Parnassus*, I would like to consider briefly Cervantes's tendency to use self-citation, as much as the work of others, as poetic material. It has been said that as poet, he does not seem to not have a "personal voice," at least in the judgment of as sensitive a reader of poetry as Alonso Zamora Vicente when he speaks of the "veiled voice" of Cervantes in the poem. As Blecua noted, it cannot be denied that Cervantes used entire verses of Garcilaso, but this is not so much a matter of lack of originality as of the deliberate search for the dissolution of the personal voice. In his poem, "To the Ecstasy of Our Blessed Lady Mother Theresa of Jesus," he includes three verses in which Garcilaso praises the Viceroy of Naples in his "First Eclogue":

> You who by working earned
> renown the world over
> and a rank second to none.[23]

Here he is not taking refuge in Garcilaso in order to hide his inexperience. The text is from 1615 and by then his apprentice years had passed. Perhaps the hypothesis could be put forth that with this citation, he achieved a certain impersonal generalization by neutralizing his voice among voices foreign to his, some of them incorporated from his own writings. This procedure would not be unique to his poems. Indeed, the imbrication of narrators in *Don Quijote* would likewise make the personal disappear behind the work, in order to resurface as the universal textual voice from that same work: for example, the character who reads the first part of Don Quijote's life is none other than the transcriber/adapter of a previous text of Cide Hamete Benengeli.

Cervantes neither cites sterile erudition nor does he wink at the reader. Such is also the case with *Journey to Parnassus* (1614). Its date of composition, as well as its considerable length, seem to indicate the importance which Cervantes attached to this work. In ill health, involved with the production of the second volume of *Don Quijote*, and engaged in writing *Persiles and Segismundo*, Cervantes might not have dedicated the time that was slipping away from him to a poem with the characteristics of *Journey*, if it were not because he sought to achieve something important and significant.[24]

While the *Journey* is not an essay in literary criticism per se, Cervantes humorously criticizes himself as a literary figure:

> 'Oh you!,' he said, the poets
> that you canonized from the long list
> by indirect reasons and ways.
>
> Where did you hold, evil one,
> the sharp sight of your talent, so that
> though blind, you were such a lying chronicler?[25]

Cervantes's curious affirmation "by indirect reasons and ways" can be taken as a self-vindication, for although the direct and fundamental thing to do was to speak of oneself, the primordial purpose of *Journey* was to leave to posterity an autobiography vindicating Cervantes's function as a poet. And, in truth, the only sincere praise, without the clichés of the time, are the ones dedicated to his own work:

> He who doesn't value being a poet,
> for what reason does he write and proclaim verses?
> Why does he disdain what he most esteems?
>
> I will never be contented nor satisfied
> with hypocritical fastidiousness; simply
> I wanted praise for what I did well.[26]

The plot of the book could not be more Cervantine: a) by means of memory, he leaves his country on an "ideal voyage," to cite the expression of Croce ("Due illustrazioni...") and returns to the golden Italy of his youth; b) reality is evaded by means of the representation of a mythography—evasion and improbability being constant features of his style; and c) by simultaneously doubling as narrator and character, he "leaves" himself. In this fashion, whether by his own means or by those of the god Mercury, Cervantes can say what he thought of his work and himself.

Having fulfilled these purposes, Cervantes extends the symbolic function of the poem to all of humanity and converts *Journey* into a mock-epic of the illusions and vanities of man. This is exemplified in the poets' blind zeal for glory, again uniting the particular and the universal. In some measure and without ignoring that *Don Quijote* is a work of greater substance, we could agree with Vicente Gaos that *Journey to Parnassus* is a kind of *Don Quijote* in miniature and in verse. It makes clear that man usually judges himself to be greater than his own merits and in the process he is swept along by a chimera. His self-concept and, to a certain degree, his aspirations, surpass the real possibility of satisfying them.

There is also another point of contact with *Don Quijote*. If *Don Quijote* mocks the romance of chivalry, *Journey* parodies the mythological world of Classicism that Renaissance authors had abused so much. If Don Quijote makes princesses of country girls and castles of windmills, *Journey* bring the gods down from the Olympic pedestals and grants them human stature, submerging them in an atmosphere of caricature similar to that of Velázquez's paintings, as Rodríguez Marín accurately noted.

The point of departure, according to this constant use of other people's texts for his personal work, is taken from *Viaggio in Parnaso* by Cesare Caporali—as Cervantes himself acknowledges in the first verse of his *Journey* and in the prologue to his *Exemplary Novels (Novelas ejemplares)*—although the poem is inspired by the appendix, *Notices from Parnassus (Avvisi de Parnaso)*. Besides Caporali, it is possible to indicate other Spanish sources: the *Journey to Sannio (Viage de Sannio,* 1585) of Juan de la Cueva, a couple of *romances* of the *Phoebean Choir (Coro febeo,* 1587) and some older precedents, such as *Lovers' Hell (Infierno de los enamorados)* or *The Triumph of*

Love (El triunfete de Amor) by the Marquis of Santillana. In turn, Cervantes's *Journey* was widely read in the seventeenth century. Already republished in 1624, it inspired *Crowns of Parnassus (Coronas del Parnaso)* (1635) by Salas Barbadillo and *The Daily Fare of the Salon Muses (Platos de las Musas de Salas)* (1640) by Jerónimo de Cáncer.

The utilization of the linked tercet, for which Cervantes has been criticized so much because of its monotony and failures is not gratuitous. If it is a question of putting all poets at the same level, of stacking them to show their extensive mediocrity, there was no better way than to make them indistinct and to try to put all judgments and clichés in the same verse and strophic vehicle. To speak of Cervantes's error, in this respect, as do R. Marín, and Schevill and Bonilla, is not to understand Cervantes's special constructive sense which, quite justly, Cervantes characterized as "rare inventor."

Cervantes proclaims his truth and life despite the cold reception suffered at the hands of many of his peers. Yet, the possibility that he would not be understood forced him to explain his own viewpoints and perspectives. Cervantes's linked narrative(s) of *The Deceitful Marriage (El casamiento engañoso)/ The Dialogue of the Dogs (El coloquio de los perros)* and, especially, *Don Quijote* testify to his capacity for eluding the mix that was so common in the picaresque tradition: writing and explicit construction of the self. Unlike *Lazarillo de Tormes*, for example, Cervantes did not use the "true" story of his life to answer a question not answered directly. On the contrary, he wrote a kind of literary, "fictional" story to inscribe himself in the margins, as absence. For Cervantes, life is not conceived as anecdote, but as a way of living, thinking, and writing:

> To sing with such a harmonious and live voice
> that they think I am a swan and that I am dying.

> cantar con voz tan entonada y viva
> que piensen que soy cisne y que me muero.

NOTES

¹ *Historia y relación verdadera de la enfermedad, felicísimo tránsito y suntuosas exequias fúnebres de la Serenísima Reina de España Doña Isabel de Valois, nuestra Señora.*

2 Quien goza de quietud siempre en su estado,
  y el efecto le acude a la esperanza
  y a lo que quiere nada le es trocado,
  argúyese que poca confianza
  se puede tener dél, que goce y vea
  con claros ojos bienaventuranza.
  ("Elegía," v. 133-148)

  No alcanzan perezosos,
  honrados triunfos, ni vitoria alguna,
  ni pueden ser dichosos
  los que, no contrastando a la fortuna,
  entregan, desvalidos,
  al ocio blando todos los sentidos.
  (*Don Quijote*, I, 43)

3 Desde mis tiernos años amé el arte
  dulce de la agradable poesía
  y en ella procuré siempre agradarte.
  (*Viaje del Parnaso*)

4 Yo que siempre me afano y me desvelo
  por parecer que tengo de poeta
  la gracia que no quiso darme el cielo.
  (*Viaje del Parnaso*)

5 Pasa, raro inventor, pasa adelante
  con tu sotil disinio, y presta ayuda
  a Apolo, que la tuya es importante.
  Antes que el escuadrón vulgar acuda
  de más de veinte mil sietemesinos
  poetas, que de serlo están en duda.
  (Chapter I, v. 223-228)

  ¡Cuerpo de mi con tanta poetambre!
  (Chapter II, v. 396)

  Dijo: ¿Será posible que en España
  Haya nueve poetas laureados?
  (Chapter VIII, v. 97-98, *Viaje del Parnaso*)

⁶ ...con la poca estimación que de ellos los príncipes y el vulgo hace, con sólos sus entendimientos comunican sus altos y extraños conceptos, sin osar publicarlos al mundo, y tengo para mí que el Cielo debe ordenarlo de esta manera, porque no merece el mundo ni el mal considerado siglo nuestro gozar de manjares al alma tan gustosos. (Cervantes, *La Galatea*, Chapter IV)

⁷ "Privilegios, Ordenanzas y Advertencias que Apolo envía a los poetas españoles" (Adjunta al *Viaje del Parnaso*)

Es el primero, que algunos poetas sean conocidos tanto por el desaliño de sus personas como por la fama de sus versos.

Item, que si algún poeta dijere que es pobre, sea luego creído por su simple palabra, sin otro juramento o averiguación alguna.

Ordénase que todo poeta sea de blanda y de suave condición, y que no mire en puntos, aunque los traiga sueltos en sus medias.

Item, que si algún poeta llegare a casa de algún su amigo o conocido, y estuvieren comiendo, y le convidare, que aunque el jure que ya ha comido, no se le crea en ninguna manera, sino que le hagan comer por fuerza, que en tal caso no se le hará muy grande.

Item, que el más pobre poeta del mundo, como no sea de los Adanes y Matusalenes, puedeadecir que es enamorado, aunque no le esté, y poner el nombre a su dama como más le viniere a cuento, ora llamándola Amarili, ora Anarda, ora Clori, ora Filis, o ya Juana Téllez, o como más gustare, sin que desto se le pueda pedir ni pida razón alguna.

[...]

Item, se advierte que no ha de ser tenido por ladrón el poeta que hurtare algún verso ajeno y le encajare entre los suyos, como no sea todo el concepto y toda la copla entera, que en tal caso tan ladrón es como Caco. (188-189)

⁸   Si a militar concierto se reduce
       cualquier pequeño ejército que sea,
       veréis que como sol claro reluce,
       y alcanza las victorias que desea;
       pero si a flojedad él se conduce,
       aunque abreviado el mundo en él se vea,
       en un momento quedará deshecho
       por más reglada mano y fuerte pecho.
       (Cervantes, *El cerco de Numancia*)

⁹   1) Los conocimientos de tipo intelectual, herméticos, son captados por "ingenios aptos a las cosas divinas e intelectuales y mente conservativa de las verdaderas ciencias y no corruptivas de ellas."

2) En cuanto al "provecho", es asignado a las mentes según tres grados: a) "las mentas bajas pueden tomar de las poesías solamente la historia con el ornamento del verso y su melodía."; b) "las otras más levantadas comen, además de esto, el sentido moral" and c) "otras más altas pueden comer, allende de esto, del manjar alegórico, no sólo de la filosofía natural, mas también de la astrología y la teología.
(León Hebreo, *Diálogos de amor*)

[10] I am thinking, for example, of the perfection of *The Ballad of Jealousy* (*Romance de los celos*):

> Where the sun sets
> between two boulders split asunder
> lies the entrance to the abyss,
> I mean by that a cave, etc.

> Yace donde el sol se pone
> entre dos partidas peñas
> una entrada del abismo,
> quiero decir una cueva, etc.

[11] See, respectively, the poems which say,
> Although you think that I am happy
> I carry grief within me
> (*The Baths of Algiers*)

> Aunque pensáis que me alegro
> conmigo traigo el dolor
> (*Los baños de Argel*)

> Child, you spilled the waste water
> and did not say: "There it goes."
> (*The House of Jealousy*)

> Dearramaste el agua niña
> y no dijiste: "Agua va."
> (*La casa de los celos*)

[12]
> El fruto que fue sembrado
> por mi trabajo contino,
> a dulce sazón llegado,
> fue con próspero destino
> en mi poder entregado.
> Y apenas pude llegar
> a términos tan sin par,

cuando vine a conocer
la ocasión de tal placer
ser para mí de pesar.
(Cervantes, *La Galatea*, Chapter IV, v. 474-482)

Mostróseme a la vista
un rico albergue de mil bienes lleno;
triunfé de su conquista,
y cuando más sereno
se me mostraba el hado,
vilo en oscuridad negra cambiado.
(*La Galatea*, Chapter IV, v. 557-563)

13   Cardenio:
Vuela mi estrecha y débil esperanza
con flacas alas, y aunque sube el vuelo
a la alta cumbre del hermoso cielo,
jamás el punto que pretende alcanza.
Yo vengo a ser perfecta semejanza
de aquel mancebo que de Creta al suelo
dejó, y, contrario de su padre al celo,
a la región del cielo se abalanza.

Caerán mis atrevidos pensamientos,
del amoroso incendio derretidos,
en el mar del temor turbado y frío;
pero no llevarán cursos violentos,
del tiempo y de la muerte prevenidos,
al lugar del olvido el nombre mío.
(Cervantes, *La entretenida*)

14 If, as Gerardo Diego intelligently states, Cervantes had a tin ear, "not receptive or passive, but active and thunderous" ("no receptiva o pasiva sino activa o entonadora"), how is it that, upon realizing that he was tone deaf, he persists throughout the years in his poetic work and in the orchestration of his prose?

15 Esta dificultad de las rimas, la cual como saben los que mejor escriben en este género de poesía, disturba muchas y hermosas sentencias; que no se pueden narrar con tanta facilidad y clareza.

16 Debe el poeta refirse más por el sonido, que por otra ninguna vía; y para esto suelen algunos ir cantando lo que van componiendo... Es menester que tenga para cada compostura su sonada... Cuando estudiaba me leía mi maestro a Virgilio cantando, porque decía él, que de aquella

manera se sentía mejor la suavidad del verso, y que Virgilio al tiempo que los iba componiendo, los iba también cantando.

[17] The preoccupations of treatise writers on aspects of tone and time of verse rhythm in the sixteenth century [one of whose most sublime examples is Francisco Salinas in his *De musica libri septem* (1577), the blind musician immortalized by Fray Luis) are not documented in the seventeenth century, when the problem of rhythm is reduced to a matter of meter and rhyme, e.g. in Juan Caramuel's *Rhythmica* of 1665.

[18] Pero como la belleza corpórea se divide así mesmo en dos partes, que son en cuerpos vivos y en cuerpos muertos, también puede haber amor de belleza corporal que sea bueno. Muéstrase la una parte de la belleza corporal en cuerpos vivos de varones y de hembras, y ésta consiste en que todas las partes del cuerpo sean de por sí buenas, y que todas juntas hagan un todo perfecto y formen un cuerpo proporcionado de miembros y suavidad de colores.   La otra belleza de la parte corporal no viva consiste en pinturas, estatuas, edificios, la cual belleza puede amarse sin que el amor con que se amare si vitupere. (Cervantes, *La Galatea*)

[19] Y según a mí me parece, este género de escritura y composición cae debajo de aquél de las fábulas que llaman milesias, que son cuentos disparatados, que atienden solamente a deleitar, y no a enseñar; al contrario de lo que hacen las fábulas apólogas, que deleitan y enseñan juntamente. Y puesto que el principal intento de semejantes libros sea el deleitar, no sé yo como pueden conseguirle, yendo llenos de tantos y tan desaforados disparates; que el deleite que en el alma se concibe ha de ser de la hermosura y concordancia que ve o contempla en las cosas que la vista o la imaginación le ponen delante; y toda cosa que tiene en sí fealdad y descompostura no nos puede causar contento alguno. Pues ¿qué hermosura puede haber, o qué proporción de partes con el todo, y del todo con las partes, en un libro o fábula donde un mozo de dieciseis años da una cuchillada a un gigante como una torre, y le divide en dos mitades, como si fuera de alfeñique, y cuando nos quieren pintar una batalla, después de haber dicho que hay de la parte de los enemigos un millón de combatientes, como sea contra ellos el señor del libro, forzosamente mal que nos pese, habemos de entender que el tal caballero alcanzó la victoria por sólo el valor de su fuerte brazo? Pues ¿qué diremos de la facilidad con que una reina o emperatriz heredera se conduce en los brazos de un andante y no conocido caballero? (*Don Quijote*, I, 47) (trans. 424-425)

[20]   Mira, Clemente, el estrellado velo
         con que esta noche fría
         compite con el día

de luces adornando el cielo;
y en esta semejanza,
si tanto tu divino ingenio alcanza,
aquel rostro figura
donde asiste el extremo de hermosura.
(*La Gitanilla*, v. 108-116)

[21] Despabilé los ojos, limpiémelos, y vi que no dormía, sino que realmente estaba despierto; con todo esto me tenté la cabeza y los pechos, por certificarme si era yo mismo el que allí estaba, o alguna fantasma vana y contrahecha; pero el tacto, el sentimiento, los discursos concertados que entre mí hacía, me certificaron que yo era allí entonces el que soy aquí ahora. (*Don Quijote*, II, 23) (trans. 615)

[22]   Elicio:
Esle tan fácil a mi corta suerte
ver con la amarga muerte
junta la dulce vida
y estar su mal a do su bien se anida,
que entre contrarios veo
que mengua la esperanza, y no el deseo.
(*La Galatea*, v. 43-48)

Saavedra:
El la veloz carrera apresuradas
las horas del ligero tiempo veo
contra mí con el cielo conjuradas
queda atrás la esperanza, y no el deseo.
(*El trato de Argel*, I)

[23]   Tú que ganaste obrando
un nombre en todo el mundo
y un grado sin segundo
("A los éxtasis de Nuestra Beata Madre Teresa de Jesús")

[24] His purpose was not to duplicate what he had already achieved in "Caliope's Song" ("Canto de Calíope"), of *La Galatea*. As José Manuel Blecua noted, it is not only a matter of praising contemporary poets, but something much more profound and serious. Neither was it a matter, as Menéndez y Pelayo stated, of "an elegant/ingenious and discreetly critical poem" (un elegante/ingenioso y discreto poema crítico"). Scholars have usually compared *Journey* with Lope de Vega's *The Laurel of Apollo (Laurel de Apolo)*, judging Lope's version to be superior. Yet, it is clear that those two works do not have much in common and that *Journey* should be related to the rest of Cervantes's production.

According to F. Rodríguez Marín, Cervantes conceived his *Journey* both as escape to a nostalgic past and to celebrate, in passing, his contemporary poets.

25   ¡Oh tú —dijo— que los poetas
        canonizaste de la larga lista,
        por causas y por vías indirectas!

        ¿Dónde tenías, magancés, la vista
        aguda de tu ingenio, que así ciego
        fuiste tan mentiroso cronista?
        (*Viaje del Parnaso*, IV, v. 490-495)
        (trans. 337-342)

26   Aquel que de poeta no se precia,
        ¿para qué escribe versos y los dice?
        ¿Por qué desdeña lo que más aprecia?

        Jamás me contenté ni satisfice
        de hipócritos melindres; llanamente
        quise alabanzas de lo que bien hice.
        (*Viaje del Parnaso*, Chapter IV, 337-342)
        (trans. 337-342)

WORKS CITED

Alborg, Juan Luis. "La poesía de Cervantes." *Cervantes*. Madrid: Gredos,1966.

Blecua, José Manuel. "Garcilaso y Cervantes." *Cuadernos de Insula*. Madrid, 1947. 141-150.

————. (with the pseudonym Joseph M. Claube) "La poesía lírica de Cervantes." *Cuadernos de Insula*. Madrid, 1947. 151-187.

Castro, Adolfo. "Cervantes, ¿fue poeta o no fue poeta?" Introduction to *Biblioteca de autores españoles*, XLII.

Castro, Américo. *El pensamiento de Cervantes*. Barcelona: Noguer, 1925, rpt. 1972.

————. *Hacia Cervantes*. Madrid: Taurus, 1967.

————. *Hacia Cervantes*. Madrid: Taurus, 1967.

Cernuda, Luis. "Cervantes, poeta." *Poesía y Literatura II*. Barcelona: Seix-Barral, 1964.

Cervantes Saavedra, Miguel de. *The Adventures of Don Quijote*. Trans. J. M. Cohen. Baltimore: Penguin, 1950.

————. *Obras completas de Cervantes*. Ed. Cayetano Rosell. Vol. III. Madrid: Rivadeneyra, 1864. vol. VIII.

————. *Obras completas de Miguel de Cervantes Saavedra*. Ed. Rodolfo Schevill and Adolfo Bonilla. Madrid: Gráficas Reunidas, 1922.

————. *Obras completas*. Ed. Angel Valbuena Prat. Madrid: Aguilar, 1943.

————. *Obras menores de Cervantes*. Ed. J. Givanel Mas. Vol. II. Barcelona: Antonio López. 1905.

————. *Poesías de Cervantes*. Ed. Vicente Gaos. Madrid: Taurus, 1970.

————. *Poesía*. Ed. Adriana Lewis. Zaragoza: Ebro, 1972.

————. *Poesías de Cervantes*. Ed. Ricardo Rojas. Buenos Aires: Coni Hermanos, 1916.

————. *Poesías completas II*. Ed. Vicente Gaos. Madrid: Castalia, 1981.

————. *Viaje del Parnaso*. Ed. Vicente Gaos. Madrid: Castalia, 1974.

————. *The Voyage to Parnassus*. Trans. G.W.J. Gyll. London: Alex, Murray and Son, 1870.

Croce, Benedetto. "Due illustrazioni al *Viaje del Parnaso* di Cervantes." *Homenaje a Menéndez Pelayo I*. Madrid, 1899.

Diego, Gerardo. "Cervantes y la poesía." *RFE*, XXXII. 1948.

Gaos, Vicente. "Cervantes, poeta." *Claves de literatura española*. Vol. I. Madrid: Guadarrama, 1971.

López-Estrada, Francisco. *"La Galatea" de Cervantes: Estudio crítico*. La Laguna de Tenerife, 1948.

Menéndez Pelayo, M. "Cervantes, considerado como poeta." *Estudios y discurso de crítica literaria I*. Madrid: C.S.I.C., 1941.

Orozco Díaz, Emilio. *Manierismo y Barroco*. Salamanca: Anaya, 1970. 2nd ed: Madrid: Cátedra, 1975.

Querol, Miguel. "Cervantes y la música." *RFE*, XXXII. 1948.

Riley, E.C. *Cervantes's Theory of the Novel*. Oxford: Oxford University Press, 1962.

Rodríguez Marín, F. "Prologue "to *Viaje del Parnaso*. Madrid: C. Bermejo, 1935.

Rojas, Ricardo. *Cervantes*. Buenos Aires: Losada, 1948.

Salazar, Adolfo. "Música, instrumentos y danzas en la obra de Cervantes." *NRFH*, II. 1948.

Selig, Karl. " Concerning the Structure of Cervantes' *La Gitanilla*." *Romanistisches Jahrbuch*, XVIII. 1962.

Zamora Vicente, Alonso."La 'Epístola a Mateo Vázquez'." Madrid: Cuadernos de Insula, 1947.

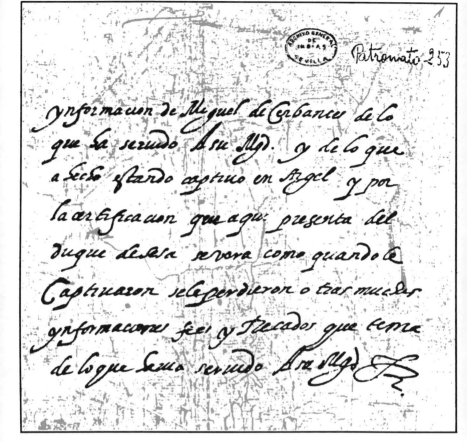

ynformacion de Miguel de Cerbantes de lo
que a seruido a su Mgd. y de lo que
a hecho estando captiuo en Argel y por
la certificacion que aqui presenta del
duque de sesa se vera como quando le
Captiuaron se le perdieron o tras muchas
ynformaciones fees y recados que tenia
de lo que hauia seruido a su Mgd.

Appendix

CURRICULUM VITAE*
MIGUEL DE CERVANTES SAAVEDRA

Ynformacion de Miguel de Cerbantes de lo que ha servido a su magestad y de lo que a hecho estando captivo en Argel y por la certificacion que aqui presenta del duque de Sesa se vera como quando le captivaron se le perdieron otras muchas ynformaciones fées y recados que tenia de lo que havia servido a su magestad.

Miguel de Cerbantes Sahavedra sobre que se le haga merced attento a las causas que refiere de uno de los officios que pide

　　　—contaduria del nuebo reyno
　　　—gobernacion de Soconusco
　　　—contador de las galeras de Cartagena
　　　—corregimiento de La Paz

El Relator doctor Nuñez　　　Juan de Ledesma

　　　—que a servido de 22 años a esta parte en la batalla naval alli de un arcabuçaço perdio una mano
　　　—el año siguiente fue a Navarino despues a Tunez y La Goleta
　　　—binyendo a esta corte para que su magestad le hiciese merced fue captivo en la galera del Sol con un su hermano que juntos habian servido en las dichas jornadas fueron llevados a Argel donde gastaron su patrimonio en su rescate y la hacienda de su padre y las doctes de dos hermanos
　　　—ya rescatados fueron a servir a Portugal y a la tierra con el marques de Sancta Cruz
　　　—aora el uno dellos sirve de alferez en Flandes
　　　—que este Miguel de Cerbantes bino con cartas del alcaide de Mistayta y fue a Oran con orden de su magestad

*Archivo General de Indias, Sevilla. Patronato Real, Legajo 253, Ramos 1 y 2, Tira 1.
Nota: La cursiva que aparece en la transcripción indica texto ilegible por deterioro del manuscrito original.—M. G-M.

—despues a asistido en Sevilla en negocios del armada con horden de Antonio de Guebara

—suplica se le de la contaduria del nuebo reyno
o la gobernacion de Soconusco
o la contaduria de las galeras de Cartagena
o el corregimiento de La Paz

es benemerito para qualquier officio y dara buena quenta

[al margen]

una certificacion del duque de Alba [sic] en que dice sus servicios en la naval y perdio la mano

en consideracion se dio licencia de mercaderias de Balencia a Argel para que sirviesen para el rescate

una informacion de servicios de pedimiento del padre estando el hijo captibo ante un alcalde año 1578

la informacion de lo que paso en la captividad y costas y gastos de rescate hecho ante un redemtor de captibos en Argel y de sus servicios

[Certificación del duque de Sessa]

El Duque de Sessa

Por haverme pedido por parte y en nombre de Miguel de Cerbantes que para que a su merced le conste de la manera que le a servido le conviene que yo le de fee dello por la presente certifico y declaro que ha que le conozco de algunos años a eta parte en servicio de su magestad y por informacion que dello tengo se y me consta que se hallo en la batalla y rota de la armada del turco en la qual peleando como buen soldado perdio una mano y despues le vi servir en las demas jornadas que huvo en Levante asta tanto que por hallarse estropeado en servicio de su magestad pidio licencia al señor don Juan para venirse en España a pedir se le hiziese merced y yo entonces le di carta de recomendacion para su magestad y ministros y habiendose embarcado en la galera Sol fue preso de turcos y llevado a Argel donde al presente esta esclavo haviendo peleado antes que le captivasen muy bien y cumplido con lo que debia y de manera que assi por haver captivado en servicio de su magestad como por haver perdido una mano en el dicho servicio meresce que su magestad le haga toda merced y ayuda para su rescate y porque las fees cartas y recaudos que traya de sus servicios los perdio todos el dia que le hizieron esclavo para que conste dello di la presente firmada de mi mano y sellada con el sello de mis armas y refrendada del secretario infrascripto. Dada en Madrid a 25 de jullio 1573

El duque [firma]

Por mandado de su excelencia

Juan de León [rúbrica]

ojo a la glosa que va abaxo de la que se le a dado por merced [rúbrica]

Su merced a suplica de doña Leonor Cortinas y en *consideracion* de lo en esta certificacion contenido hizo merced de dar licencia *para que* del reyno de Valencia se pudiesen llevar a *Argel dos* mile ducados de mercaderias no prohividas con que *el* dicho beneficio de la dicha licencia sirviesen de rrescate de Miguel *de* Cerbantes en esta fee contenido y asi se dio el *derecho* a las partes que es fecha en Madrid a XVII de henero de *1580*

[rúbrica] esta merced desta cedula no esta aun despachada ni vendida
                porque no dan por ella sino sesenta ducados

Fee de bienes [roto lo que sigue]

Informacion de servicios.   En Madrid a 29 de mayo de
1590
ante un alcalde 1578   se presenta [rúbrica]

—En la villa de Madrid a diez e siete dias del mes
de março de mile e quinientos e setenta y ocho años ante
el ilustre señor licenciado Ximenez Hortiz del consejo de
su magestad alcaldes en su casa e *corte* e por [quanto] ante
my Francisco de Yepes escrivano de su majestad e de
probincia en esta corte parescio presente Rodrigo de
Cerbantes e presento en pedimiento e ynterogatorio de
preguntas que su tenor de lo cual es como se sigue
—Illustre señor Rodrigo de Cerbantes estando en
esta corte digo que a Miguel de Cerbantes my hijo que al
presente esta cautibo en Argel y a mi como su padre
conbiene averiguar y probar como el dicho Miguel de
Cerbantes my hijo a serbido a su magestad de diez años a
esta parte hasta que abra dos años que le cautibaron en la
galera del Sol *en que* benia Carrillo de Quesada y por que
en todas las ocasiones que en el dicho tienpo se ofrescieron
en Italia y en la Goleta y Tunez y en la batalla nabal en la
cual salio herido de dos arcabuzazos y estropeado la mano
hizquierda de la cual no se puede serbir en lo cual hiço
como muy buen soldado sirbiendo a su magestad a vuestra
merced pido e suplico mande rescibir la dicha
ynformacion de lo susodicho y rescibida me la mande dar
signada en la forma en manera que haga fee para la
presentar ante quien y con derecho deba e pidio justicia e
para ello etc Rodrigo de Cerbantes

—E visto por el dicho señor alcalde mando se tome
e resciban al tenor del dicho pedimiento los testigos que el
dicho Rodrigo de Cerbantes presentare y lo que dixeren
expusieren se lo mando dar signado en publica forma en
manera que haga fee para el hefeto que lo pide y lo firmo
de su nonbre testigos Naba e Sosa escrivanos de probincia
Francisco de Yepes

—Por estas preguntas pido sean esaminados los
testigos que son o fueren presentados por parte de Rodrigo
de Cerbantes estante en esta corte sobre la ynformacion

que a pedido sobre el rrescate de Miguel de Cerbantes su
hijo

I   Primeramente sean preguntados si conoscen al dicho
Rodrigo de Cerbantes y al dicho Miguel de Cerbantes su
hijo catibo

II   Si saben etc que el dicho Miguel de Cerbantes cativo es
hijo legitimo del dicho Rodrigo de Cerbantes y de doña
Leonor de Cortinas su muger legitima abido e procreado
de legitimo matrimonio y por tal a ser criado y alimentado
se nonbra y es abido e tenido y comunmente reputado
entre todas las personas que los conoscen y dellos an
tenido o tienen noticia e ansi es publico e notorio

III   Si saben etc que el dicho Miguel de Cerbantes es *de*
hedad de treynta años poco mas o menos y de diez años a
esta parte a serbido como muy buen soldado a su magestad
el Rey don Felipe nuestro señor en las guerras que a
tenydo en Italia y la Goleta y en Tunez y en la batalla nabal
que el señor don Juan de Austria tubo con el armada del
turco de donde salio herido de dos arcabuzazos en el pecho
y otro en la mano hizquierda que quedo estropeado della
digan lo que saben

IIII   Si saven etc que la dicha batalla nabal se rreconoscio el
armada del turco estava el dicho Miguel de Cerbantes con
calentura y unos amigos suyos le dixeron que pues estava
tan malo que se metiese debaxo de la cubierta de la galera
pues no estaba sano para pelear y el dicho Miguel de
Cerbantes respondio que no haçia lo que debia metiendose
so cubierta sino que mejor hera morir como buen soldado
en el serbicio de Dios e del rrei y asi peleo como baliente
soldado en el lugar del esquife como su capitan le mando y
despues de la batalla sabido por el señor don Juan de
Austria quan bien le abia serbido le acrecento quatro
ducados mas de su paga

V   Si saben etc que podria aver dos años poco mas o
menos que binyendo de Italia a España en la galera del Sol
en que benia Carrillo de Quesada catibaron turcos de Argel

al dicho Miguel de Cerbantes a donde al presente esta cautibo

VI   Si saben etc que el dicho Rodrigo de Cerbantes es honbre hijo dalgo y muy pobre que no tiene bienes ningunos porque por aver rrecatado a otro hijo que ansi mesmo le cautibaron la mesma ora que al dicho su hermano quedo sin bienes algunos

Testigo

En Madrid a veynte dias del mes de março de myle e quinientos y setenta e ocho años el dicho Rodrigo de Cerbantes para la dicha ynformacion presento por testigo a Mateo de Santisteban alferez de la conpañya del capitan Alonso de Carlos uno de los capitanes probeidos por su magestad en este año de setenta e ocho y nattural que es este testigo de Tudela de Nabarra estante en esta corte del qual fue tomado e rescibido juramento en forma debida e de derecho e quedo de descir berdad e preguntado por el ynterrogatorio presentado por el dicho Rodrigo de Cerbantes dixo lo siguiente

I   A la primera pregunta del dicho ynterrogatorio dixo que conosce al dicho Rodrigo de Cerbantes contenido en la pregunta e ansi mesmo conosce a Miguel de Cerbantes su hijo cautibo que esta en la ciudad de Argel a los quales conosce al dicho Rodrigo de Cerbantes de dos años a esta parte e al dicho Miguel de Cerbantes de ocho años a esta parte

Generales

Fue preguntado por las preguntas generales de la lei dixo que es de hedad de treynta años poco mas o menos e no es pariente de ninguno de los contenidos en la primera pregunta ny le toca ninguna de las preguntas generales de la lei que le fueron hechas

II   A la segunda pregunta del dicho ynterrogatorio dixo que a oydo descir para publico e notorio en esta corte de dos años a esta parte que el dicho Miguel de Cerbantes cautibo es hijo legitimo del dicho Rodrigo de Zerbantes e de la dicha doña Leonor de Cortinas su muger e por tal es abido e tenido e comunmente reputado lo qual a oydo descir a los dichos sus padres e a otras personas de crédito en esta corte que no se acuerda de sus nombres por lo qual le tiene este testigo al dicho Miguel de Cerbantes por hijo legitimo de los dichos sus padres que corresponde a la pregunta

III   A la tercera pregunta dixo que abra ocho años poco mas o menos que este testigo bio e començo a conoscer al dicho Miguel de Cerbantes que fue el dia que el señor don Juan dio batalla a la armada del turco en la mar a las bocas de Leopant y entonces podia ser de hedad el dicho Miguel de Cerbantes de hasta veynte e dos o veynte e tres años e agora podra tener treynta años o treynta e un años poco mas o menos que el dicho dia de la batalla que el dicho señor don Juan de Austria dio a la armada turquesca este dia bio que el dicho Miguel de Cerbantes sirbio en la dicha batalla y era soldado de la conpañia del capitan Diego de Urbina en la galera Marquesa de Juan Andrea en el cuerno de tierra y que un año antes abia que el dicho Miguel de Cerbantes serbia en la dicha conpañia porque lo bio asi mismo este testigo en el cual dicho tienpo e batalla bio este testigo que el dicho Miguel de Cerbantes de la dicha batalla nabal salio herido de dos arcabuzaços en el pecho y en una mano yzquierda o derecha de que quedo estropeado de la dicha mano y este testigo bio que el dicho Miguel de Cerbantes sirbio en la dicha batalla a su magestad como buen soldado porque este testigo se hallo presente asi mismo por ser soldado de la misma conpañya

IIII   A la quarta pregunta del dicho ynterrogatorio de lo que save que es verdad que quando se rreconoscio el armada del turco en la dicha batalla nabal el dicho Miguel de Cerbantes estava malo y con calentura y el dicho su capitan y este testigo e otros muchos amigos suyos le dixeron que pues estava enfermo y con calentura que se estubiese quedo a bordo en la camara de la galera y el dicho Miguel de Cerbantes respondio que que dirian del e que no hacia lo que debia e que mas queria morir peleando por Dios e por su rei que no meterse so cubierta e que su salud e asi bio este testigo que peleo como baliente soldado con los dichos turcos en la dicha batalla en el lugar del esquife como su capitan le mando y le dio horden con otros soldados y acabada la batalla como el señor don Juan supo y entendio quan bien lo abia hecho y peleado el dicho Miguel de Cerbantes le acrecento y le dio quattro ducados mas de su paga y este testigo lo save por lo aber visto por vista de ojos e por aver sido soldado con el dicho Miguel de Cerbantes en una capitanya y esto responde a la pregunta

V   A la quinta pregunta dixo que sabe que abra dos años y medio o tres poco mas o menos que estando este testigo en Napoles estava el dicho Miguel de Cerbantes en la dicha ciudad que abia de benir a España y le pregunto que en que galera abia de benir e le dixo que en la galera del Sol con Carrillo de Quesada y ansi se partio de este testigo diziendo se benia a España y despues de alli a tres meses supo y entendio este testigo de personas ciertas e berdaderas que la dicha galera del Sol abian tomado turcos y abian cautibado al dicho Miguel de Cerbantes con ottros soldados e llebado los a Argel adonde despues a entendido por cosa muy cierta que estava cautibo en la dicha ciudad de Argel y a dicho Grabiel de Castañeda soldado e otros que an benido de Argel e que le bieron cautibo aya en Argel al dicho Miguel de Cerbantes y esto rresponde a la pregunta y ansi este testigo le tiene por honbre que al presente esta cautibo porque no a oydo descir sea ya rrescatado

VI   A la sesta pregunta dixo que este testigo tiene al dicho Rodrigo de Cerbantes por tal persona como la pregunta lo dize e que es muy pobre e no tiene vienes con que poder rrescatar al dicho Miguel de Cerbantes su hijo porque por aver rrescatado a otro hijo que le cautibaron en la dicha armada quedo sin vienes algunos porque ansi es publico e notorio a este testigo por los conoscer como los conosce del tienpo aca que dicho tiene y esto es la verdad e lo que save para el juramento que hiço e firmo lo de su nonbre Mateo de Santisteban poso ante mi Francisco de Yepes

En este dia para la dicha ynformacion el dicho Rodrigo de Cerbantes presento por testigo al alferez Grabiel de Castañeda natural de la montaña del balle de Cariedo del lugar de Salaya estante en esta corte del qual fue rrescibido juramento en forma de derecho e quedo de descir berdad e preguntado por las preguntas de su ynterrogatorio dixo e depuso lo siguiente

I   A la primera pregunta dixo que conosce al dicho Rodrigo de Cerbantes de tres años a esta parte e conosce al dicho Miguel de Cerbantes su hijo de siete años a esta parte e que esta cautibo en Argel

Generales

Fue preguntado por las preguntas generales de la lei dixo que es de hedad de veynte e cinco años poco mas o menos e que no es pariente de los susodichos ny le toca ninguna de las preguntas generales de la lei que le fueron hechas

II   A la segunda pregunta dixo que este testigo tiene al dicho Miguel de Cerbantes cabtibo por hijo legitimo del dicho Rodrigo de Cerbantes e de la dicha doña Leonor de Cortinas su muger por que asi se lo oyo descir al dicho Miguel de Cerbantes en la ciudad de Argel do esta cautibo y en esta corte a personas que los conoscen y esto es publico e notorio

III   A la tercera pregunta del dicho ynterrogatorio dixo que el dicho Miguel de Cerbantes al parescer de este testigo sera de hedad de treynta años poco mas o menos e tal paresce por su aspecto y que este testigo save que el dicho Miguel de Cerbantes a serbido a su magestad en todas las ocasiones de guerra que se an suscedido ansi en la batalla nabal que tubo el señor don Juan con la armada turquesca como en las demas partes e lugares que se an ofrescido ansi en la Goleta como en otras partes que a abido ocasion porque este testigo lo a bisto e conoscio en la dicha armada e guerra nabal y en La Goleta de los siete años a esta parte poco mas o menos que le conosce y esto rresponde a la pregunta

IIII   A la quarta pregunta del dicho ynterrogatorio dixo que save este testigo e bio que al tienpo e saçon que se rreconoscio el armada del turco por nuestra armada española el dicho Miguel de Cerbantes estava malo con calentura y este testigo bio que su capitan e otros amigos suyos le dixeron que pues estava malo no pelease e se rretirase e baxase debaxo de cubierta de la dicha galera porque no estava para pelear y entonces bio este testigo que el dicho Miguel de Cerbantes respondio al dicho capitan e a los demas que le abian dicho lo susodicho muy enojado señores en todas las ocasiones que asta oi en dia se an ofrescido de guerra a su magestad y se me a mandado e serbido muy bien como buen soldado y ansi agora no are menos aunque este enfermo e con calentura mas bale pelear en serbicio de Dios e de su magestad e morir por ellos que no baxarme so cubierta e que el capitan le pusiese en la parte e lugar que fuese mas peligrosa e que alli estaria e moriria peleando como dicho tenia y ansi el dicho capitan le entrego el lugar del esquifee con doze soldados adonde bio este testigo que peleo muy balientemente como buen soldado contra los dichos turcos hasta que se acabo la dicha batalla de donde salio herido en el pecho de un arcabuçaço y de una mano de que salio estropeado y sabido por el dicho señor don Juan quan bien lo abia hecho le acreecento quattro o seis escudos de bentaja de mas de su paga y esto save este testigo por averse allado presente en la dicha armada y aberlo bisto y esto rresponde a la pregunta

V   A la quinta pregunta del dicho ynterrogatorio dixo que abra dos años poco mas o menos que estando este testigo cautibo en Argel fue cierto que un capitan turco de Argel topo e cautibo la galera del Sol que la pregunta dize y truxo cabtibo al dicho Miguel de Cerbantes e a otros muchos soldados españoles y al presente esta cautibo el dicho Miguel de Cerbantes en la dicha ciudad de Argel el mesmo capitan que tomo la dicha galera el qual tiene en mucho su rrescate por averle hallado al dicho Miguel de Cerbantes cartas de su alteça del señor don Juan para su magestad en que le suplicaba le diese una conpañia de las que se hiciesen en España para Italia pues hera honbre de merito y serbicios porque este testigo las leyo en Argel al tienpo que le cautibaron y este testigo le dexo cautibo abra dos años poco menos porque luego como el dicho Miguel de Cerbantes fue cautibo de alli a pocos dias se rrescato este testigo e traxo del cartas para sus padres y esto rresponde a la pregunta

VI A la sesta pregunta dixo que este testigo tiene al dicho Rodrigo de Cerbantes por hijodalgo e que es muy pobre que no tiene bienes ningunos porque por aver rrescatado otro hijo que asi mysmo le cautibaron el mismo dia que al dicho Miguel de Cerbantes quedo pobre e sin bienes algunos y esto save por los conoscer como los conosce este testigo de tienpo que dicho tiene e tanbien bio cautibo en Argel otro hermano del dicho Miguel de Cerbantes que agora an rescatado y esta es la verdad e lo que save deste caso para el juramento que hiço y firmolo de su nonbre Grabiel de Castañeda paso ante mi Francisco de Yepes

Testigo

Este dicho dia mes e año susodicho el dicho Rodrigo de Cerbantes para la dicha ynformacion presento por testigo a Antonio Godinez de Monsalbe natural e vezino desta villa e Sargento de Don Juan de la Carzel capitan de ynfanteria por su magestad

Testigo susodicho del qual fue rrescibido juramento en forma de derecho e quedo de descir berdad e preguntado por el dicho ynterrogatorio dixo lo siguiente

I A la primera pregunta dixo que conosce al dicho Rodrigo de Cerbantes de cinco meses a esta parte e conosce al dicho Miguel de Cerbantes de cinco años a esta parte que fue desde la jornada de Tunez el qual esta cautibo al presente si de cinco años a esta parte no se a librado

Generales

Fue preguntado por las preguntas generales de la lei dixo que es de hedad de veynte e cinco años poco mas o menos e no le ba ynteres en esta ynformacion

II   A la segunda pregunta dixo que este testigo tiene al dicho Miguel de Cerbantes cautibo por hijo legitimo del dicho Rodrigo de Cerbantes e de doña Leonor de Cortinas su muger e por tal es abido e tenido por las personas que le conoscen e conoscen a los dichos sus padres como este testigo

III   A la tercera pregunta dixo que al parescer deste testigo el dicho Miguel de Cerbantes podra aver e ser de hedad de treynta años poco mas o menos e que a oido descir este testigo a personas de credito soldados y capitanes que el dicho Miguel de Cerbantes a serbido a su magestad de diez años a esta parte en todas las ocasiones de guerra que se an ofrescido ansi en Italia como en la batalla nabal e jornada de Nabarino y este testigo le bio serbir en la jornada de Tunes que el señor don Juan hiço abra cinco años al qual le bio serbir como buen soldado en la dicha guerra e que este testigo a bisto al dicho Miguel de Cerbantes una mano estropeada el qual le dixo que en la dicha batalla nabal le abian dado un arcabuzaço e tanbien lo a oydo descir a otras muchas personas que se hallaron en la dicha batalla nabal como el dicho Miguel de Cerbantes abia peleado muy balientemente en la dicha batalla e que della abia salido herido del dicho arcabuçaço en la dicha mano y esto rresponde a la pregunta

IIII   A la quarta pregunta dixo que dize lo que dicho tiene en la pregunta antes desta a que se rrefiere e que todo contenido en la pregunta lo a oydo descir aver sido berdad lo en ella contenido a muchas personas soldados e capitanes que lo bieron que de sus nonbres no se acuerda
V   A la quinta pregunta dixo que es berdad que el dicho Miguel de Cerbantes fue cautibo del capitan del mar turco e del imam y otro capitan de otra galera que rresidian e rresiden en Argel abra dos años e medio poco mas o menos e le cautibaron quando tomaron los dichos

capitanes turcos la dicha galera del Sol que la pregunta dize
y este testigo le bio traer cautibo juntamente con ottro
hermano suyo que se dize Rodrigo de Cerbantes e que abra
cinco meses poco mas o menos que este testigo bino de
Argel rrescatado porque ansi mesmo estava cautibo
quando el dicho Miguel de Cerbantes e Rodrigo de
Cerbantes su hermano los traxeron [a] Argel cautibos los
dichos turcos y este testigo le dexo al dicho Miguel de
Cerbantes cautibo de un turco que hera el propio capitan
del mar e agora a sabido que esta en poder de Cenaga rrey
de Argel por lo qual sino se a librado de los cinco meses a
esta parte que este testigo le dexo cautibo esta al presente
cautibo en la dicha ciudad de Argel y esto es publico y
notorio

VI   A la sesta pregunta dixo que save que el dicho Rodrigo
de Cerbantes es onbre hijo dalgo e muy pobre e que por
aver rrescatado al dicho Rodrigo de Cerbantes su hijo que
bino rrescatado con este testigo no tiene bienes algunos de
que poder rrescatar al dicho Miguel de Cerbantes cautibo e
si los tubiera este testigo lo supiera y entendiera por le
conoscer como le conosce muy bien e sabe la hazienda que
tiene que no tiene ninguna para poder hazer el dicho
rrescate y esto es la verdad para el juramento que hiço e
firmolo Antonio Godinez de Monsalbe paso ante mi
Francisco de Yepes

Testigo

En la villa de Madrid a primero dia del mes de abrile de
myle e quinientos y setenta e ocho años el dicho Rodrigo
de Zerbantes para la dicha ynformacion presento por
testigo a don Beltran del Santo e de Castilla rresidente en
esta corte del qual fue rrescibido juramento en forma de
derecho e quedo de descir berdad e preguntado por las
preguntas de su ynterrogatorio dixo e depuso lo siguiente

I   A la primera pregunta dixo que conosce al dicho
Rodrigo de Cerbantes e conosce al dicho Miguel de
Zerbantes su hijo cautibo a los quales conosce al dicho

Rodrigo de Cerbantes de un año a esta parte y al dicho Miguel de Cerbantes su hijo de tres años a esta parte

Generales

Fue preguntado por las preguntas generales dixo que es de hedad de veynte e ocho años poco mas o menos e no es pariente de los dichos Rodrigo ni Miguel de Zerbantes ny le ba ynteres en esta ynformacion

II   A la segunda pregunta del dicho ynterrogatorio dixo que tiene al dicho Miguel de Cerbantes por hijo legitimo del dicho Rodrigo de Cerbantes e doña Leonor de Cortinas su muger e por tal es abido e tenido y ansi es publico e notorio

III   A la tercera pregunta del dicho ynterrogatorio dixo que este testigo tiene al dicho Miguel de Cerbantes cautibo por de hedad de treynta años que la pregunta dize e tal paresce por su aspecto quando le dexo este testigo cautibo que abra un año e que a oydo descir a soldados y capitanes que de sus nonbres no tiene memoria que el dicho Miguel de Cerbantes a serbido a su magestad de diez años a esta parte en todas las ocasiones de guerra que se le an ofrescido ansi en la dicha batalla nabal que obo por el señor don Juan con la armada del turco adonde el dicho Miguel de Cerbantes salio herido de una mano de tal manera que esta manco della y que este testigo le a bisto que de la dicha mano hizquierda esta manco de tal manera que no la puede mandar

IIII   A la quarta pregunta del dicho ynterrogatorio dixo que todo lo contenido en la dicha pregunta lo a oydo este testigo descir a capitanes e soldados principales que se hallaron en la batalla nabal que la pregunta dize e que paso por el dicho Miguel de Cerbantes todo lo en ella contenido como en ella lo declara e que por raçon de aberlo hecho tan bien el dicho Miguel de Cerbantes en la dicha batalla e peleado como buen soldado el dicho señor don Juan le abia acrescentado quatro ducados mas de paga y esto rresponde a la pregunta

V   A la quinta pregunta dixo que abra quatro años que a
este testigo cautibaron en la goleta turcos a donde fue
llebado a Argel y abiendo estado cautibo un año bio que el
dicho Miguel de Cerbantes bino cautibo de turcos a la dicha
ciudad de Argel que le abian cautibado en la galera del Sol
que la pregunta dize y este testigo le ablo e trato tienpo de
obra de un año e medio en la dicha ciudad de Argel a
donde le dexo como benia de Italia e que en la dicha galera
que la pregunta dize le abian cautibado y este testigo abra
un año que se rrescato del dicho cautiberio y al tienpo que
se bino para España dexo cautibo al dicho Miguel de
Cerbantes en la dicha ciudad de Argel en poder de un turco
llamado Arnaurio Mami capitan en la dicha ciudad de
Argel el qual le tenia en mucha estima por rrespeto de
ciertas cartas de recomendacion que le abia hallado al
dicho cautibo del señor don Juan y duque de Cesar para
que su magestad le hiciese merced ofreciendose de una
conpañia como persona que lo merescio muy bien y por
este rrespeto le tienen en posesion de honbre de mucho
rrescate y esto lo save por lo aber bisto y este testigo cree y
tiene entendido y es cierto que si de un año a esta parte no
se a rrescatado que todabia y al presente esta cautibo por
averle dexado como dicho tiene este testigo abra un año
cautibo en Argel en poder del turco que dicho tiene y
despues aca a sabido y entendido que el rrey de Argel le a
tomado e le tiene por le tener por honbre de gran rrescate
por rrespeto de las cartas que se le hallaron como dicho
tiene del dicho señor don Juan e del duque de Cesar y esto
responde a la pregunta

VI   A la sexta pregunta dixo que tiene al dicho Rodrigo de
Zerbantes por honbre hijo dalgo como la pregunta lo dize
e que tanbien save que es muy pobre e que por aver
rescatado a otro hijo suyo que se dize Rodrigo de Cerbantes
que tanbien le cautibaron el propio dia que al dicho Miguel
de Cerbantes a quedado sin bienes algunos para poder
rescatar al dicho Miguel de Cerbantes e si los tubiera este
testigo lo supiera y entendiera por tener noticia de su
hacienda conoscimyento y esto es la verdad para el

juramento *que* hiço e firmolo de su nonbre don Beltran
del Salto y de Castilla

Paso ante my Francisco de Yepes. / E yo Francisco de Yepes
escrivano de su magestad y de probincia en esta corte y
presente fui a lo que dicho es en uno con los dichos
testigos y de pedimiento del dicho Rodrigo de Cerbantes [la
siguiente leyenda junto con la rúbrica se encuentran
insertas en medio del párrafo en el original] el licenciado
Ximenez Ortiz [rúbrica] [continúa el texto normal] e por
mandado del dicho señor alcalde que aqui firmo su
nombre lo fize escrivir y fize aqui my sig*no* que es atras *en*
testimonio *de* verdad

Francisco de Yepes

[rúbrica]

Informacion de como fue cabtivo y lo esta y como a
servido a su magestad en la guerra e de su probanza

Probanza de Miguel de Cerbantes

A su merced a suplicacion de doña Leonor Cortinas y en
consideracion de lo en esta ynformacion y en una fee que
dio el duque de Sesar contenido hizo merced de dar
licencia para que del reyno de Valencia se pudiesen llebar a
Argel dos mille ducados de mercaderias no prohividas con
que el dicho beneficio de la dicha licencia sirviese para su
rrescate de Miguel de Cerbantes su hijo en esta
ynformacion contenido y asi se dio el despacho a las partes
de que se da esta fee. Fecha en Madrid a XVII de henero de
1580

[rúbrica]

CURRICULUM VITAE[*]
MIGUEL DE CERVANTES SAAVEDRA

Information concerning Miguel de Cervantes, of how he has served His Majesty and of what he has done while being held captive in Algiers. And by the Duke of Sesa's certification here presented, it which will show that when they [the Turks] captured him, he lost much information, documents, and papers he carried regarding his service to His Majesty.

Miguel de Cervantes Saavedra requests favorable consideration regarding one of the positions he is seeking:

—accountancy of the New World
—home office of Soconusco
—auditor of the galleys of Cartagena
—magistracy of La Paz

Doctor Nuñez, narrator   Juan de Ledesma

    —He has served for the last 22 years; in the naval battle there, he lost a hand when he was shot with an arquebus.
    —The following year he went to Navarino, and later to Tunez and La Goleta.
    —While on his way to this court, so that His Majesty might favor him, he was captured on the galley Sol, together with his brother, with whom he had served in said campaigns, and taken to Algiers, where they spent his patrimony, his father's estate, and the dowries of two brothers on his ransom.
    —Once ransomed, they went to serve in Portugal, together with the Marquis of Santa Cruz.
    —One of them currently serves as a lieutenant in Flanders.

*Archivo General de Indias, Seville. Patronato Real, Legajo 253, Ramos
    1 and 2, Tira 1.
The italics appearing in the transcription indicate illegible text due to
    a damaged original.—M. G.-M.

—This Miguel de Cervantes arrived with letters from the mayor of Mistayta, and went to Oran by order of His Majesty.

—Later,in Seville, he took part in business regarding the fleet, by order of Antonio de Guebara.

—He requests that he be granted the accountancy of the New World

or the home office of Soconusco,

or the accountancy of the galleys of Cartagena,

or the magistracy of La Paz

He is well-qualified for any position and will give a good accounting.

[in the margin]

A certification from the Duke of Alba [sic] containing an account of his naval services and of the loss of the hand.

To that effect, he gave permission for merchandise to be sent from Valencia to Algiers to serve as ransom.

A report on the request for assistance by his father before a mayor in 1578, while his son was being held captive.

Information on what happened to him in captivity, as well as the costs and expenses of the ransom, presented to a redeemer of captives in Algiers and of his services.

[Certification of the Duke of Sessa]

The Duke of Sessa

Having asked me on behalf of, and in the name of, Miguel de Cervantes, that I indicate to His Grace the manner in which he has served him, it is to his benefit that I testify of it: I hereby certify and declare that I have known him for several years regarding his service to His Majesty, and from the information I possess, I know, and make known, that he was present at the battle and defeat of the Turkish fleet in which, while fighting as a good soldier, he lost a hand and, later, I saw him serve in other campaigns that took place in Levante until such time as he found himself crippled in the service of His Majesty, and asked permission of don Juan to return to Spain to request that he be granted a favor, and I, then, gave him a letter of recommendation for His Majesty and his ministers. And having embarked on the galley Sol, he was captured by the Turks and taken to Algiers, where he is presently a captive. Having fought valiantly before they captured him, and having fulfilled his obligations, so that now, having been captured in the service of His Majesty, and for having lost a hand in said service, he deserves that His Majesty grant him all possible favor and help with his ransom. And because the documents, letters and papers he carried regarding his tour of duty were all lost the day he was captured, in order to vouch for this, I delivered this document, signed by my hand, and sealed with the seal of my arms, and witnessed by the undersigned secretary. Executed in Madrid, 25 July, 1573.

The Duke [signature]

By order of His Excellency.

Juan de Leon [rubric]

Attention to the gloss appearing below that which has been mercifully granted him [rubric].

His Grace, at the request of doña Leonor Cortinas, and with due *consideration* of the contents of this certificate, mercifully granted the petition *so that* the kingdom of Valencia might send to *Algiers two* thousand ducats of non-prohibited merchandise, so that benefit of said petition might serve as ransom for Miguel *de* Cervantes, mentioned in this document, and thus the petition of the parties was granted. Executed in Madrid, 17 January, 1580.

[rubric] The granting of this petition is not yet dispatched or sold because they will only give sixty ducats

List of property [the rest of the document is damaged]

Information concerning services   In Madrid, 29 May,
                                   1590.
Before a mayor   is presented. [rubric]

—In the city of Madrid, 17 March, 1578, before the illustrious licentiate, Ximenez Hortiz, of His Majesty's council, the mayors of his house *and court*, and, also, before me, Francisco de Yepes, scrivener to His Majesty and to the province. Rodrigo de Cervantes was present in this court and submitted a request and inquiry, as follows:

—The illustrious Rodrigo de Cervantes, appearing before this court: "I declare concerning Miguel de Cervantes, my son, presently being held captive in Algiers, that I, as his father, am constrained to find out and prove how said Miguel de Cervantes, my son, has served Your Majesty for the last ten years, until two years ago when they captured him on the galley Sol *on which* Carillo de Quesada traveled, and because on all occasions of war that presented themselves during said time period in Italy, the Goleta, and Tunez, and in the naval battle in which he [Miguel de Cervantes], while performing as a very good soldier in the service of His Majesty, was wounded by two arquebus shots, which crippled his left hand, rendering it useless, I [therefore] request and supplicate His Majesty to obtain the said information regarding the aforementioned, and, once received, have it sent to me, signed in the form which certifies it for the presentation to whomever it may and should concern, and who sought justice concerning it, etc." Rodrigo de Cervantes.

—Once [the document] is seen by said mayor, I order that he take it and that the witness receive it in accordance with said petition that said Rodrigo de Cervantes will present; and whatever they say and explain, I order to be handed over, signed in public form, so that it may be certified for the effects required. The witnesses, Naba and Sosa. Scrivener of the province, Francisco de Yepes.

—Concerning these questions, I request that the *witnesses* be examined that are or will be presented on behalf of Rodrigo de Cervantes, in attendance in this court, regarding the information that has been requested concerning the ransom of Miguel de Cervantes, his son.

I First, they need be asked if they know said Rodrigo de Cervantes and said Miguel de Cervantes, his captive son.

II If they know, etc., that said captive Miguel de Cervantes is the legitimate son of said Rodrigo de Cervantes and of doña Leonor de Cortinas, his legitimate wife, had and conceived in lawful marriage, and so being raised and nurtured, was named; and it is given and understood and generally known among all people who know them and have had or have news of them; it is therefore public and well known.

III If they know, etc., that said Miguel de Cervantes is approximately 30 years old, and that as of the last ten years since this report, he has served as a very good soldier to His Majesty, King Phillip, Our Lord in the wars he has waged in Italy, the Goleta and Tunez, and in the naval battle that His Grace Juan de Austria fought against the Turkish fleet, where he [Miguel de Cervantes] was wounded by two arquebus blasts, one in the chest and the other in the left hand, which has rendered him disabled. Let them speak that which they know.

IIII If they know, etc., that in said naval battle, that when the Turkish fleet was sighted said Miguel de Cervantes had a fever, and some of his friends told him that since he was so sick, he should stay below deck, for he was too sick to fight; and said Miguel de Cervantes answered that he would not be doing his duty by staying below deck, and that it was better to die as a good soldier in the service of God and the king, and so he fought as a valiant soldier near the skiff, as his captain had commanded him, and after the battle, once it was known by Juan de Austria how well he had served, he increased his pay by four ducats.

V If they know, etc., that approximately two years could have passed since [the time when] Miguel de Cervantes, while coming from Italy to Spain in the galley Sol, in which Carrillo de Quesada traveled, was captured by Turks of Algiers, and he is presently being held captive there.

VI   If they know, etc., that said Rodrigo de Cervantes is a gentleman hidalgo and so poor that he does not have any property, since he has already ransomed another son who they [the Turks] had captured in the same way and at the same time as the said brother, and he [the father] was left without any property.

Witness

In Madrid, 20 March, 1578, said Rodrigo de Cervantes presented as a witness for said information Mateo de Santisteban, lieutenant in the company of Captain Alonso de Carlos, one of the captains appointed by His Majesty in this year of '78.   This witness is a native of Tudela of Navarre in attendance in this court, from whom testimony was taken and received in the prescribed and lawful manner.   And he swore to tell the truth and, when questioned according to the interrogatory put forth by said Rodrigo de Cervantes, he [Mateo de Santisteban] said the following:

I   To the first question of said inquiry, he declared that he knows said Rodrigo de Cervantes mentioned in the question, and he also knows Miguel de Cervantes, his son, held captive in the city of Algiers;   he has known said Rodrigo de Cervantes for the last two years, and said Miguel de Cervantes for the last eight years.

Generalities

He was asked the general questions of the law, and said the he was approximately 30 years old, and is not related to either of the aforementioned in the first question, and that no additional general law questions posed to him concerned him.

II   To the second question of said inquiry, he replied in this court that he has heard said publicly and openly that for the last two years said Miguel de Cervantes, captive, is the legitimate son of said Rodrigo de Cervantes and said doña Leonor de Cortinas, his wife, and as such is had and held and is commonly known, and this has been stated by his aforementioned parents and by other reliable people in this court, whose names he does not recall. Thus, this witness holds that said Miguel de Cervantes is the legitimate son of said parents, as put forth in the question.

III   To the third question he said that approximately eight years ago, this witness saw and began to know said Miguel de Cervantes, and that it was the day that don Juan engaged the Turkish fleet on the sea at the mouth of Leopant, and at that time it was possible that Miguel de Cervantes could have been 22 or 23 years old, and now he could be approximately 30 or 31 years old, and that said day of the battle on which said don Juan de Austria fought the Turkish fleet, [Mateo de Santisteban] saw that said Miguel de Cervantes served in said battle, and that he was a soldier in the company of Captain Diego de Urbina on the galley Marquesa of Juan Andrea of the horn of land and that one year earlier, said Miguel de Cervantes served in said company, because it was seen to be so by this same witness; at the said time and battle, this witness saw that said Miguel de Cervantes in said naval battle was wounded by two arquebus blasts, one in the chest and one in either the left or right hand, which was left crippled, and this witness saw that said Miguel de Cervantes served as a good soldier in said battle for His Majesty, because this witness was likewise present, being a soldier in the same company.

IIII   To the fourth question of said inquiry concerning what he knows to be the truth, when the Turkish fleet was sighted in said naval battle, said Miguel de Cervantes was sick with a fever, and said captain and this witness and many other friends of his told him that since he was sick with a fever that he should stay below board in the cabin of the galley, and said Miguel de Cervantes responded [by asking] what they would say of him, [by saying] that he would not be doing his duty, and that he would rather die fighting for God and his king than than go below deck, and

[also] that his health was as mentioned. And this witness saw that he fought near the skiff as a valiant soldier against said Turks in said battle, as his captain commanded him and gave him orders, along with the other soldiers. And once the battle was over, and don Juan had discovered and understood how well said Miguel de Cervantes had performed and fought, he increased his pay by four ducats. And this witness knows it, having seen it with his own eyes and having been a soldier with said Miguel de Cervantes in a captaincy and this answers the question.

V   To the fifth question he said that he knows that approximately two and a half or three years ago, while this witness was in Naples, said Miguel de Cervantes was in said city and was to go to Spain, and he asked him in which galley he was to travel, and he told him that [he would travel] in the galley Sol with Carrillo de Quesada, and he thus he took leave of this witness, saying that he was going to Spain. Three months later this witness found out and understood from reliable and trustworthy people that said galley, the Sol, had been captured by the Turks, and that they had captured said Miguel de Cervantes, along with other soldiers, and had taken them to Algiers where [this witness] has heard for certain that he was captive in said city of Algiers. And the soldier Grabiel de Castañeda has said, along with others who came from Algiers, that they witnessed the said Miguel de Cervantes prisoner there in Algiers, and this answers the question. And so this witness considers his still captive, not having heard anything about his being ransomed.

VI   To the sixth question, he said that this witness considers said Rodrigo de Cervantes to be that person to whom the question refers, and that he is very poor and does not have the means by which to ransom said Miguel de Cervantes, his son, having ransomed his other son, who was captured in said fleet, and was left without anything. And this is common knowledge to this witness, since he has known them well during the aforesaid time. And this is the truth and that which he knows for the testimony he gave, and he signed his name, Mateo de Santisteban. Appeared before me, Francisco de Yepes.

On this day, said Rodrigo de Cervantes presented as a witness for the said information lieutenant Grabiel de Castañeda, originally of the mountain of the valley of Cariedo in the area of Salaya, in attendance in this court, from whom testimony was received in the prescribed manner, an he swore to tell the truth, and upon being questioned according to the inquiry, he said and declared the following:

I   To the first question, he said that he has known said Rodrigo de Cervantes for the past three years, and that he has known said Miguel de Cervantes, his son, for the past seven years and that he [Miguel de Cervantes] is a captive in Algiers.

Generalities

He was asked the general questions of the law, and said that he was approximately 25 years old, and that he was not a relative of the aforementioned parties, and that none of the general questions of the law asked him were pertinent.

II   To the second question, he said that this witness considers said Miguel de Cervantes, captive, to be the legitimate son of said Rodrigo de Cervantes and of said doña Leonor de Cortinas, his wife, because this is how he heard it said by Miguel de Cervantes in the city of Algiers, where he is being held, and in this court by people who know them, and this is public and well known.

III   To the third question of said inquiry, he declared that said Miguel de Cervantes, in the opinion of this witness, is approximately 30 years old, and so his appearance would indicate, and that this witness knows that said Miguel de Cervantes has served His Majesty on all occasions of war that have come to pass, including the naval battle that don Juan waged against the Turkish fleet, as well as in other areas and places, including the Goleta and other areas

274 MIGUEL DE CERVANTES SAAVEDRA

where there have been confrontations because this witness has seen it, and knows that in said fleet and naval war and in the Goleta and during the past seven years, approximately, he has known him, and this answers the question.

IIII To the fourth question of said inquiry, this witness replied that he knows and saw that when the Turkish fleet was recognized by our Spanish fleet, said Miguel de Cervantes was sick with a fever, and this witness saw that his captain and other friends told him that since he was sick, he should not fight, but, rather, he should go below deck of said galley because he was not in condition to fight. And then this witness saw that said Miguel de Cervantes responded very angrily to said captain and to the others who had said this to him: "Gentlemen, on all occasions of war that until now have presented themselves to His Majesty, I have been ordered and have served very well as a good soldier and so now I will do no less, although I be sick and with a fever. It is better to fight in the service of God and of His Majesty and die for them than to go below deck." And [he requested] that the captain put him in the area and place of greatest danger, and there he would remain and die fighting as he had said. And so said captain assigned him to the area of the skiff with a dozen soldiers, where this witness saw that he fought valiantly as a good soldier against said Turks until said battle was over, in which he was disabled, having been wounded in the chest and in one hand by an arquebus shot. Once don Juan knew how well he had performed, he granted him a bonus of four or six escudos in addition to his regular pay, and this is known by the witness, since he was present in said fleet and saw it, and this answers the question.

V To the fifth question of said inquiry, he declared that approximately two years ago, this witness being held captive in Algiers, it was certain that a Turkish captain of Algiers came upon and captured the galley Sol that the question mentions, and captured said Miguel de Cervantes, along with many other Spanish soldiers, and at present said Miguel de Cervantes is held captive in said city of Algiers. The same captain that captured said galley is holding Miguel de Cervantes for a very high ransom, having found on him letters of His Highness from don Juan for His Majesty, in which he asked to be given a company among those formed in Spain and destined for Italy, since he was a man of merit and accomplishments. This witness knows this to be true, as he read them in Algiers at the time they captured him, and this witness left him there in captivity two years ago, or a little less, since just as said Miguel de Cervantes was taken captive, a few days later this witness was ransomed, and he brought letters from him to his parents, and this answers the question.

VI   To the sixth question, he said that this witness considers said Rodrigo de Cervantes as an hidalgo, and that he is very poor and has no possessions whatsoever, having already ransomed his other son, who was also taken captive on the same day as was said Miguel de Cervantes; he was left poor and without any possessions. And this he knows because this witness has known them well during the time in question. And he also saw captive in Algiers— although he has not been ransomed—the other brother of Miguel de Cervantes. And this is the truth and what he knows of this case for the testimony he gave, and he signed his name, Grabiel de Castañeda. Appeared before me, Francisco de Yepes.

Witness

On this aforementioned day, month, and year, the said Rodrigo de Cervantes presented as witness for said information Antonio Godinez de Monsalbe, a native resident of this city and a sergeant of don Juan de la Carzel, infantry captain to His Majesty.

The aforementioned witness was sworn in legally and swore to tell the truth, and when questioned according to said inquiry, declared the following:

I   To the first question, he said that he has known said Rodrigo de Cervantes for the past five months, and has known said Miguel de Cervantes for the past five years, that is, since the campaign of Tunez, and he is being held captive if, during the last five years, he has not been freed.

Generalities

He was asked the general questions of the law, and said that he was approximately 25 years old, and [that the rest] had no bearing on this information.

II   To the second question, he said that this witness considers said Miguel de Cervantes, captive, to be the legitimate son of said Rodrigo de Cervantes and of doña Leonor de Cortinas, his wife, and he is recognized as such by people acquainted with him and with his parents, as in the case of this witness.

III   To the third question, he said that, in the opinion of this witness, said Miguel de Cervantes could be approximately 30 years old, and that this witness has heard it said by reliable people, soldiers and captains, that said Miguel de Cervantes has served His Majesty during the past 10 years in all conflicts that have arisen, in Italy, as well as in the naval battle and campaign of Nabarino; and this witness saw him serve in the campaign of Tunez that don Juan waged five years ago, in which he witnessed him serve as a good soldier in said war, and that this witness has seen said Miguel de Cervantes with a crippled hand, which he said was the result of an arquebus shot during said naval battle; and he has also heard it said by many other people who were present at said naval battle how said Miguel de Cervantes had fought most valiantly in said battle, and that he had been wounded in the hand by said arquebus shot and this answers the question.

IIII   To the fourth question, he refers to what he already said in the previous question, and said that he has heard everything contained in the question to be considered true by many people, soldiers and captains, who saw him

[Miguel de Cervantes], but that he does not remember their names.

V   To the fifth question, he said that it is true that said Miguel de Cervantes was taken captive about two and a half years ago by a Turkish sea captain and an imam and another galley captain who resided and reside in Algiers. And said Turkish captains took him captive when they seized said galley Sol, to which the question refers, and this witness saw him taken into captivity, along with another brother of his, named Rodrigo de Cervantes, and that approximately five months ago, this witness, having been ransomed, came from Algiers, where he also had been held captive when said Miguel de Cervantes and Rodrigo de Cervantes, his brother, were taken captive to Algiers by said Turks. And this witness left said Miguel de Cervantes in the hands of the Turks, the aforementioned sea captain, and now he has heard that he is held by Cenega, king of Algiers, and if he has not been freed during the past five months, when this witness last saw him in captivity, then he must presently be held in said city of Algiers, and this is public and well known.

VI   To the sixth question, he said that he knows that said Rodrigo de Cervantes is an hidalgo and very poor, having ransomed said Rodrigo de Cervantes, his son, who was ransomed together with this witness.   He has no possessions with which to ransom said Miguel de Cervantes, captive, and if he did have any, then this witness would know it and be aware of it, since he knows him very well, and is acquainted with his estate, which is insufficient to effect said ransom.   And this is the truth of the testimony he gave, and he signed it Antonio Godinez of Monsalbe.   Appeared before me, Francisco de Yepes.

Witness

In the city of Madrid, 1 April of 1578, said Rodrigo de Cervantes presented as a witness for said information don Beltran del Santo y de Castilla, in attendance of this court, who gave testimony in the prescribed manner and swore to tell the truth, and when asked the questions of the inquiry, he said and declared the following:

I   To the first question, he declared that he knows said Rodrigo de Cervantes and said Miguel de Cervantes, his son, captive. He has known them both, said Rodrigo de Cervantes for the past year, and said Miguel de Cervantes, his son, for the past three years.

Generalities

He was asked the general questions, [and] said that he was approximately 28 years old, and that he is not related to said Rodrigo or Miguel de Cervantes, nor does he have any vested interest in this information.

II   To the second question of said inquiry, he declared that he considers said Miguel de Cervantes to be the legitimate son of said Rodrigo de Cervantes and doña Leonor de Cortinas, and as such he is held and known, and it is public and well known.

III   To the third question of said inquiry, he declared that this witness considers said Miguel de Cervantes, captive, to be approximately 30 years old, as mentioned in the question, and so his appearance would indicate when he left him [Miguel de Cervantes] in captivity a year ago, and he has heard it said by soldiers and captains, whose names he does not recall, that said Miguel de Cervantes has readily served His Majesty during the last 10 years on all occasions of war, and as such he participated in said naval battle that don Juan waged against the Turkish fleet, where said Miguel de Cervantes was wounded in the hand and has thus been crippled, and this witness has seen that he is crippled in the left hand, such that it cannot be used.

IIII   To the fourth question of said inquiry, he declared that this witness has heard everything included in said question to have been uttered by high-ranking captains and soldiers present at the naval battle mentioned in the question, and that what happened to said Miguel de

Cervantes, all of which is contained in the question, is as declared, and that because Miguel de Cervantes had performed so valiantly in said battle, and had fought as a good soldier, said don Juan increased his pay by four ducats, and this answers the question.

V   To the fifth question, he said that four years ago Turks captured this witness in La Goleta, from whence he was taken to Algiers, and, having been held captive one year, he saw said Miguel de Cervantes brought in captivity by the Turks to said city of Algiers, for they had captured him on the galley Sol, referred to in the question. And this witness spoke and dealt with him for the period of a year and a half in said city of Algiers, where he left him. As he was coming from Italy, they [the Turks] captured him on said galley, referred to in the question, and this witness was ransomed a year ago from said captivity, and when he returned to Spain, he left said Miguel de Cervantes in said city of Algiers in the power of a Turk named Arnaurio Mami, captain in said city of Algiers, who held him in high regard because he had discovered on said captive certain certain letters of recommendation from don Juan and the Duke of Cesar, requesting that His Majesty favor him [Miguel de Cervantes] by offering him a company, as he is a most deserving individual. And because of this esteem, they consider him to be a person worthy of a large ransom, and this he [the witness] knows for having seen it. And this witness believes and understands and holds it to be certain that if during the past year he has not been ransomed, then he is presently in captivity, as this witness declares, having left him one year ago in captivity in Algiers in the hands of the Turk, as he declares. And since then he has heard and become aware that the king of Algiers has taken him [Miguel de Cervantes] and now holds him, and believes him to be deserving of a large ransom, because of the letters from said don Juan and the Duke of Cesar that were found on him, as he has declared, and this answers the question.

VI   To the sixth question, he said that he considers said Rodrigo de Cervantes to be an hidalgo as the question indicates, and also that he knows that he is very poor, having ransomed his other son, named Rodrigo de Cervantes, who they captured the same day as said Miguel de Cervantes, and, as a result, he has no possessions left with which to ransom said Miguel de Cervantes; and if he did have them, then this witness would know and be aware of them, since he is acquainted with his estate. And this is the truth concerning the testimony he gave, and he signed in his name, Beltran del Salto y de Castilla.

Appeared before me, Francisco de Yepes. / And I, Francisco de Yepes, scrivener to His Majesty and of the province, in attendance in this court, declare that what I have said accords with the said witnesses and the petition of said Rodrigo de Cervantes [the following words, together with the rubric are inserted in the middle of the paragraph of the original]. The licentiate Ximenez Ortiz [rubric], and by order of said mayor, who signed his name here. I ordered it written, and I made my sign here, on the reverse, in witness of the truth.

Francisco de Yepes

[rubric]

Information on how he was taken captive, how he still is, and how he has served His Majesty in the war, and the proof.

Proof of Miguel de Cervantes

To His Grace, in response to the request of doña Leonor Cortinas, and in consideration of the contents of this information and of the document executed by the Duke of Sesar, generously grants the petition, so that 2000 ducats of non-prohibited merchandise might be sent from the kingdom of Valencia to Algiers, so long as the said benefits of said petition serve to ransom Miguel de Cervantes, her son, mentioned in this information. And thus the issues in this document are resolved. Executed in Madrid, 17 January, 1580.

[rubric]

CONTRIBUTORS

PATRICK H. DUST. Associate Professor of Spanish at
Carleton College. Along with articles on Benito Pérez
Galdós, Federico García Lorca and Jorge Guillén, he
has published primarily in the areas of Literary
Theory and Criticism, and the philosophy of José
Ortega y Gasset. He is currently working on a book
titled (provisionally) *The Ego Between Eros and
Society: Hispanic Forms of Love from The Celestina
to Lorca.*

RUTH EL SAFFAR. Professor of Spanish Literature at
Northwestern University. Author of numerous
essays, especially on the early modern period in
Spain, and four books on Cervantes including
*Distance and Control in Don Quixote: A Study in
Narrative Technique* (1975) and *Beyond Fiction: The
Recovery of the Feminine in the Novels of Cervantes*
(1984).

EDWARD H. FRIEDMAN. Professor of Spanish at Arizona
State University. Author of studies on Spanish
Golden Age literature and contemporary narrative.
His books include *The Unifying Concept: Approaches
to the Structure of Cervantes' Comedias* (1981), and
*The Antiheroine's Voice: Narrative Discourse and
Transformations of the Picaresque* (1987), and he is
co-author (with L. Teresa Valdivieso and Carmelo
Virgillo) of *Aproximaciones al estudio de la literatura
hispánica.*

ANTONIO GOMEZ-MORIANA. Professor of Comparative
Literature and Hispanic Studies, and Director of the
Comparative Literature Program at the Université de
Montréal. Director of the monographic series

"L'univers des discours" (Les Editions du Préambule, Longueuil, Québec). He has written on a wide range of topics including *Lazarillo de Tormes* and the picaresque novel, Cervantes, the Spanish "comedia," Unamuno, Ortega, text and discourse theory. His most recent books are: *La subversion du discours rituel* (Longueuil, Québec, Les Editions du Préambule, 1985) and *El Quijote, juego semiótico* (Amsterdam, Rodopi, forthcoming).

MARGARITA LEVISI. Professor of Spanish Literature at the Ohio State University. She has published articles on Golden Age prose and poetry. Her current research is focused in the area of autobiographical narrative on which she has written a book, *Autobiografías del Siglo de Oro* (1984).

GEORGE MARISCAL. Assistant Professor of Literature at the University of California-San Diego. He has published essays on Calderón, Cervantes and Avellaneda, Spanish and English theatrical practice in the early modern period, and the Chicano novel. He is currently completing a book-length study entitled *The Subject of Seventeenth Century Spain*.

HELEN H. REED. Associate Professor of Spanish at the State University of New York, Oneonta. Author of *The Reader in the Picaresque Novel* (1984) and various essays on the picaresque, reader-response theory, Cervantes, and other Golden Age writers. She is currently working on a biographical and literary study of Ana de Mendoza, the Princess of Eboli.

NICHOLAS SPADACCINI. Professor of Hispanic Studies and Comparative Literature at the University of Minnesota. He has written on Cervantes, the picaresque novel, and Spanish Golden Age drama; has edited a number of Spanish classics including Cervantes's *Entremeses* (1982), and has co-edited *La vida y hechos de Estebanillo González*, 2 vols. (1978), Cervantes's *El Rufián dichoso* and *Pedro de Urdemalas* (1986), *Literature among Discourses. The Spanish Golden Age* (1986) and *The Institutionalization of Literature in Spain* (1987).

JENARO TALENS. Professor of Literary Theory at the Universidad de Valencia, Spain. He has published several books of poetry, has translated into Spanish a number of European classics, including Shakespeare, and has authored many books of criticism and literary theory. Among them are *Novela picaresca y práctica de la transgresión* (1975), *La escritura como teatralidad* (1977), *Escriptura i ideología* (1979), and *Elementos para una semiótica del texto artístico* (1978). Recently his interest in film has been highlighted by a book on Buñuel, *El ojo tachado* (1986).

ANTHONY N. ZAHAREAS. Professor of Hispanic Studies and Comparative Literature at the University of Minnesota. He has written essays on various periods of Spanish literature and culture and is the author of several books and editions, among them, *The Art of Juan Ruiz* (1965), *Visión del esperpento* (with R. Cardona, 1971), *La vida y hechos de Estebanillo González*, 2 vols. (with N. Spadaccini, 1978), and *Plays and Playhouses in Imperial Decadence* (1986). His most recent work on *The Historical Function of Juan Ruiz's Libro de Buen Amor*, 3 vols. is forthcoming from The Hispanic Seminary of Medieval Studies at the University of Wisconsin.

CONTRIBUTING EDITORS TO THE *CURRICULUM VITAE* OF
MIGUEL DE CERVANTES SAAVEDRA

Transcription by:
MARIO GOMEZ-MORIANA. Educational advisor at the Junta
de Andalucía and Director of the Pedagogic Section of
the Museo de Bellas Artes, Sevilla.

Translation by:
DWAYNE E. CARPENTER. Associate Professor, Dept. of
Spanish and Portuguese, Columbia University. He
has done extensive work on Alfonsine legal texts
(*Siete partidas*) and the legal status of Jews in
Medieval Spain, and published several articles on
Medieval and Renaissance literature. He is currently
working on Jewish-Christian polemics in Medieval
Spain, and has recently published *Alfonso X and the
Jews* (1986).

PAUL E. LARSON. Doctoral Candidate, Dept. of Spanish and
Portuguese, Univ. of Minnesota. His areas of interest
include Medieval and Renaissance Spanish literature
and historiography.

Editorial corroboration by:
OSCAR PEREIRA. Doctoral Candidate, Dept. of Spanish and
Portuguese, Univ. of Minnesota. His areas of interest
include Nineteenth and Twentieth Century Spanish
Philosophy. He recently published an article entitled
"Desintegración social y sensibilidad pastoril bajo el
régimen fascista chileno" in *Poética de la población
marginal: sensibilidades determinantes* (1988).

INDEX

292